Best of FamilyFun
Cooking&Parties

This book is dedicated to
the readers of *FamilyFun* magazine.

Most of the recipes, party ideas, and photographs in this book
were previously published in *FamilyFun* magazine. These pages were excerpted from *FamilyFun Cookbook* and *FamilyFun Parties*.

FamilyFun magazine is a division of Disney Publishing Worldwide.
To order a subscription, call 800-289-4849.

Family Fun Magazine
BOOK EDITORS: Deanna F. Cook, Alexandra Kennedy, and Cindy Littlefield
MANAGING EDITOR: Priscilla Totten
PRODUCTION EDITOR: Paula Noonan
EDITORIAL ASSISTANTS: Katherine Eastman, Megan Fowlie, Grace Ganssle, Jean Graham,
Debra Liebson, and Julia Lynch
PRODUCTION EDITORS: Martha Jenkins, Jennifer Mayer, and Dana Stiepock
ART DIRECTORS: David Kendrick and Mark Mantegna
TECHNOLOGY COORDINATORS: Luke Jaeger and Tom Lepper

Impress, Inc.
DESIGNERS: Carolyn Eckert, Howard Klein. James McDonald,
ASSISTANT DESIGNERS: Leslie Tane and Katie Winger
ART ASSISTANTS: Tobye Cook, Jen Darcy, and Kathryn Ellsworth

The staffs of **Family Fun** and **Impress, Inc.**
conceived and produced *Best of FamilyFun Cooking & Parties* at
244 Main Street, Northampton, Massachusetts 01060.

In collaboration with
Disney Editions, 114 Fifth Avenue, New York, New York 10011

Special thanks to all the *FamilyFun* writers and readers for their wonderful recipes and party ideas from *FamilyFun Cookbook* and *FamilyFun Parties*. With gratitude to all the staff of *FamilyFun*'s art and editorial departments, who directed much of the original work. Also, special thanks to all the photographers, stylists, and models for their excellent work.

Library of Congress Cataloging-in-Publication Data

ISBN 0-7868-5901-6
First Edition

FamilyFun
Cookbook

Irrestible Recipes for You and Your Kids **4**

FamilyFun
Parties

Party Plans for Birthdays, Holidays, & Every Day **158**

FamilyFun
Cookbook

By Deanna F. Cook
and the Experts at FamilyFun Magazine

EDITIONS

New York

Contents

Fluttery Creations:
Page 57

PHOTOGRAPHS ON TABLE OF CONTENTS: LIGHTWORKS PHOTOGRAPHIC

CHAPTER 1

Getting Ready

A S THE FOOD EDITOR of Disney's *FamilyFun* magazine, I like to root around in our file cabinets and pull out letters from our readers whenever I need a boost. Hearing a parent thank us for the recipes in the magazine is satisfying, but looking at a child's expression in the accompanying photo — holding up a Father's Day cake or a homemade apple pie — makes my day. A child's excitement as he offers up a slightly lopsided creation is proof that cooking is about family, about making something good to eat in the kitchen, and sharing it with someone you love. Forget the flowers — say it with spaghetti and cupcakes.

Since we started *FamilyFun* in 1991, families have come to rely on us for our cooking tips and recipes. They've clipped and saved and spilled flour all over them — the mark of good recipes. We decided it was about time to gather our most popular recipes in one place for the busy parents who want to put good meals on the table and enjoy them with their kids. In this cookbook, you will find recipes for real food, meals parents actually make and kids actually eat. And they're fun, from the preparation to the table.

Over the years, our contributors and readers have shared their tricks for satisfying every eater at the table. I am relieved to report that none of them involve preparing a different meal for each family member — a strategy some exasperated parents resort to. A couple of the tricks appeal particularly to kids. For starters, the names of the recipes are clever — Carrot Stick Salad, Veggies in a Blanket,

Shopping Wisely: *Page 12*

Turtle Bean Burritos. This may be a small point to an adult, but to many a picky child a catchy name makes a meal more appetizing. An innovative presentation is also key to making food more tempting. We won't pretend that every mom and dad has time to carve radishes into flowers, but some simple tricks — cutting sandwiches with cookie cutters, arranging sliced fruit into faces, or serving fun pasta shapes — win over the kindergarten set.

If you have finicky eaters in your household (and who doesn't?) you can still present nutritionally balanced meals. For the child (or adult) who turns up his nose to a tomato slice tucked in a grilled-cheese sandwich, for example, we say offer him a host of healthful add-ins — avocado, salsa, onion, broccoli. After all, things taste better when you have a choice.

Try to expand your repertoire in other ways as well. When I was a kid, the most exotic thing my family ate was Swedish meatballs. Now we can't imagine a week without stir-fry. (My six-year-old nephew told me that pesto is the best thing you can eat on tortellini. Granted, he is the nephew of a food writer, but I don't think he's the only kid in his school who brings pesto for lunch.) The trend is that families in the nineties are eating out more and tasting new flavors all over town: Mexican, Chinese, Japanese, Thai, Italian, Greek, Caribbean. As our palates become more sophisticated — more receptive to a broad range of ingredients and cooking methods — we are expanding our choices. Grocery stores have responded, too, with shelves stocked with fresh herbs, specialty vegetables, and seafoods unheard of a generation ago. This recipe collection takes advantage of our global education with easy-to-follow recipes that introduce exotic foods in not too exotic ways.

Although most families' lives are

too overscheduled for three-course dinners every night, the special occasions call for extra effort. For those days, we have included some of my favorite holiday recipes. I always marvel at the fact that when my family reminisces, the conversation often comes back to food — especially the traditional dishes. For my younger sister it might be the memory of the green cupcakes my mom made for her St. Patrick's Day birthday; for my older sister it is the baklava my grandfather made at Christmas. Holiday recipes make parents (and grandparents) heroes in the eyes of their kids, and they create traditions our children insist we maintain year after year.

The kitchen is the family room — the core of the home, where everyone gravitates, not just for eating, but for learning and growing as a family. We hope these recipes will bring your family as many happy memories in the kitchen as they have brought the readers of *FamilyFun*. Now get ready to share some deliciously good times.

Eat dinner together. For many busy families, the evening meal is often the only time of day the crew gets to spend together. It is a good time to share ideas, catch up on news, and enjoy each other's company, and it may be the only time your kids get your undivided attention. Make sure the television is off and that all phone calls will be returned after dinner is over. At the dinner table, the best family entertainment can happen spontaneously through storytelling, laughter, and the appreciation of a good meal shared.

Plan menus ahead and save time. An hour spent planning meals on a Sunday will save you time all week long. Brainstorm new recipe ideas, try a more ambitious Sunday meal (with enough leftovers for lunch), or cook a sauce for a spaghetti dinner, freezing half for

Table Topics

When Karen Telleen-Lawton of Boulder, Colorado, wanted to make dinner a more fulfilling time for her family, she inaugurated Table Topics, a list of subjects in a basket on which they could speak extemporaneously. There are only two rules: You can choose to talk about whatever you wish rather than the topic drawn; and the speaker is allowed uninterrupted time, until he or she requests comments. Karen found that whether the assignment was to discuss something fun they had done in the last few days or to talk about something embarrassing that happened, her kids reveled in the undivided attention. Best of all, their practice of regular communication taught them a lot about each other.

Getting Ready

later. If you need ideas, peruse the chapters with your kids and involve them in the selection process; kids who participate in menu planning are more likely to eat the meals. Make a menu plan out of construction paper or create one on your word processor, then post it on the refrigerator. Be sure that each meal is complete — with a protein, grain, vegetable, and dessert. When you have a menu, you can compile a grocery list and avoid the tedious daily trips to the market.

Shop wisely. Although your kids might say "there's nothing to eat" unless you buy bags of junk food, it's important to have the following basics on hand for snacks, lunches, and last-minute dinners:

☛ Vegetables: Scan the produce aisle for the freshest vegetables — usually those that are in season. Some staples you want to keep in your crisper or pantry are lettuce, onions, garlic, mushrooms, broccoli, cauliflower, peppers, tomatoes, squash, carrots, potatoes, peas, and corn on the cob. During off-seasons, pick up frozen peas, corn, and green beans, which taste better and are more nutritious than produce shipped thousands of miles.

☛ Fruits: Besides standbys such as oranges and apples, take advantage of berries, grapes, melons, and tropical fruits. Always have a lemon on hand for fresh lemon juice.

☛ Grains: Fiber is an important part of any diet, so pick up whole grain cereals and breads and replenish your supply of whole wheat and all-purpose flour, popcorn, rice, couscous, cornmeal, and rolled oats.

☛ Dairy: This primary source of calcium is most healthful when it is low- or no-fat. Try skim milk and low-fat yogurt and eat low-fat cheese, if your kids are game. Butter and margarine are too high-fat to be worthwhile sources of calcium.

Eggs, another dairy case staple, are healthful in moderation.

☞ Pasta: You can stock your shelves with everything from dry bow ties to wagon wheels. In the freezer, keep on hand fresh tortellini and ravioli.

☞ Meats and poultry: For fast dinners, pick up fish, chicken, ground beef and turkey, sausages, or tofu. Many grocers now carry free-range meats, which are more expensive, but leaner and chemical-free.

☞ Baking essentials: For impromptu baking projects, stock up on baking powder, baking soda, yeast, honey, granulated, brown, and confectioners' sugar, salt, vanilla extract, dried fruits and nuts, flavored and unflavored gelatin, food coloring, sprinkles, baking chocolate, cocoa powder, and chocolate chips.

☞ Sauces and condiments: Be sure to have in your refrigerator salsa, mustard, mayonnaise, catsup, chutney, relish, and soy sauce, as well as barbecue and spaghetti sauce.

☞ Oils and vinegars: Invest in virgin olive oil, as well as vegetable oil, and in red wine, white, and balsamic vinegars.

☞ Canned foods: Although canned goods once had a bad name, they are excellent time-savers. Try canned beans, such as chickpeas and kidney beans, canned tomatoes, and canned fruits in their juice.

☞ Stocks: Bouillon cubes and chicken broth are great for instant soups.

☞ Herbs and spices: Grow or pick up fresh herbs to snip over food and use as a garnish. Have the following dried herbs and spices on hand: cinnamon, basil, bay leaves, thyme, parsley, oregano, rosemary, dill, curry powder, chili powder, cumin, and any other favorites.

☞ Nuts and nut butters: Peanut butter, sesame

Grocery Savings

Buy in bulk: Pick up extra-large packages of frequently used items like cereal and juices.

Take advantage of special sales: Stock up on nonperishable items, such as canned goods and paper products.

Check the newspaper: Food sections will keep you up-to-date on the best produce buys.

Shop at double-coupon stores: Some stores will give you twice the face value of your coupons — a substantial savings.

Buy produce at local food stands: It eliminates the cost of a middleman —and lets you support local business.

Grow your own: For less expensive, better-tasting produce, plant some vegetables and herbs.

When *FamilyFun* reader Lori Nienau's son and daughter began to show an interest in food preparation, she organized a kids cooking class, held in her Kirkland, Washington, home. Lori collected recipes and asked both kids to invite a friend to attend their course. Their one-and-a-half-hour sessions took place one day a week after school and ran for four weeks. Lori began introducing the young chefs to the four food groups, cooking terminology, and the importance of a clean kitchen. After the kids learned to make an item, they placed the recipe in a three-ring binder and took home samples of their creations to share.

seeds, sunflower seeds, and walnuts add protein to sandwiches and salads.

Be prepared. The better equipped you are, the more likely you can efficiently whip up dinners, desserts, and other involved dishes. Consider the following checklist:

☞ Pots and pans, including a non-stick frying pan and small, medium, and large saucepans with fitted lids, a large soup pot, and a roasting pan.

☞ Utensils, such as a wooden spoon, whisk, garlic press, slotted spoons, spatula, ladle, rubber spatula, pastry brush, and pot holders.

☞ Small, medium, and large mixing bowls, as well as dry and liquid measuring cups.

☞ Baking tools — a rolling pin, pastry wheel, cookie cutters (regular, mini, and giant cutters, as well as aspic cutters, which are available at specialty shops and well worth the investment), pastry bag and decorator's tips, and Popsicle sticks.

☞ Baking pans, including two cookie sheets, a 13- by 9- by 2-inch pan, two 8- or 9-inch round cake pans, 9-inch pie pans, an 8½-inch and a 5-inch loaf pan, muffin tins (mini, regular, and giant) and paper liners, and a wire cooling rack.

☞ Appliances — an electric mixer, food processor or blender, and a microwave oven.

Raise healthy eaters. The key to good nutrition is not counting every calorie or avoiding all fatty foods: It's eating small portions of a variety of foods. In other words, it's okay to serve your child a cupcake as long as you also serve a healthy sandwich, carrot sticks, and a glass of skim milk. Be sure to set a good example by eating healthy foods yourself. Many of the recipes in this book are for special occasions — so eat those in moderation. And don't deprive your kids of their favorite foods; just be sure to dole them out carefully. Good tastes are linked with happy childhoods.

Introduce one new food every week. Taste is a learned behavior. It's tempting to serve hamburgers and pizza seven nights of the week, but it's more important to educate your children's palates so they can learn to love a wide range of foods. Introduce a new fruit or vegetable on a regular basis, and if your children don't like it, reintroduce it a few months later. Kids' tastes change over time. Try sneaking a new food into a dish they love or offer it as an optional topping. For inspiration, see some of the creative recipes in this book, such as the Broccoli Trees, page 104, or the Ziti with Ricotta and Spinach, page 94.

Eat out one night a week. Eating out can be a fun way to spend time together. *FamilyFun* reader Shelly Cronin, who is from the magazine's hometown of Northampton, Massachusetts, reserves Friday nights for eating out with her family and Saturday nights for eating out with her husband. She says this tradition is a wonderful way to enjoy her kids' company and to maintain a close relationship with her husband. If you can, make a point of taking each of your children out to breakfast or lunch once a month and let him or her be the center of attention.

Teach your kids to cook, set the table, and clean up. Learning to cook is an important life skill and a great hobby to get your kids hooked on. In each chapter, our simple recipes will help you introduce young chefs to the right way to cook. Encourage your children to be creative in the kitchen — to smell fresh herbs and decide whether to add them to the soup, for example — and to enjoy the process of making something to eat. Let your kids thumb through the pages in this cookbook and pick out the recipes they want to try. For a cooking class, pick one recipe to try per week, then enlist the kids' help with the cleanup afterward.

Designer Table Setting

In *FamilyFun* reader Nancy Weber's household, table setting is transformed from a chore into an art form. The person setting the table gets to set it any way he or she sees fit — as long as four people can dine with the result. Sometimes they have plates under the chairs and all the knives and forks in a pile in the middle of the table; other times they have origami napkin swans; sometimes everyone has a different shape and color glass, and the napkins are tied around the rungs of the chairs. And one night Dad made a model of the starship *Enterprise* using forks, knives, and plates.

Step 1. Arrange a napkin on the diagonal and pull one layer down.

Step 2. Flip the napkin over and fold in the two sides.

Step 3. Turn it over again and fill with silverware.

Getting Ready

CHAPTER 2

Breakfast: Rise and Shine

To a child, Sunday breakfast is the best meal of the week. You get to sleep late, read the Sunday comics, and eat in your pajamas. The fare is as sweet as dessert: Maple syrup poured over a stack of pancakes, warm blueberry muffins, or cinnamon rolls straight from the oven. Weekday breakfasts, however, bear little of that romantic charm. The morning becomes a rush hour, and some kids (and parents) would rather just not bother fixing breakfast or eating, despite the knowledge that the first meal of the day is the most important. So, how can you turn breakfast into a favorite meal every day without getting up before dawn to start baking?

On weekdays, make it fast and eat slow. Fill your freezer with whole grain cereals, breads, and other nutritious baked goods. Keep a supply of fresh fruits (cut into bite-size pieces), low-fat milk, and juices in the refrigerator. Store cereal on a shelf your children can reach, so they can help themselves. For a real time-saver, set the table for breakfast each night as soon as the dinner dishes are cleared.

Bake breakfast treats on the weekends. Muffins, scones, and homemade pancake mixes all can be made ahead to save time. Let your child browse through this chapter and pick a recipe to try each week; if invited to help make it, he might also be more inclined to eat it.

Serve small portions. You don't want to load your child up on heavy breakfast foods before school, or it will slow him down. Serve a variety of lighter foods, including protein, starches, fiber, and fat:

If your kids need to dash off with a lunch box in one hand and breakfast in the other, here are some manageable quickies:

Warm yesterday's pancakes or waffles in the toaster and serve with jam.

Make a peanut butter and banana sandwich on toast.

Fill a pita with a scrambled egg and a slice of ham.

Mix ricotta cheese with cinnamon and sugar and serve with sliced apples inside a whole wheat pita.

Mix granola into a container of yogurt.

Blend a banana with a little milk or OJ and pour into a thermos.

fruit and milk on a high-fiber cereal, for example, or a batch of scrambled eggs with whole wheat toast.

If your child can't eat first thing in the morning, brown-bag her breakfast. If your child honestly can't bear the idea of breakfast — and the only way to keep her at the breakfast table is forcibly — pack her a school breakfast that includes a juice box, a muffin or high-quality cereal bar, and an easy-to-eat piece of fruit, such as a banana or an apple.

Define breakfast loosely. Nowhere is it written that breakfast must consist of eggs, pancakes, and sausage. If your child prefers cold pizza or tuna fish sandwiches for breakfast, just consider yourself lucky that he doesn't start the day with a cola.

Enjoy weekend breakfasts. If eating dinner together every night is unrealistic, plan on eating breakfast together on a weekend morning. Turn off the TV, make a big breakfast or brunch, and catch up on the busy week.

Sunday Morning Omelets

Kids like to choose their own fillings for this classic egg dish. Encourage them to invent combinations from whatever leftover vegetables, spreads, cheeses, and meats you have on hand. How about a jelly and cream cheese omelet?

½ tablespoon butter or margarine
2 eggs
1 tablespoon water
  Salt and pepper to taste
Filling options:
1 tablespoon grated cheese, such as Cheddar or Mozzarella
1 tablespoon cottage cheese, Boursin, or flavored cream cheese
2 tablespoons diced, cooked chicken
1 tablespoon crispy bacon pieces
2 teaspoons jam or jelly
2 sliced mushrooms
2 cherry tomato halves
1 tablespoon diced green or red pepper
1 tablespoon diced onion

In a large, nonstick frying pan, melt the butter or margarine over medium-high heat. Beat the eggs with a fork in a small bowl and stir in the water, salt, and pepper. Pour the egg mixture over the butter, swirling the egg until you have coated the pan with a thin layer of uncooked egg. Sprinkle the desired fillings over the omelet and cook for 1 to 3 more minutes, or until desired doneness. To serve, hold the pan at a 45-degree angle and, with a spatula, gently fold the omelet in half. Makes 1 generous omelet.

Breakfast Burrito

The morning after a Mexican meal, I use up my leftover tortillas, grated cheese, chopped onion, and salsa in this delicious roll-up sandwich.

1 tablespoon butter
6 eggs, beaten
4 to 6 8-inch flour tortillas
Filling options:
½ cup grated Monterey Jack cheese
1 plum tomato, chopped
1 small onion, diced
¼ green or red pepper, chopped
½ avocado, diced
  Salsa
  Sliced olives

Over medium-high heat, melt the butter in a large, nonstick frying pan and scramble and cook the eggs to your liking. Meanwhile, warm the tortillas for a few minutes on the rack of a 250° oven, then fill with the egg and your choice of ingredients. Fold into a burrito (see page 99 for directions) Serves 4.

Breakfast Burrito

EGG HEADS

For a silly activity that makes terrific use of eggshells, you can make Egg Heads with wild grass-dos. For each, you'll need a raw egg, a needle, grass seed, and potting soil. First, use the needle to make a hole about the size of a quarter in one end of an egg, then drain the contents and rinse out the shell. Gently draw or paint faces on the shell and set in an egg carton to dry. Spoon soil into the shell, then plant the grass seeds according to package instructions. Moisten, cover with plastic wrap, and place in a sunny window until the seeds sprout — about one week. When the Egg Heads have a thick head of hair, remove the covering and style with scissors. Water your Egg Heads regularly.

Well-Timed Eggs

Soft-Boiled Eggs:
In a saucepan, cover eggs with water and bring to a boil. Reduce the heat to a simmer and cook for 2 to 3 minutes more. Remove each soft-boiled egg and let sit until it is cool enough to handle.
Hard-Boiled Eggs:
Cook eggs as you would for soft-boiled, but simmer for 15 minutes. Plunge into cold water to halt the cooking and make peeling easier.
Note: Add 2 minutes to cooking times if the eggs are straight from the refrigerator.

Royal Ham 'n' Eggs

This dish is a favorite at my mother's inn in Woodstock, Vermont. The vegetables listed can be substituted with ½ cup of sliced mushrooms, chopped broccoli, shredded zucchini, or cubed boiled potatoes; instead of ham or sausage, you can add strips of prosciutto or bacon pieces.

- 1½ cups French bread cubes
- ½ pound cooked ham or sausage, cubed
- 1 8-ounce package frozen chopped spinach, thawed and drained
- 12 cherry tomatoes, sliced in half
- 8 ounces Cheddar cheese, grated
- 8 eggs
- 1 teaspoon dried mustard
- ¼ teaspoon pepper
- 1 cup milk

Preheat the oven to 350°. Butter a 13- by 9- by 2-inch baking dish and line with the bread cubes. Cover with layers of ham or sausage, chopped spinach, cherry tomatoes, and grated cheese. In a separate bowl, whisk the eggs, dried mustard, pepper, and milk. Pour the mixture over the casserole. Bake for 30 minutes, then broil for 2 minutes, or until the cheese turns golden brown. Makes 8 to 10 servings.

Breakfast Pizza

Better known as a frittata, this egg dish can be topped with everything your kids like on pizza. Prepare it the night before and serve at room temperature.

- 4 eggs, beaten
- ¼ to ½ cup grated mild Cheddar or Monterey Jack cheese
- ¼ cup diced ham, pepperoni, mushrooms, or other pizza topping
- 1 tablespoon butter or margarine

Preheat your broiler. In a medium-size bowl, mix the eggs, cheese, and pizza toppings. Melt the butter in an 8-inch frying pan with a metal handle over medium heat. Pour in the egg mixture and cook until the bottom is golden, about 7 minutes. Remove the pan from the stove and place it under the broiler for about 3 minutes, or until the top has puffed up and lightly browned. Cool slightly and cut into wedges. Makes 1 frittata.

Royal Ham 'n' Eggs

The Best Way to Nuke Bacon

☛ Microwave slices of bacon between 2 paper towels so you can throw the mess away. For crispy bacon, heat 4 slices on high for 4 minutes.

Pancakes & Waffles

The Perfect Pancake Mix

FamilyFun contributor Becky Okrent developed this vitamin-packed mix to encourage her family to make pancakes in short order.

- 3   cups all-purpose flour
- 3   teaspoons baking soda
- 4½ teaspoons baking powder
- 1½ teaspoons salt
- 1   tablespoon sugar (optional)
- 2   cups whole wheat or oat flour, or a combination
- 1   cup seven whole grain cereal (available at health food stores)
- 1   cup cornmeal
- 4   tablespoons wheat germ (optional)

In a large mixing bowl, sift the all-purpose flour with the baking soda, baking powder, salt, and optional sugar. Drop in the remaining flour, cereal, cornmeal, and wheat germ and stir until thoroughly blended. Store in an airtight container and, if using wheat germ, refrigerate. Makes 7½ cups, enough for 15 batches of 5 pancakes.

Perfect Pancakes:

You can store leftover batter in the refrigerator for two days and reheat leftover pancakes in a toaster.

- 1   tablespoon butter
- 1   egg
- ½   cup nonfat yogurt, buttermilk, sour cream, or milk
- ½   cup Perfect Pancake Mix

Set a griddle or skillet over medium heat and melt the butter. Lightly beat the egg with the yogurt, buttermilk, sour cream, or milk. Add the pancake mix and stir just until smooth.

Ladle the batter onto the skillet. Turn the pancakes when you see air bubbles on the surface (about 1 minute). Serve with maple syrup, jam, yogurt, or confectioners' sugar. Makes about 5 medium pancakes.

Perfect Blueberry Pancakes:

Stir ½ cup fresh or frozen blueberries into the batter before cooking.

Pancake Specials

Apple-Walnut Pancakes: Toss chopped walnuts, sliced apples, and ½ teaspoon cinnamon into your batter.

Cranberry-Orange Pancakes: Add ½ cup cranberries, 1 tablespoon orange juice, and 1 teaspoon orange zest to the batter.

Banana Pancakes: Top pancakes with sliced bananas before flipping.

Pumpkin Pancakes: Mix 2 tablespoons of mashed pumpkin and 1 teaspoon of allspice into the batter.

Personalized Pancakes: Shape the batter on the griddle into animals, cartoon characters, or your child's initials.

Perfect Blueberry Pancakes

Great Toppings for Pancakes, Waffles, and French Toast

Children love the opportunity to get creative with toppings. Here are some ideas:

- Confectioners' sugar
- Cinnamon Sugar (see page 36)
- Strawberry jam
- Unsweetened yogurt
- Sliced fresh fruit or berries
- Honey
- Lemon Curd (see page 35)
- Cream cheese and jelly
- Flavored butters (see pages 36 and 52)
- Vanilla yogurt and granola
- Raspberry Syrup (see page 24)
- Applesauce and cinnamon

Waffles on the Run

The next time you pull out the waffle iron, remember to make an extra batch for mornings when your family needs to grab a quick bite. Cook the waffles, leaving them slightly lighter than usual, cool, then place in a sealable plastic bag and freeze. To reheat, pop one in the toaster, then garnish with your favorite toppings or one of the suggestions above.

Sunday Waffles

The leisurely pace of Sundays means extra time for *FamilyFun* contributor Becky Okrent and her family to make waffles, using her Perfect Pancake Mix.

> 2 eggs, separated
> 1 cup milk
> 3 tablespoons vegetable oil or melted butter
> 1 cup Perfect Pancake Mix (see page 21)

In a bowl, combine the egg yolks, milk, and oil or butter. Stir in the Perfect Pancake Mix. Beat the egg whites until stiff and gently fold into the batter. Cook on a greased waffle iron until lightly browned. Makes 4 to 6 waffles.

Banana Split Waffles:

Top a waffle with 1 tablespoon of plain or vanilla yogurt, sliced banana, and a sprinkle of granola.

Poppy Seed Waffles:

Add 1 tablespoon of poppy seeds to the batter before cooking.

Strawberry Cream Cheese Waffles:

Spread store bought strawberry cream cheese on a waffle and cut into pie-shaped wedges.

Pick an Orange Orange?

Because most oranges are dyed to improve their appearance, don't judge an orange by its color. Pick a sweet orange by examining the navel: the bigger the better. For 1 cup of juice, you will need 3 sweet medium juice oranges.

Breakfast Milk Shake

This make-ahead healthy shake is so thick, some kids insist on calling it banana ice cream.

> 2 bananas
> 5 to 10 whole strawberries (optional)
> ¼ cup blueberries (optional)
> ½ cup milk or orange juice

Slice the bananas into 1-inch chunks. Wash and stem the berries. Seal the fruits in a plastic bag and freeze for 3 hours or overnight. Place the frozen fruits in a blender or a food processor (if they are rock hard, let them slightly defrost). Add the milk or orange juice and puree or process until smooth and thick. Pour into a glass, bowl, or mug and serve with spoons or straws. Serves 2.

Muffins

![Good Morning Muffins and Best Apple Butter]

Good Morning Muffins and Best Apple Butter

Hot Mulled Apple Cider

Combine a gallon of cider with 4 cinnamon sticks, a few cloves, ¼ teaspoon of ground nutmeg, and several orange slices. Gently warm over medium heat. Strain and transfer to mugs. For extra flavor, add a cinnamon stick and orange slice to each serving.

Good Morning Muffins

Thanks to these nutritious muffins, my brother gets his kids to eat apples and carrots for breakfast.

3   eggs
½   cup sugar
½   cup vegetable oil
1   cup grated apples
1   cup grated carrots
1   cup whole wheat flour
1   cup all-purpose flour
1   tablespoon baking powder
¼   teaspoon salt
1   teaspoon cinnamon

Preheat the oven to 375°. Lightly grease a 12-cup muffin tin or line it with paper liners and set aside. Blend the eggs, sugar, and oil until well combined. Stir in the grated apples and carrots. In a separate bowl, sift the flours, baking powder, salt, and cinnamon. Blend the dry ingredients with the apple mixture until just combined. Spoon the batter into the muffin tins and bake for 25 minutes, or until golden brown. Makes 12 muffins.

Best Apple Butter

As I learned from my mother, who created this recipe, the best part of making apple butter is that your house fills with a sweet, cinnamon aroma. It isn't a lot of work, but it takes a long time to bake, so plan to make it when you are working around the house. Nothing is better when spread on muffins, scones, or toast.

9   to 10 apples, peeled, cored, and cut into 1-inch chunks
1   cup apple cider
2   teaspoons apple pie spice (available in the spice rack at your grocer's)

Place the apples in a large, nonreactive saucepan with the cider. Cover the pot and cook for about 30 minutes over low heat, or until the apples are soft. Cool, divide into two batches, and puree each in the bowl of a food processor or blender. Pour all of the pureed fruit into a 13- by 9- by 2-inch baking dish, sprinkle with the apple pie spice, and stir well.

Stirring every 20 minutes, bake in a preheated 300° oven for 2 to 3 hours, or until your apple butter is deep brown and thick. Cool and then scoop it into a clean jar with a sealable lid. It will keep for up to 2 months in your refrigerator. Makes 1½ cups.

P B & J Surprise Muffins

The inspiration of *FamilyFun* contributor Beth Hillson, these moist peanut butter muffins hide a secret jelly or jam filling. She lets her son pick the flavor and puts him in charge of spooning the surprise into the batter. Her advice: Make a batch on a Sunday so your child can enjoy them as breakfast treats all week long.

1¾   cups all-purpose flour
⅓   cup sugar
2½   teaspoons baking powder
½   teaspoon salt
½   cup creamy peanut butter
1   large egg
¾   cup milk
⅓   cup butter, melted
½   cup strawberry, raspberry, or
      grape jelly or jam

Preheat the oven to 375°. Line a 12-cup muffin tin with paper liners. In a large bowl, combine the flour, sugar, baking powder, and salt. In a separate bowl, mix the peanut butter with the egg; add the milk, a little at a time, then add the butter. Mix well. Pour the wet batter into the bowl with the dry ingredients and stir gently to combine (the batter will be stiff).

Put a heaping tablespoon of batter in the bottom of each muffin cup. Use a finger to make an indentation in the center and put a teaspoon of jelly in the hole. Cover with another heaping tablespoon of batter, or enough to fill each cup about two thirds full. Spread the top batter gently until no jelly is visible. Bake for 20 minutes, then turn the muffins onto a wire baking rack to cool. Be careful — the jelly centers can get hot. Makes 12 muffins.

PB & J Surprise Muffins

Very Blueberry Whole Wheat Muffins and Blueberry Buckle

2½ cups blueberries, washed
    and stems removed

Preheat the oven to 375° and line a 12-cup muffin tin with paper liners. In a large bowl, cream the butter and sugar. Add the eggs, and stir in the milk and vanilla extract. In another bowl, sift the dry ingredients. Stir them into the butter and sugar mixture, then fold in the blueberries. Fill the muffin cups almost to the top and bake for 25 minutes, or until light brown. Makes 12 muffins.

Blueberry Buckle

This foolproof coffee cake is a specialty in Maine, America's blueberry capital.

Topping:

⅓	cup sugar
½	cup all-purpose flour
1½	teaspoons cinnamon
¼	cup butter, softened

Batter:

¼	cup butter
¾	cup sugar
2	eggs
½	cup milk
2	cups all-purpose flour
½	teaspoon salt
2	teaspoons baking powder
2	cups blueberries, washed and stems removed

To make the topping, stir the dry ingredients and butter with a fork until the mixture crumbles. Set aside.

Preheat the oven to 350° and grease a 9-inch square pan. In a mixing bowl, cream the butter and sugar, add the eggs, and stir in the milk. Mix until smooth. Sift the flour, salt, and baking powder into a separate bowl. Gradually stir it into the batter. Fold in the blueberries, then spread the batter in the pan. Sprinkle the topping over the batter. Bake for 35 to 40 minutes, or until a toothpick inserted in the middle comes out dry. Serves 8.

GO BLUEBERRY PICKING

For the sweetest blueberries, head to a local farm and pick your own. To find a blueberry farm in your area, call your county extension service or state department of agriculture. Be sure to pick extra for freezing — just toss them in a sealable plastic container. You'll welcome the berry taste in the middle of winter.

Very Blueberry Whole Wheat Muffins

If you are trying to introduce your kids to whole grain flours, a basket of these sweet blueberry muffins is convincing evidence that unprocessed flours taste the best.

6	tablespoons butter, softened
¾	cup sugar
2	eggs
½	cup milk
1	teaspoon vanilla extract
1	cup all-purpose flour
1	cup whole wheat flour
1	tablespoon baking powder
¼	teaspoon salt

Strawberry-Almond Muffins

Fresh strawberries and slivered almonds are excellent flavor companions, but if your kids rank among the many who are not nut fans, you can substitute Grape Nuts cereal for the almonds.

½   cup butter, softened
¾   cup sugar
2   eggs
½   cup milk
1½ teaspoons almond extract
1½ cups all-purpose flour
½   cup whole wheat flour
1   tablespoon baking powder
¼   teaspoon salt

2   cups strawberries, chopped
¾   cup slivered almonds

Preheat the oven to 375° and line a 12-cup muffin tin with paper liners (a good job for kids). In the bowl of an electric mixer or food processor, cream the butter and sugar. Add the eggs, one at a time, and blend until fluffy. Mix in the milk and the almond extract. In a separate bowl, sift the flours, baking powder, and salt. Add the flour mixture to the milk mixture and blend until just combined. Fold in the strawberries and almonds. Fill the muffin cups to the top and bake for 30 minutes, or until golden brown. Makes 12 muffins.

STRAWBERRY SLUSH

Strawberries stack up third, right behind papaya and cantaloupe, on a list of the most nutritious fruits compiled by the Center for Science in the Public Interest. That's because they are so high in vitamin C (ounce per ounce, they outrank even oranges).

6 ice cubes
16 strawberries
½ cup frozen
  concentrated limeade
½ cup water

Place the ice cubes in a blender or food processor and pulse until crushed. Add the strawberries, limeade, and water. Puree until smooth and thick. Pour into tall glasses with flexi-straws. Serves 2.

FunFact
To dream of strawberries is a sign of good things to come.

Strawberry-Almond Muffins and Strawberry Slush

27

CHAPTER 3

Lunch Specials

COMING UP with creative lunch ideas for kids five days a week, nine months out of the year, is no easy feat. You're not alone if your child sometimes eighty-sixes your latest healthy concoction in favor of a hot dog from the school cafeteria. What we perceive as a delicious, well-balanced lunch box full of goodies may seem boring, weird, or just plain gross to kids.

FamilyFun contributor Becky Okrent says it's important to be sensitive to your child's style when packing a lunch from home. "I have two kids who are exact opposites. My son refuses to take anything conspicuous, such as a chicken drumstick, and if I pack anything so garish as a slice of homemade bread, he will think I'm trying to humiliate him in front of his friends. My daughter wants all the frills. She finds crustless sandwiches cut into heart shapes a testament of my love."

The challenge is to prepare lunches that are nourishing, palatable, and appealing to each child. So, exactly how do you do that, especially when you aren't at school at lunchtime to see how your efforts are paying off? These tips from Okrent and other *FamilyFun* contributors are key.

Make lunches at home. Although many school lunch programs have lightened up their menus, it's smart to make your lunches at home where you can save money and control the nutritional value. If that isn't realistic, call the school cafeteria and find out its nutritional guidelines. School lunch programs vary from school system to school system — some prepare all their foods from scratch, and others offer vended meals. Keep a copy

Chinese Sesame Noodles: *Page 42*

A Week of Lunches

Monday:
SuperSub (page 32), Mini Chocolate Chip Cookies (page 121), juice box

Tuesday:
PB and Jellyfish sandwich (page 31), bug juice, gummy worms

Wednesday:
Chinese Sesame Noodles (page 42), orange wedges, iced tea, fortune cookies

Thursday:
Chicken Nuggets (page 42), Home-made Tortilla Chips (page 50), Cub-cakes (page 124)

Friday:
Customized Egg Salad (page 35), potato chips, milk

them. They can help with everything from shopping to cooking to packing. **Make lunches the night before.** In most homes, it's too hectic on school mornings to make lunches, but it can be a fun collaborative project the night before. Over the weekends, you can also make lunch-box treats — muffins, cookies, or a pot of soup — to enjoy all week.

Serve small portions. Many parents make the mistake of sending too much food to school with their children. Try small amounts of a variety of foods.

Get creative with your presentation. One way to make lunches enticing is to come up with clever packaging ideas. Pack the fixings for a sandwich and let your child assemble it at school, or send sesame noodles in a Chinese take-out container with chopsticks.

Remember that lunchtime is social time. Don't send anything too conspicuous in your kids' lunch boxes, such as foods with strong odors, without running it by them first.

Send a little bit of home in the lunch bag. Pack a lunch-box surprise, such as a note, sticker, or lollipop. It's a simple gesture that will let your kids know your thoughts are with them even when you're not.

of the weekly menu posted on your refrigerator and discuss the healthy choices with your children.

Start with the lunch box. In September, let your children pick out favorite lunch boxes or reusable bags that they feel express their individuality. Be sure lunch boxes include or can accommodate a thermos with an opening wide enough for a spoon (for soup, pasta, or yogurt). A mini ice pack is also a worthwhile accessory.

Plan well-balanced menus ahead of time. Before you go shopping, agree on the lunches for the week and post the list on the refrigerator. You might even allow one day for leftovers and another, as a treat, for a school lunch.

Involve the kids in preparing their lunches. If they have a little time invested, they will be more likely to eat

Sandwiches

Something Fishy

Even picky preschoolers won't throw back this clever lunch. Serve it with Goldfish crackers and gummy worms.

- 2 slices whole wheat or white bread
- 1 6-ounce can tuna in water, drained
- 2 tablespoons mayonnaise
  Lettuce
- 1 tomato, thinly sliced

Stack the bread slices and cut out the fish shape below, or use a fish-shaped cookie cutter. Make a tuna salad with the tuna and mayonnaise, then layer it with the lettuce and tomato. Serves 1.

PB and Jellyfish:

For variety, try a peanut butter and jelly sandwich on the precut, fish-shaped bread.

Mini Muffuletta

Salami fans always order up this smaller take on the New Orleans classic.

- 1 small hard roll
- 2 slices salami
- 2 slices ham
- 1 slice provolone
  Diced onion (optional)
  Sliced olives (optional)
  Sliced radishes (optional)
  Olive oil
  Vinegar

Cut the roll in half and place the salami, ham, and provolone on the bread. Add the onion, olives, and radishes, if desired. Drizzle the bread with olive oil and a splash of vinegar (too much will make it soggy). Serves 1.

Easy Lunch-box Stuffers

- ☞ Carrots, celery sticks, or broccoli florets with a small container of salad dressing for dipping. (To prevent the veggies from drying out, wrap them in a damp paper towel.)
- ☞ Fresh fruit: Try sliced apples rubbed with lemon juice, fresh or canned pineapple chunks, melon in season, fruit salad, or a fruit smoothie.
- ☞ Pretzels, salted peanuts, or popcorn
- ☞ Celery sticks filled with cream cheese or peanut butter and raisins
- ☞ Fruit yogurt packed in a thermos
- ☞ Crackers served plain or sandwiched with peanut butter, jelly, or cheese
- ☞ Mozzarella sticks or string cheese
- ☞ Graham crackers, plain or sandwiched with peanut butter
- ☞ Dried fruit: Raisins, apricots, apples, or pineapples
- ☞ Tortilla chips with a small jar of salsa
- ☞ Pasta salad or soup in a thermos
- ☞ Pickles, olives, or hard-boiled eggs
- ☞ Stickers or a note from you

Something Fishy

Lunch Specials

SuperSub

The Yumbrella

While your kids are out splashing in the rain, you can prepare them a healthy lunch that looks like an umbrella.

- 1 slice of bread
  Mayonnaise, mustard, or butter
- 1 slice of cheese or salami
  Red or green pepper
- 1 radish or carrot
  Parsley or bean sprouts

Spread the bread with mayonnaise, mustard, or butter. Cut the cheese or salami slice into the shape of an umbrella (a round slice should give you two umbrella tops). For the umbrella handle, cut a ¼-inch slice straight through the red or green pepper and use the natural curve at the bottom for the handle (one slice will yield two handles). Add squirts of mustard on the umbrella for raindrops. Surround the umbrella with radish or carrot flowers and parsley or bean sprout grass. Place the bread on a plate and squirt more mustard raindrops around it. If it's especially wet outside, you can complete the meal with a cup of hot soup. Serves 1.

The Yumbrella

SuperSub

Faster than a hot dog, stronger than spicy mustard, SuperSub gives the basic hero extra-special powers by adding kids' favorite fixings — onions, peppers, black olives, or sweet pickles.

- 1 medium hero roll
- 4 to 6 slices of thinly cut cheese
     and/or luncheon meats
- 4 thin tomato slices
- ½ cup shredded lettuce
- 2 teaspoons vegetable oil
- 2 teaspoons red wine vinegar
     Salt and pepper to taste
     Special fixings

Slice the hero roll in half lengthwise. Line the roll with the cheese and luncheon meat. Top with the tomato and lettuce. Sprinkle with the oil and vinegar and season with salt and pepper and any special additions. Close up the sandwich, then cut it in half and wrap it in plastic wrap. Makes 1 large sub.

Happy Lunches

Kathy Bostrom's kids enjoy getting children's meals at fast-food restaurants, but it isn't always economical. So now she makes her own. While Kathy fixes lunch, she lets the kids color a white paper lunch bag. For the ever-popular toy, she saves cereal box prizes and buys gumball trinkets. Her kids pretend to drive through the kitchen, picking up their lunches at the counter.

Sprout Your Own

For a healthy crunch on your child's sandwich, try this indoor gardening project. Measure ½ cup of dried beans (alfalfa, radish, wheat berry, mung, lentil, or adzuki) into a 2-quart, widemouthed plastic jar. Cover with nylon mesh or cheesecloth and secure with a rubber band. Fill halfway with cool water and set the jar away from direct sunlight for 8 hours. Gently drain the water through the mesh cover and return the jar to its shady spot. Twice a day for the next three days, fill the jar with tepid water, drain the water, then set the jar back in the shade. By the fifth day, your crop should be ready to harvest. Your sprout growers need only to reach into the jar and gently pull out handfuls of the mature sprouts. Toss them with salad dressing or stuff them into a sandwich and enjoy. To store leftover sprouts, wrap them in a double thickness of paper towel and refrigerate in a plastic bag.

Sailboat Sandwiches

These novel sandwiches — filled with tuna salad and topped with Cheddar cheese sails — give kids a real feel for the seashore. Set these treats in a plateful of blue corn tortilla chips to complete the nautical theme.

    4   dinner rolls
    1   cup tuna salad
    4   slices Cheddar cheese
    8   toothpicks

Slice the tops off the dinner rolls and hollow them out. Fill the rolls with the tuna salad or any other filling your kids like. Slice the Cheddar cheese into rectangles about ⅛ inch thick and cut the rectangles on the diagonal to make triangles. Insert a toothpick into each triangle to make little sails and add them to the top of your "boats." Makes 4.

Veggies in a Blanket

The young *FamilyFun* readers Ian and Abigail Rowswell entered this burrito-like concoction in our Kids' Snack-off Contest, and their recipe got rave reviews. The siblings, ages nine and six, from Medina, New York, say the sandwich is kind of like a wrapped-up salad.

    2   6-inch flour tortillas
    2   tablespoons cream cheese
    1   medium carrot, grated
    2   lettuce leaves

Wrap each tortilla in a paper towel and microwave for 15 seconds (or warm in a cast-iron pan on low). Spread 1 tablespoon cream cheese over each tortilla, add carrot and lettuce, and roll. Makes 2.

Peanut Puzzler

(caption) Peanut Puzzler

Peanut Butter & Banana Bread Sandwich

Banana bread is the secret ingredient in this twist on the old standby. (For a terrific recipe, see page 63.)

2 slices of banana bread
   Peanut butter
1 banana or apple, sliced

Spread peanut butter on one slice of banana bread. Layer with the banana or apple slices and top with the second bread slice. In a matter of seconds, you've put together a nutritious sandwich that has a sweet dessert flavor. Serves 1.

Peanut Butter and...

Even the most devoted PB & J fans enjoy a little variety. Try combining one of the following ingredients with peanut butter for a novel sandwich.

☛ **Sliced bananas or apples**
☛ **Fresh berries**
☛ **Maple syrup**
☛ **Crispy bacon**
☛ **Raisins, dried apricots, or dried apple rings**
☛ **Chopped, pitted dates**
☛ **Grated carrots**
☛ **Wheat germ and honey**
☛ **Apple butter**

Peanut Puzzler

This spread is great with fresh fruit, such as a few halved grapes, apple slices, or banana slices. For added enticement, you can use a cookie cutter to shape the sandwich into puzzle pieces.

1 cup peanut butter, creamy or chunky
3 tablespoons toasted sesame seeds
¼ cup honey

Mix together all the ingredients and spread on bread or fruit. Makes 1¼ cups.

FunFact
The average American child will eat 1,500 peanut butter sandwiches by high school graduation.

Personalized Lunch Bags

Pick up reusable, nylon lunch bags and some bright puffy paints at a discount or craft supply store and let your kids decorate their own lunch bags. Chances are there will be no mistaking whose lunch is inside.

Salami Snake

A salami snake, slithering across the table, makes an excellent centerpiece for a party spread.

- 1 loaf of French bread
- 14 salami slices
- 14 Provolone or American cheese slices
-      Lettuce
-      Sliced tomato
-      Mayonnaise
-      Carrot strips, broccoli florets, radish, and red pepper

Make a large salami and cheese sandwich with lettuce, tomato, and mayonnaise on the bread, reserving the bread heels for later use. Cut the sandwich into 2-inch pieces. Arrange these in a snake curve on a platter. For the head, halve one heel and open it to make the snake's mouth.

Wedge 2 carrot strip "fangs" into the mouth to hold it open. Cut a piece of red pepper into a tongue shape and set it between the fangs. Add broccoli florets for eyes and radish slices for eyebrows. Use the remaining heel at the tip for a tail. Serves 8.

Salami Snake

Customized Egg Salad

This outstanding egg salad comes from *FamilyFun* contributor Vivi Mannuzza.

- 6 eggs, hard-boiled
- 2 tablespoons mayonnaise
-      Salt and pepper to taste
- 6 tablespoons of finely chopped add-ins, such as radishes, sweet pickles, scallions, red onions, peppers, celery, chives, parsley, cilantro, olives, capers, steamed asparagus, peas, fresh spinach, pulverized anchovies

Carefully peel chilled, hard-boiled eggs. Mash with the mayonnaise and mix in your choice of chopped add-ins just before serving. Serves 4.

Lunch Specials

Spreads

From top to bottom:
Real Peanut Butter;
Quick Boursin; and
Hummus

Hummus

This chickpea spread makes a wholesome vegetarian sandwich. On wheat bread, top a layer of hummus with grated carrot, bean sprouts, and cheese.

- 1   15-ounce can chickpeas, drained
- 1   to 2 crushed garlic cloves
- ¼   cup lemon juice
- ¼   cup tahini paste
- 2   tablespoons olive oil

Place all the ingredients, except the olive oil, in the bowl of a food processor or blender and puree. If necessary, add 1 to 2 tablespoons of water to make creamy. Pour the olive oil over the spread before refrigerating so the hummus does not dry out. Makes 1½ cups.

Baba Ghanouj

For a Mediterranean sandwich, cover a pita pocket with this smooth eggplant dish and add tomatoes, cucumbers, and olives.

- 1   large eggplant
- 1   crushed garlic clove
- 2   tablespoons tahini paste
- 2   tablespoons lemon juice
- ½   teaspoon salt
- 2   tablespoons olive oil

Preheat the oven to 350°. Remove the stem from the eggplant, poke the skin with a fork, and bake on a cookie sheet for 45 minutes, or until soft. Cool thoroughly. Scoop out the flesh and place it in a food processor or blender with the garlic clove, tahini, lemon juice, salt, and olive oil. Puree until smooth and refrigerate. Makes 1½ to 2 cups.

Real Peanut Butter

Nothing beats the all-natural taste of peanut butter when you make it at home with no preservatives or sugar.

- 2   cups unsalted roasted peanuts
- 1   tablespoon vegetable oil
    Salt to taste

Puree the shelled peanuts and vegetable oil in a food processor or blender until smooth, about 3 minutes. For chunky peanut butter, stir in ¼ cup chopped peanuts. Add salt to taste and store in the refrigerator. Makes 1 cup.

Real Cashew Butter:

Puree 2 cups unsalted, roasted, or plain cashews with 4 tablespoons of vegetable oil. Store in the refrigerator.

Real Almond Butter:

Puree 2 cups unsalted, blanched almonds with 2 tablespoons of vegetable oil; if necessary, add more oil. Store in the refrigerator.

Quick Boursin

This flavored cream cheese, mixed with fresh herbs, makes a wonderful sandwich spread.

- 1   4-ounce package cream cheese
- 2   tablespoons butter
- 2   tablespoons fresh chopped dill, basil, chives, or a combination
- 1   crushed garlic clove
    Salt and pepper to taste

Place the cream cheese and butter in a bowl or a food processor and let soften. Add the herbs and garlic and stir or puree until smooth. Season with salt and pepper. Makes ⅔ cup.

Grilled-Cheese
Sandwich: The
Next Generation

Grilled-Cheese Sandwich: The Next Generation

This sandwich from *FamilyFun* contributor Mollie Katzen is a far cry from the grilled cheese on buttered white of our youths. Open-faced and open to experimentation, this healthy lunch is a favorite in her household.

½   cup olive oil
1   small red onion, chopped
1   medium stalk broccoli, in small
      florets
   Salt to taste
   Dried thyme
8   slices sourdough, rye, or wheat
      bread
2   cups grated Cheddar cheese

Heat 2 tablespoons of the olive oil in a frying pan over medium heat and wait 30 seconds. Add the onions and cook for 2 minutes. Add the broccoli, sprinkle with salt and 2 pinches of thyme, and cook, stirring, for 8 to 10 minutes. Transfer the vegetables to a bowl and set aside.

Using a pastry brush, paint the bread slices lightly on both sides with the remaining olive oil (a good job for kids). Heat the pan on medium-low, add a few bread slices, and cook until golden brown. Flip the bread and reduce the heat to low. Place a small pile of broccoli florets and chopped onion on the center of each piece of bread. Sprinkle cheese over the vegetables and cover the pan until the cheese melts. Let the cheese cool a bit before serving. Serves 4.

Lunch Specials

Designosaur a Pizza

Young *FamilyFun* reader Jacob Sandmire of Sandy, Utah, gets such a kick out of helping his mom make dinosaur-shaped pizzas that he forgets the vegetables he's using for eyes and mouths are destined to be eaten. By the time the pizzas are done, the veggies are buried under melted cheese, and Jacob's raring to dig in. (Many grocers sell bread dough in the frozen food section, or you can make your own with the recipe on page 72.)

- 2 pounds bread dough
- 1 large dinosaur cookie cutter (available at kitchen supply and and craft stores)

Toppings:
- ½ cup pizza or spaghetti sauce
- ½ cup grated carrots
- ½ cup steamed broccoli florets
- 1½ to 2 cups grated mix of Colby and Monterey Jack cheeses
- ½ cup chopped ham or pepperoni
- ½ cup chopped green pepper
- ½ to 1 cup sliced black olives
- ½ cup chopped onions
- ½ cup sliced mushrooms
- ½ cup chopped tomatoes

Preheat the oven to 350°. Roll out, stretch, and press the dough ¼-inch thick, then cut it into dinosaurs. Line up the shapes on a lightly greased cookie sheet and let your kids spread on the sauce and toppings of their choice. Make eyes, mouths, and spikes down the backs with larger olive pieces. Bake for 15 to 20 minutes, or until the edges lightly brown. Makes 8 mini pizzas.

Croque Monsieur

For a welcome change to the everyday grilled cheese, try this classic French alternative.

- 2 slices wheat bread
- 2 teaspoons butter
- 2 slices American cheese
- 1 slice ham

Spread butter on one side of each piece of bread. In a frying pan over medium-low heat, place one piece of bread, butter side down, then layer with cheese, ham, then cheese. Top with the remaining slice of bread and grill until the cheese melts and the bread is lightly browned. Flip the sandwich over to brown the other side. Serves 1.

GRILLED CHEESE AND...

Jazz up your grilled cheese with the following:
- Sliced tomatoes
- Salsa
- Sliced onions
- Fresh dill or basil
- Sliced apple
- Sliced green pepper
- Grated carrot
- Finely diced cucumber
- Olives

Try some different cheeses for a whole new flavor:
- Mozzarella
- Brie
- Monterey Jack
- Muenster
- Swiss

Turkey Meatball Sub

For a low-fat alternative to the traditional meatball sub, try this turkey version. It will stand up to a slathering of tomato sauce, onions, peppers, and melted Mozzarella cheese.

Meatballs:
- 1 pound ground turkey
- 1 egg, beaten
- ¼ cup minced onion
- 1 teaspoon oregano
- 1 teaspoon basil
  Salt and pepper to taste
- 3 tablespoons bread crumbs

Subs:
- 3 to 4 sub rolls
- 1 small onion, sliced and sautéed (optional)
- 1 green pepper, sliced and sautéed (optional)
- 2 cups tomato sauce
- 1½ cups grated Mozzarella cheese (optional)

Preheat your oven to 350°. In a large bowl, break up the turkey meat. Blend the egg with the onions, oregano, basil, and salt and pepper and thoroughly mix into the turkey. Sprinkle with bread crumbs and mix. Roll the meat into 2-inch balls and bake on a jelly roll pan for about 25 minutes, turning occasionally until light brown and completely cooked. (Alternatively, you can pan-brown the 2-inch balls in a lightly oiled, large skillet, turning them until completely cooked. Drain on paper towels.)

To build a sub, set two to three meatballs into a roll and layer on the sautéed onion and green pepper. Spread with the tomato sauce and top with the grated Mozzarella. Warm in the oven until the cheese melts and then serve. Makes 3 to 4 subs.

Lunch Specials

Pizza Men

These two cheery designs are offered as a suggestion, not a blueprint — children tend to be inventive when creating faces! (See the recipe for Designosaur a Pizza, opposite, for other topping options that may inspire your kids.)

- 2 tablespoons tomato sauce
- 1 English muffin, split and toasted
- ⅓ to ¼ cup grated Mozzarella cheese
- 3 olives, cut in half
- 1 slice red pepper
- 1 slice green pepper

Spread tomato sauce on both English muffin halves. Sprinkle grated cheese all over one half. Add olive halves for eyes and a nose, and a red pepper slice for a mouth. On the other muffin half, use olive slices for eyes and a nose, a green pepper for a mouth, and the remaining cheese for hair. Broil in a toaster oven for 5 minutes. Makes 2 individual pizzas.

Pizza Men

How To Make Bread Crust Croutons

Don't toss those crusts — they make great croutons. Each day, place them into a sealable bag and store it in the refrigerator. At the end of the week, cube the collection of crusts, toss them with melted butter, and arrange them on a baking sheet. Sprinkle with herbs, such as oregano, parsley, and paprika. Bake in a 350° oven for 20 minutes, or until the crusts are lightly toasted. Serve over fresh green salad or as a soup garnish.

Quesadilla

This is my favorite weekend lunch or light dinner. Essentially Mexican grilled-cheese sandwiches, these treats have tons of kid appeal. Quesadillas can really heat up inside, so slice them into wedges before serving to your kids.

- 2   6-inch flour or corn tortillas
- 2   tablespoons grated cheese
      Salsa and/or sour cream
      (optional)

Place 1 tortilla on an ungreased skillet over medium heat. Sprinkle lightly with grated cheese and top with a second tortilla. Cook for about 2 minutes on each side, or until the cheese melts. Let cool for 2 minutes, then cut into wedges, pie style. Serve with salsa and sour cream. Serves 1.

Spinach Quesadilla:

Add 1 to 2 tablespoons of chopped spinach, cooked and drained, between 2 layers of cheese.

Black Bean Quesadilla:

Layer refried beans or your own black bean filling between cheese layers. To make your own bean filling, sauté 2 tablespoons of cooked black beans with 2 teaspoons onion and taco seasoning.

Beef Quesadilla:

Top your quesadilla with leftover taco-seasoned meat.

Chicken Quesadilla:

Sauté shreds of chicken with taco seasoning or chili powder for a nutritious filling.

Veggie Quesadilla:

Sauté shredded carrot and zucchini or summer squash and season with chili powder. Then add 1 tablespoon of the mixture along with the cheese filling.

Mexican Tuna Melt

This mayo-free tuna salad is made with the flavors of Mexico — lime juice, avocado, and fresh cilantro.

- 2   6-ounce cans white tuna in water
      Juice of 1 lime
- 1   tablespoon chopped fresh cilantro
- 1   tablespoon minced onion
- 1   avocado, chopped
- 1   plum tomato, chopped
      Minced jalapeño to taste
- 4   bagels, sliced
- 8   slices Monterey Jack cheese

Gently toss the tuna, lime juice, cilantro, onion, avocado, tomato, and jalapeño in a bowl. Spoon the salad on top of the bagel halves and top with a slice of cheese. Toast in a toaster oven until the cheese melts. Serves 4.

Bumpy Road

Cheese and pepperoni are delicious toppings for slices of crusty French bread. Once broiled, the cheese melts and the pepperoni pokes up so that the treat resembles a bumpy road. You can also use chopped vegetables or crumbled bacon.

- 2   6-inch pieces of French bread
     Grated cheese (a mix of Cheddar and Mozzarella is good)
- ¼   cup diced pepperoni or Genoa salami
- ⅛   cup black olives (optional)

Preheat the oven or toaster oven to 375°. Slice the bread in half lengthwise to form the "roads." Generously layer cheese and salami over the olives on the bread slices. Bake for 5 to 10 minutes, or until the cheese has melted. Cool for 2 minutes before serving. Makes 4.

Falafel Flying Saucers

For out-of-this-world taste, let your kids help make these vegetarian sandwiches. (Our testers particularly liked shaping the "flying saucers.") Falafel is sold premixed in boxes and in bulk.

Falafel:
- 1   cup falafel mix
- ⅔   to ¾ cup water
     Peanut oil

Dressing:
- ¾   cup plain yogurt
- ¼   cup tahini
- ½   lemon, juiced

Sandwich:
- 1   tomato, diced
- 1   cucumber, peeled and sliced
- 1   small red onion, diced (optional)
- 2   cups shredded lettuce
- 1   carrot, grated (optional)

Falafel Flying Saucers

- ½   cup alfalfa sprouts (optional)
- 2   to 3 8-inch pitas, sliced in half

Mix the falafel and water together and let sit for 15 minutes. In the meantime, prepare your choice of vegetables and make the dressing. For the dressing, combine the yogurt, tahini, and lemon juice (thin with water if necessary).

Heat ½ inch of the peanut oil in a frying pan. To shape the "flying saucers," roll 1½-inch balls of the falafel mix and flatten slightly. Fry in oil until lightly browned on each side, about 3 minutes. Drain on paper towels.

To assemble the sandwich, spread the dressing in half a pita, layer two to three falafel flying saucers with the vegetables, and top with more dressing. Serves 4 to 6.

Veggie Tic-Tac-Toe

Get your kids to munch down veggies with this edible tic-tac-toe. Use aspic cutters (tiny cookie cutters) to cut the vegetables into shapes.

Chinese Sesame Noodles

Chicken Nuggets

These nuggets may be packed for a school lunch as finger food, gathered on skewers, or stuffed in a pita pocket.

1   whole skinless, boneless chicken
    breast, cut into 1-inch cubes
2   teaspoons paprika
1   teaspoon salt
½   cup all-purpose flour
¼   cup sesame seeds
    Black pepper to taste
    Garlic salt or granules to taste
    (optional)
1   cup vegetable oil

Shake the chicken cubes (you can also use skinned drumsticks) in a sealable plastic bag with the seasonings. Heat the vegetable oil in a pan and fry the nuggets until golden brown. Drain well on paper towels to remove excess oil. These nuggets can be stored in the refrigerator and reheated in a microwave on paper towels. You can also send these off to school with a bit of Honey Mustard Dip or soy sauce for dipping. Wrap them in foil before packing in a lunch box. Serves 4.

Honey Mustard Dip:

In a small bowl, mix ¼ cup Dijon mustard, 1 tablespoon honey, and 1 tablespoon water with a fork until smooth. Serve with the Chicken Nuggets for dipping.

Oodles of Noodles

When you're serving spaghetti for dinner, cook extras. The noodles, spirals, and bow ties, with or without the sauce, make great leftovers for lunch. Add the following to plain pasta:
☞ **Parmesan cheese and butter**
☞ **Olive oil, basil, and diced tomato**
☞ **Raw vegetables and salad dressing**
☞ **Cubed roast chicken, salad dressing, and peppers**

Chinese Sesame Noodles

This dish may sound exotic, but it pleases peanut-lovers. (You can substitute Italian spaghetti for the noodles.)

¼   cup creamy peanut butter or
    sesame paste
½   cup hot water
⅓   cup soy sauce
2   teaspoons honey
1   crushed garlic clove
1   tablespoon chopped fresh ginger
1   pound cooked Chinese noodles
4   scallions, cut in ½-inch pieces
    Mung bean sprouts
    Chopped peanuts

In a large bowl, mix the peanut butter or sesame paste with hot water until creamy. Whisk in the soy sauce, honey, garlic, and ginger. Add the noodles. Top with scallions, sprouts, and peanuts. Serve warm or cold. Serves 6 to 8.

Miniature Quiches

With bits of red pepper and kernels of corn peeking through the custard, these child-size variations of the French dish make an attractive addition to a lunch buffet. Preparing the quiche pastry for the muffin tins takes a little extra time, but it's a fun way for young chefs to practice rolling, cutting, and shaping pie crusts. If you're in a rush, use store-bought pastry dough.

Pastry:

- 1½ cups all-purpose flour
- 1 teaspoon sugar
- ¼ teaspoon salt
- ½ cup cold butter
- 4 to 5 tablespoons ice-cold water

Filling:

- 2 teaspoons butter
- ½ small onion, minced
- ½ small sweet red pepper, minced
- ½ cup frozen corn
- ½ cup milk
- 1 egg
- ⅓ cup grated Cheddar cheese
  Salt and pepper to taste
  Paprika

To make the pastry, mix the dry ingredients in a medium bowl. Using a pastry cutter (or a fork and knife), cut the butter into the dry ingredients until the mixture resembles a coarse meal. Add the water, tablespoon by tablespoon, mixing well, until the dough holds together. Gently knead the dough, then gather it into a ball. Cover it in plastic wrap and chill for about 30 minutes.

While the dough chills, sauté the onion in the butter over medium heat for 5 minutes, or until translucent. Add the red pepper and corn and sauté for an additional 5 minutes, or until both the pepper and the corn are tender. Remove from the heat and set aside to cool. Meanwhile, in a medium bowl,

Miniature Quiches

whisk together the milk and egg, add the cheese, and salt and pepper to taste. Stir the red pepper and corn mixture into the milk and egg mixture until evenly combined.

Preheat the oven to 350°. To assemble the quiche, roll out the dough on a lightly floured surface to a ⅛-inch thickness. Using a widemouthed cup or glass (at least 4 inches in diameter), cut the dough into 12 circles. Place the circles into a 12-cup muffin tin, shaping the pastry to fit the mold and crimping the edges as you go. For crisper shells, prick the pie dough with a fork and prebake for about 5 to 10 minutes. (If the dough falls, gently press the sides back up.) Let them cool, then pour the quiche mixture almost to the top of each muffin cup. Place the tin on the middle rack of the oven. Bake for 20 to 25 minutes, or until the custard has puffed up and a toothpick inserted in the middle comes out clean. To remove them from the pan, run a sharp knife around the edge of each quiche. Sprinkle with paprika before serving. Makes 12.

Leftover Lunches

- ☞ Pizza slices
- ☞ Sliced London broil on toast
- ☞ Roast chicken: Toss cubed chicken with salad dressing and refrigerate in a plastic container. Pack along with a bag of greens for a quick chicken salad.
- ☞ Burritos: Make extra for dinner and seal in plastic wrap. Reheat in the microwave for lunch.

Lunch Specials

CHAPTER 4

After-School Snacks

WHEN WE PUT the word out in a recent issue of *FamilyFun* that we were looking to snack, recipes from our readers' kids poured in from across the country. We tested them all in our North- ampton, Massachusetts, hometown and invited a panel of kids to give the recipes a yea or nay. To our surprise, it wasn't only the sweet stuff that scored the highest marks; it was the innovative, the silly, and the fun.

Because kids are the experts on snack- ing, we have taken our cue from them when selecting and developing recipes for this chapter. These suggestions should help your family bridge the snack gap — finding something between the parent- approved carrot stick and the child- approved marshmallow surprise. Con- sider, too, some of the following rules:

Invention makes everything taste better. Even those dreaded good-for-you foods are a hit when cleverly disguised. Encourage your kids to arrange fresh fruits and vegetables in creative ways. They can create funny fruit faces, cars with wheels, and veggie landscapes.

Snacks should not take longer to make than to eat. Those that do may taste sublime, but practical- ly speaking, they are just too labor- intensive to become a standard in your family's repertoire. The exceptions to this rule are cookies, granola bars, and other baked goods that can be made ahead in batches and stored.

Don't eat snacks with a fork. It's a proven fact that anything eaten with fin- gers tastes better.

Edible collage: *Page 58*

Snacks in Seconds

☞ **A bowl of cereal**

☞ **Orange wedges, blueberries, melon balls, frozen grapes, or other bite-size fruits**

☞ **Mini veggies, such as baby carrots, short celery sticks, broccoli florets, or cherry tomatoes**

☞ **Dried fruits – figs, apricots, apples, and raisins (let your kids pick favorites from the dry bins at the grocery store)**

☞ **Low-fat cookies and skim milk**

☞ **Cheese cut into fun shapes (use cookie cutters) on whole grain crackers**

☞ **Yogurt with smoosh-ins – granola, fruit, raisins, and carob chips**

If you think your kids are snacking nonstop, don't worry, be happy. Because kids get a good percentage of their daily calories from snacks, these mini meals are an important part of their diet. When planning snacks, keep this in mind, trying not to serve too many sweets. (A few sugary items are okay, as long as they are figured into the overall intake for the day.) And if all they want is the sweet stuff, be sure they skip dessert after dinner and brush their teeth after snacking.

Designate a space for parentally approved snacks. Keep a drawer in the refrigerator, a canister on the counter, or a space in the freezer filled with snacks for your kids. (See Snacks in Seconds, at left, for ideas.) Whatever you provide should be something that you don't mind the kids having at any time of day without first asking you for permission. It's one of life's great simplifiers.

Turn the kids into snack chefs. Children who become creatively involved with food are less likely to engage in junk-food frenzies, and the best time for them to cook is after school or on a weekend afternoon, before the rush for dinner begins. Together, flip through the chapter for recipe ideas and do the grocery shopping as a team. You can then be cooking coach, overseeing the chef. (The no-bake recipes, such as Peanut Butter Balls and Spider Pretzels on page 49, are the fastest and safest.) The benefits teaching kids to cook are tremendous — kids learn a sense of responsibility, are introduced to basic cooking skills, and feel a great deal of pride when they have something to show, and eat, for their efforts.

Cucumber Dipping Sauce: *Page 52*

Healthy Snacks

Apple Rings

As a child, I painstakingly hung apples to dry by the fireplace until they turned leathery (a trick I learned at Old Sturbridge Village in Massachusetts). Drying apples naturally concentrates their sweetness and nutrition, which made them a hit for the Colonists and for me.

> 4 apples (McIntosh and Golden Delicious work well)
> 1 tablespoon lemon juice
> 3 tablespoons water
> Sturdy thread or twine

Peel, core, and slice the apples into rings about ⅛ inch thick. Mix the lemon juice and water in a shallow dish. To prevent discoloring, dip each ring into the mixture, then pat dry with a paper towel.

String the fruit through the center of each ring and hang in a dry, warm place (near a fireplace or sunny window is ideal). The rings will take 1 to 2 weeks to dry, depending on the room conditions. Kids can periodically taste them to determine if they are ready (dry rings will have a chewy, almost leathery texture).

To expedite the process, dry the apples in a warm oven. Instead of stringing the rings, place them on a wire cooling rack that rests on a baking tray (so the air can circulate). Put the tray in a 150° oven and allow the rings to dry for about 4 hours, turning once midway through. When the rings have no moisture left, remove them from the oven and eat, or cool before placing them in small bags for storing. Makes about 30 rings.

Apple Rings

Juicy Fruit Salad

Call this a soup or call it a salad, the Field sisters (Shanden, twelve, and Lauren, ten), of Petaluma, California, can't get enough of this clever fruit combo. They won 10th place in *FamilyFun*'s Snack-off contest.

> 1 cup shredded apples
> ½ cup diced strawberries
> ⅓ cup diced peaches
> ¼ cup chopped grapes
> ¾ cup orange juice
> 1 tablespoon lemon juice
> Juice of half a grapefruit

Stir the shredded apples, strawberries, peaches, and chopped grapes in a medium-size bowl. Pour the orange, lemon, and grapefruit juice over the fruit and stir well. Serves 3 to 4.

Snacking Apples

- McIntosh
- Empire
- Golden Delicious
- Cortland
- Winesap
- Jonathan

APPLE RINGS

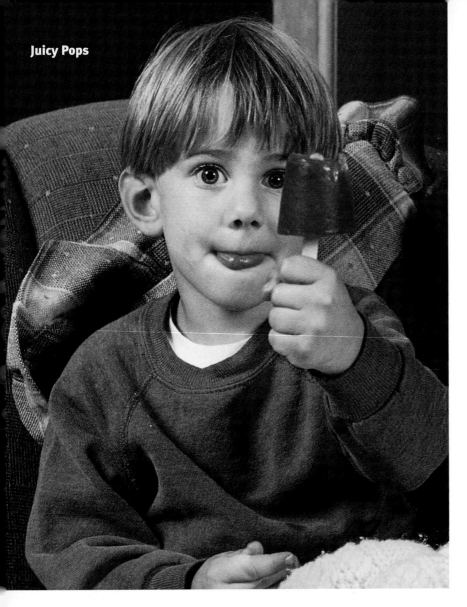

Juicy Pops

For this frozen treat with a surprise in the middle, choose a juice and fruit combination that you know will be a hit — orange juice with pineapple chunks or cranberry-apple juice with whole strawberries.

12   fruit pieces
36   ounces fruit juice

Press one piece of fruit onto the top of a Popsicle stick and place the stick, fruit side down, in a 3-ounce paper or plastic cup. Fill the cup with juice and cover with tinfoil, making sure to push the free end of the stick through the center of the foil (this will help the stick freeze upright). Freeze the pops for about 4 hours, or until solid. To serve, gently squeeze the sides of the plastic cup until the pop is loosened or peel away the paper cup. Makes 12.

Fast Fruit Freezes

In the steamy heat of summer, cool off with these healthy treats. Make them out of whatever fruit you have on hand — strawberries, pineapple, melon, bananas, or plums. To assemble, slide a Popsicle stick or toothpick into a piece of fruit. Cover with a sandwich bag or plastic wrap and freeze for at least 4 hours.

MINI FRUIT POPSICLES

When a bite is just enough, fill an ice tray with juice, cover with tinfoil, and stick a toothpick through the foil into the center of each cube. Freeze for about 3 hours, or until solid.

Smoothie Pops

FamilyFun reader Mallory Wright, age eleven, of San Luis Obispo, California, likes to make homemade vanilla ice cream, but smoothies on sticks are her real claim to fame.

5   strawberries, washed and hulled
1   medium banana
4   ice cubes, crushed
1   cup strawberry yogurt
½   cup milk
½   cup fruit juice

Mix all the ingredients in a blender until smooth. Pour into 3-ounce paper cups, cover with plastic wrap, and insert Popsicle sticks upright through the plastic. Freeze for 5 hours. Makes 9.

Peanut Butter Balls

Rolling up these no-cook treats gives kids a legitimate excuse for playing with their food. For a deluxe version, toss the finished balls in shredded coconut, carob chips, or chopped peanuts and call them "meteorites."

1¼ cups confectioners' sugar
1 cup creamy or chunky peanut butter
1 cup powdered milk
1 cup honey

In a medium-size bowl, combine all the ingredients. Roll the dough into 1-inch balls and set on waxed paper. Refrigerate until firm. Makes 30 to 36 balls.

Sawyer's Celery Logs

Fill celery with a crunchy mix and you'll be snacking healthy all afternoon. Sawyer Paull-Baird is a four-year-old smart eater from Milan, Michigan.

2 stalks celery
6 tablespoons cream cheese
¼ cup granola
Raisins (optional)

Wash and dry the celery. Cut each stalk into three even lengths. Spread 1 tablespoon of cream cheese on each of the celery pieces and top with granola (press it down). Add raisins, if desired. Makes 6 pieces.

Spider Pretzel

It's easy to make this arachnid treat, and it looks positively lifelike crawling on the table.

For each:
2 round crackers
2 teaspoons creamy peanut butter
8 small pretzel sticks
2 raisins

Make a cracker sandwich with the peanut butter. Insert the pretzel "legs" into the filling. With a dab of peanut butter, set raisin eyes on top. Makes 1.

Rice Cakes and...

☞ **Real Peanut, Almond, or Cashew Butter (see page 36) and jam**
☞ **Honey and sliced apple, pear, or peach**
☞ **Cream cheese and jelly**
☞ **Hummus (see page 36) and cucumber slices**
☞ **Cream cheese and tomato slices**
☞ **Peanut butter and honey**
☞ **Turkey slices and honey mustard**

FunFact **It takes about 540 peanuts to make a 12-ounce jar of peanut butter.**

Quick Peanut Butter Snacks

Spread peanut butter in the center of a piece of celery and top it with several raisins to create Ants on a Log.

Stir peanut butter with a little honey to make a healthy dip for carrot or celery sticks, apple slices, and whole grain crackers.

Sandwich peanut butter between graham crackers or other crackers (this makes a nice surprise in your kids' lunch boxes).

Crunchy Snacks

Tortilla Chips

Homemade Tortilla Chips

FamilyFun contributor Cynthia Caldwell's baked tortilla chips have been the hit of many family parties. Her advice: Don't toss leftover flour tortillas; turn them into chips.

- 2 8-inch flour tortillas
- 2 tablespoons olive oil
   Coarse salt

Preheat your broiler. Cut each tortilla into 8 wedges and lightly brush both sides with the oil. Arrange them on a jelly roll pan. Broil, flipping once when they begin to brown. When brown on both sides, remove and lightly sprinkle with salt. Serves 1.

Parmesan Chips:

Instead of salt, sprinkle with 1 to 2 teaspoons grated Parmesan cheese.

Garlic Chips:

Crush 1 clove of garlic and add to oil before brushing on tortillas.

Herb Tortillas:

Add 1 tablespoon chopped fresh herbs (parsley, cilantro, basil, or dill) to the oil, then brush on the tortillas.

TORTILLA TIP

To recrisp store-bought chips, microwave on high for 10 to 40 seconds.

Crunchy Teaser

Here's a Chinese stick puzzle you can solve and eat. Instead of using the traditional wooden sticks, try carrot sticks. Arrange eighteen into nine triangles as shown. The challenge: remove three sticks to change the pattern into six triangles. Like any good brainteaser, this puzzler has several solutions. How many can your family find?

Nuke-able Nachos

The following makes enough for two to four kids, depending on their size and appetite. They will undoubtedly stretch and snap the gooey cheeses.

- 2 cups nacho chips
- 1 cup grated cheese (Monterey Jack, Cheddar, and/or Muenster)
- ½ cup diced tomatoes
   Leftover hamburger, refried beans, onions, jalapeño peppers, and olives (optional)
   Mild salsa and/or plain yogurt to taste

Place chips on a dinner plate. Sprinkle with the cheese, tomatoes, and the optional items if desired. Microwave on high for 1½ minutes. Serve with salsa and yogurt for dipping. Serves 2 to 3.

Potato Chip Nachos:

Substitute potato chips for tortilla chips.

Hit-the-Trail Mixes

Whether you call it gorp, birdseed, or trail munchies, it's all the same — high-energy food that can be eaten on the run. Let your child fill a sealable plastic bag with a handful of his or her favorite dried fruits and nuts (buy them in bulk at a health food store). You'll need ½ cup of mix per child.

Gorp:

An acronym for "good old raisins and peanuts," gorp is a camping trip essential. Mix peanuts, raisins, and M&M's.

Rain Forest Munch:

The fruits of the rain forest give this combination its name. Mix dried pineapple, dried papaya, unsweetened coconut flakes, macadamia nuts, cashews, and chocolate chips.

Birdseed:

Here's a bird food for humans: combine hulled sunflower seeds, raisins, peanuts, and dried dates (the pellet-shaped ones, rolled in dried milk).

Morning Sunburst:

Mix up an all-fruit mix with dried apples, pineapples, cranberries, and cherries, as well as banana chips and raisins (eating 1 cup of this will fulfill two out of the five daily minimum servings of fruits and vegetables).

FunFact
A large sunflower, with a 2-foot-wide bloom, can produce up to 2,000 sunflower seeds.

Curveball Crunch

Half the fun of going to the ballpark is snacking on popcorn and peanuts, but it can get expensive. Here's an irresistible stadium treat to make at home.

- 8 cups popped popcorn
- 3 cups mini pretzels
- 1 cup roasted peanuts
- 2 tablespoons margarine or butter
- ½ cup brown sugar
- 1 tablespoon maple syrup

Measure the popcorn, pretzels, and peanuts into a large mixing bowl. Meanwhile, make a toffee syrup by melting the margarine or butter in a saucepan over low heat. Use a wooden spoon to stir in the brown sugar and continue stirring until the mixture bubbles. Remove from the heat and stir in the maple syrup. (The toffee should be smooth.)

Next, drizzle the toffee onto the dry mixture, tossing to distribute the glaze evenly. Once cool, immediately wrap portions in plastic. Makes 12 cups.

Trail Mix Extras

Variety is the key to a good trail mix; it enables kids to explore new tastes.

- ☛ **Banana chips**
- ☛ **Dried apricots or apples**
- ☛ **Corn nuts**
- ☛ **Mini pretzels**
- ☛ **Cereal**
- ☛ **Pumpkin, sunflower, or sesame seeds**
- ☛ **Walnuts**
- ☛ **Butterscotch or carob chips**

Curveball Crunch

Big Dips

Peanut Butter Dip

Great Dippers

- Bread sticks
- Raw veggies
- Leftover chicken and steak
- Grilled vegetables
- Cheese cubes
- Apple slices
- Bagel chips
- Crackers
- Pretzels or potato chips
- Tortilla chips
- Pita bread, toasted

Peanut Butter Dip

Tricia Vega of Port Chester, New York, says her children, Torrai and Briana, love this dip — a variation on an Asian recipe — with everything from grilled meats to raw vegetables or as a sauce on rice and noodles.

½ cup chicken broth
½ cup milk
4 tablespoons peanut butter
3 tablespoons grated green pepper
1 teaspoon soy sauce
1 crushed garlic clove
½ teaspoon sugar
  Salt and pepper to taste
2 tablespoons chopped scallions
  (optional)

In a heavy saucepan, mix all the ingredients except the scallions and cook over low heat until the sauce thickens. Stir often for about 15 minutes. Sprinkle with scallions and serve hot surrounded by your choice of dippers. Makes 1 cup.

Cheese-Lover's Dip

Many finicky eaters live by the philosophy, "If I can dip it, I'll try it." This dip is fun to serve in a bowl shaped from a hollowed-out loaf of pumpernickel bread.

2 8-ounce packages cream
    cheese, softened
2 tablespoons mayonnaise
1 tablespoon heavy cream
1 tablespoon grated onion
1 teaspoon Worcestershire sauce

Beat all the ingredients together until smooth and chill until ready to serve. Present with carrot and celery sticks, broccoli florets, or bagel chips. Makes 2 cups.

Cucumber Dipping Sauce

This healthy dip has a robust flavor that all of our adult taste-testers (and some of the kids) raved about. You can skip the garlic for a subtler flavor.

1 medium cucumber, peeled, halved
    lengthwise, seeded, and cut into
    1-inch pieces
¼ cup chopped fresh parsley
1 medium scallion, thinly sliced
¼ cup plain yogurt or cottage
    cheese
2 tablespoons fresh lemon juice
1 tablespoon cider vinegar or white
    wine
1 crushed garlic clove
    Pepper to taste

Process all the ingredients in a blender or food processor until creamy and smooth. Store in the refrigerator for at least 10 minutes before serving. This dip is delicious when served with crackers. Makes ¾ cup.

Nachos with Salsa Fresca

Chunky Guacamole

Your kids can use a table knife to dice the avocado — the remaining ingredients just need to be measured and stirred.

> 3 ripe avocados, peeled and diced, one pit reserved
> 2 tablespoons fresh lime juice
> 1 cup Salsa Fresca

Sprinkle the chopped avocado with lime juice, stir in the salsa, and place the mixture in a bowl lined with lettuce leaves. If you don't plan to serve it immediately, place an avocado pit in the bowl to prevent browning and cover it tightly with plastic wrap. Store in the refrigerator. Makes 4 cups.

Salsa Fresca

Otherwise known as *pico de gallo* (beak of the rooster), this bright red salsa can be used as a dip as well as a topping. The key ingredient is fresh cilantro (aka coriander) — a flavor that makes any dish taste Mexican.

> 2 garlic cloves
> 4 jalapeño peppers, sliced in half, seeded, and veined
> 1 medium onion, quartered or 1 bunch of scallions, chopped
> ¼ cup cilantro leaves
> 2 large tomatoes or 6 small ones, cored and quartered

Chop the ingredients in the order listed above. Drop each ingredient into a food processor with the blades running, turning the machine off between additions (avoid liquefying the tomatoes). If you plan to store the sauce in the refrigerator, place it in a jar and pour a tablespoon of vegetable oil over the top. Makes 3 cups.

exican Hot ocolate

xicans make their hot colate with tablets that flavored with cinnamon orange rind. For this que flavor, combine up water and 2 ounces hsweet chocolate in a cepan. Cook over medi- heat, stirring, until lted. Bring to a boil for inutes, then stir in ps milk, and simmer for 7 minutes. Add a dash innamon and grated nge rind. Serves 4.

Chile Con Queso

This famous chip dip will whet your family's appetites for a Tex-Mex dinner. You can make it with bottled salsa or homemade Salsa Fresca.

> ¾ pound Monterey Jack or mild Cheddar cheese, cubed
> 1 cup salsa

In a 1-quart microwave-safe bowl, mix the cheese cubes and salsa. Cover and cook on medium for 5 minutes, or until the cheese melts (halfway through the cooking time, stir the mixture). Serve the dip in the bowl with a basket of tortilla chips. You can also offer sliced raw vegetables, such as red and green peppers or broccoli spears, for dipping. Makes 2¼ cups.

Sweet Snacks

Choc-o-bananas

Choc-o-bananas

With no stove-top cooking or chopping required, this frozen banana recipe is truly for children. The chocolate hardens quickly, so work fast.

- 3 bananas
- 6 Popsicle sticks
- 3 1.5-ounce chocolate bars
- 1 tablespoon nut topping, crispy rice cereal, granola, or shredded coconut (optional)

Peel the bananas and remove any stringy fibers. Cut them in half, widthwise, and push a Popsicle stick through the cut end of each half. Cover them in plastic wrap and freeze for about 3 hours.

Place the chocolate bars in a microwave-proof bowl and cook on high for about 2 minutes, or until the chocolate melts (check after 1 minute). Stir in the nuts, cereal, or coconut. Using a butter knife, spread the chocolate mixture over the frozen bananas to coat them completely. Kids can roll them in more topping, but this is messy! Rest the pops on a plate covered with waxed paper and freeze until ready to serve. These keep in the freezer for 1 to 2 weeks. Makes 6.

Delectable Dominoes

Kids won't bother adding up the dots on these edible game pieces before popping them down the hatch. Spread graham crackers with a thin layer of cream cheese or peanut butter, then arrange chocolate, butterscotch, and white chocolate chip dots in domino patterns.

Chocolate Quicksand

There is really no need to measure the chocolate for this — just squirt to taste.

- 1 banana, peeled
- 1 cup vanilla or chocolate ice cream or frozen yogurt
- ½ cup milk
- ¼ cup chocolate syrup

In the morning, slice the banana, place it in a plastic lunch bag, and freeze. After school, place all the ingredients in a blender and process until smooth. Makes 1½ cups.

Chocolate Peanut Butter Cups

Chocolate Peanut Butter Cups

A homemade version of one of the most popular treats of all time (you know which one we mean). The calorie count is high, so eat this one in moderation.

- 1 tablespoon chocolate chips
- 1 heaping tablespoon peanut butter (creamy or chunky)

Place half the chips in a double paper muffin cup and microwave on high for 1 minute. Stir, then repeat for 30 seconds, or until chips are completely melted. Place the cups in the freezer for 5 minutes. Spoon the peanut butter on top of the chocolate, then sprinkle with remaining chips. Microwave on high for another minute. Stir and swirl with a butter knife. Microwave for 30 seconds more, or until chips are completely melted. Freeze for 5 minutes; remove and eat. Makes 1 muffin cup so rich it can be shared.

Chocolate Peanut Butter Pizza

Nine-year-old Sherri Maunsell of Brandon, Manitoba, Canada, spends her summers cranking out chocolate candies. Here's one from the chocolate connoisseur that took first place in the *FamilyFun* Snack-off.

- 1 6-ounce package chocolate chips
- 1 6-ounce package peanut butter chips
- 2 ounces white baking chocolate
  Candies for decoration

Microwave the chips in a microwave-safe dish on high for 1 minute, stir, and microwave for 1 more minute. Grease a 12-inch pizza pan and spread on the melted chips with a spatula. Microwave the white chocolate for 1 to 2 minutes, or until melted, and drizzle over the pizza to look like cheese. Decorate with candy and refrigerate for 20 minutes. Cut into 12 wedges. Serves 12.

Almost S'mores

Lose the marshmallow, says Alexa Scally. Her minimalist creation introduces a nouveau classic that's a big hit at her preschool in Macomb, Michigan.

Graham crackers
Chocolate frosting

Break each cracker into four sections and spread frosting on two. Place the other two crackers on top to make sandwiches. Soften overnight in an airtight container, if desired. Make as many as you like.

Peanut Butter Clay

With this edible play dough, you can invite your kids to play with their food. Stir 1 cup creamy peanut butter, 1½ cups instant powdered milk, and 3 tablespoons honey in a medium-size bowl until the dough is smooth (if it's dry, add more honey; if it's too moist, add more powdered milk). Kids can form it into critters of their choice, from snakes to monsters, then decorate their artwork with peanuts, raisins, chocolate chips, and coconut. Store the unused dough in the refrigerator. Makes about 10 creatures, depending on their sizes.

Chilly Yogurt Sandwiches

For a quick frozen treat, put a scoop of frozen yogurt between two graham crackers, wrap in plastic, and freeze.

Chocolate Chip Ice-Cream Sandwiches

FamilyFun contributor Barbara Albright (former editor of *Chocolatier*) keeps a stash of these frozen delights in her freezer for a cool way to satisfy a chocolate attack. The small amount of corn syrup and vegetable oil in the dough prevents the cookies from becoming rock hard.

2⅓ cups all-purpose flour
1 teaspoon baking powder
½ teaspoon salt
1 cup unsalted butter, softened
⅔ cup firmly packed brown sugar
½ cup sugar
1 tablespoon vegetable oil
1 tablespoon light corn syrup
1 large egg
2 teaspoons vanilla extract
1 package (10 to 12 ounces) chocolate chips or M&M's
¾ cup chopped walnuts or pecans (optional)
5 to 7 cups vanilla ice cream

Preheat the oven to 325° and adjust the shelves to the upper third of your oven. Lightly butter large baking sheets. In a large bowl, stir the flour, baking powder, and salt. In a separate bowl, combine the butter, sugars, oil, and corn syrup. Mix in the egg and vanilla extract until blended, then gradually add the flour mixture. Stir in the chocolate chips and nuts, if desired.

Pat 2 tablespoons of dough into flat circles on the prepared baking sheets, leaving 2 inches between them. Bake for 14 to 16 minutes, or until lightly browned. Remove the sheets to wire racks and cool for about 5 minutes. Using a metal spatula, transfer the cookies to racks and cool completely. Repeat until all the dough is used.

Let the ice cream soften in the refrigerator for 30 minutes. Spread ½ cup of ice cream on the bottom of one cookie. Place a second cookie on top. Wrap each sandwich in plastic wrap or foil and freeze for 2 hours, or until firm. If the sandwiches are too hard, stand at room temperature before serving. Makes 16 to 20.

An Edible Fishbowl

Dig up that old fishbowl and give it a good scrub. Then try this "sea" food that Sandy Drummond and Betsy Rhein of Holland, Michigan, adapted from a creative Jell-O advertisement.

6 3-ounce packages of blueberry gelatin dessert
1 cup blueberries or grapes
   Gummy fish

Prepare the blueberry gelatin in a large mixing bowl according to package directions and refrigerate until partially set (for an aquarium with more waves, let the gelatin thoroughly set). Make a rocky ocean floor by pouring the blueberries or grapes into the fishbowl. Spoon the blue "water" over the fruit, arranging the gummy fish into the gelatin. Chill thoroughly. Let the kids fish for the snack with a ladle and be sure to restock the aquarium with extra candies. Makes 12 cups.

An Edible Fishbowl

Fluttery Creations

Young butterfly fans will flutter at the sight of sweet, gelatin butterflies. The idea came from *FamilyFun* contributor Jean Mitchel, who made them for her daughter's butterfly-themed birthday party.

2 3-ounce packages of cherry, blueberry, or lemon gelatin dessert
1 cup boiling water
   Twisted licorice
   Shoestring licorice
   Candy dots

In a medium-size bowl, dissolve the gelatin dessert with the boiling water. Pour the mixture into an 8-inch square pan and refrigerate for at least 3 hours. Using a 2½-inch butterfly cookie cutter (available at kitchen supply stores), carefully cut out the gelatin. Alternatively, cut a butterfly stencil out of waxed paper, place it on the gelatin, and cut around it with a sharp knife. If the butterflies are difficult to remove, dip the bottom of the pan in warm water for a few seconds.

Arrange a short length of twisted licorice in the center of the wings. For antennae, insert shoestring licorice into the heads. For added color, remove several candy dots from their paper and press them into the wings. Makes 9 butterflies.

Fluttery Creations

No-Hands Jell-O Eating Contest

Every player is a winner in this birthday party or backyard carnival contest. Prepare several packages of flavored gelatin as directed. Then the judge should put 1 cup per contestant in a bowl and instruct each player to sit on his hands. When the kids hear "Go," they race to clean their bowls. The first clean plate wins, and the winner gets a full tummy.

Ice-Cream Flowerpots

Crackling Peanut Butter Balls

Our kid testers loved this messier, higher protein version of the Rice Krispies Treats classic.

¼ cup margarine
1 10-ounce package marshmallows
⅓ cup creamy peanut butter
6 cups crispy rice cereal

Melt margarine in a large saucepan over low heat. Add marshmallows and stir quickly until they are all melted (mini marshmallows melt faster). Turn off the burner and stir in peanut butter until mixed. Add the cereal and stir until coated. Butter your hands and roll the mixture into tennis ball shapes. Dry on waxed paper for 5 minutes before eating (store leftovers in plastic wrap). Makes 24 to 36 balls.

EDIBLE COLLAGES

Skip the paper and glue and let your kids use graham crackers and honey to create artwork they can eat. Fill a variety of small paper cups with goodies, such as raisins, chocolate or carob chips, carrot curls, gumdrops, gummy dinosaurs, or colored cereal. Spread a thin layer of honey (this is the glue for the collage) over the surface of a graham cracker. Using items from the cups, your kids can make any design in the honey — a rainbow, a funny face, a Matisse-like collage. When the collages are complete, the kids can dig in or save them for dessert.

Ice-Cream Flowerpots

With an ice-cream treat that looks like a flowerpot, you can invite your kids to go ahead and eat the daisies.

2 tablespoons chocolate cookie crumbs
1 scoop chocolate ice cream
Green sprinkles
Gumdrops
Cookies or peanut butter cups
Candy spearmint leaf

To make the "dirt," place 1 tablespoon of the chocolate crumbs into the bottom of a clear plastic cup. Add a scoop of softened chocolate ice cream, followed by a second layer of cookie crumbs. For grass, sow green sprinkles on the top. Place a straw (cut to a 6-inch length) into the center of the flowerpot and freeze. Meanwhile, make a flower by sticking gumdrops and cookies or peanut butter cups together with toothpicks. To serve, press the flower into the straw. Add a candy spearmint leaf. Makes 1 pot.

How To Make Ice Cream out of Snow

If you're lucky enough to be snowed in, scoop up a bowl of fresh snow and make a batch of ice cream. Place 1 pint whipping cream in a blender with ½ cup of sugar and your choice of flavoring: 1 teaspoon vanilla extract, ¼ cup chocolate syrup, 1 sliced banana, ¼ cup berries, or a few tablespoons of peanut butter. Blend on high for 3 minutes, or until the cream thickens. Meanwhile, fill a large mixing bowl with very clean snow. Pour the cream mixture over the snow, fold in crushed cookies, candies, or chocolate chips. Eat fast: it tastes best fresh. Serves 4 to 6.

After School Apple Cake

After-School Apple Cake

This moist, all-natural dessert was my mother's standby, and my siblings and I couldn't get enough of it.

- 6 apples (Cortland, Braeburn, and Empire work well)
- 2 teaspoons cinnamon
- ¾ cup vegetable oil
- 4 eggs
- 1¼ cups sugar
- 1 tablespoon baking powder
- 1 cup all-purpose flour
- 1 cup whole wheat flour

Preheat the oven to 350°. Grease and flour a 13- by 9- by 2-inch baking pan. Peel, core, and slice the apples, set them in a large bowl, and sprinkle with the cinnamon. In the bowl of an electric mixer, blend the oil, eggs, and sugar. Add the baking powder, flour, and wheat flour and blend until combined. Pour the batter over the apples, gently stirring until the apples are just coated. Pour this mix into the prepared baking pan, arranging the apples in an even layer, and bake for 35 to 45 minutes, or until a knife inserted in the center comes out clean. When the cake is cool, cut it into small squares. Makes 16 to 18 pieces.

After-School Snacks

Apple Skins a la Mode

If you polled a dozen adults on their favorite childhood dessert, eight would say apple crisp. The drawback was waiting an hour for it to come out of the oven. This version can be made in minutes in the microwave.

- 1 apple
- 1 tablespoon margarine or butter
  Cinnamon Sugar
  Granola and/or wheat germ
- 1 scoop frozen yogurt or ice cream

Quarter an apple, scoop out the seeds, and place skin side down in a microwave-safe bowl. Place a pat of butter on each quarter. Sprinkle with Cinnamon Sugar and granola or wheat germ. Microwave on high for 1 minute, or until the apple is soft. Top with ice cream or yogurt. Makes 1 large serving.

HOT WHITE COCOA

Not everyone is a chocolate-lover, so here's to vanilla fans. In a medium-size saucepan, heat 2 ounces of white baking squares and 1 cup of water over medium heat, stirring constantly. When melted, bring to a boil, then simmer for 3 minutes. Add 3 cups of milk and heat until warm. Remove from the heat and beat with a whisk until frothy. Ladle into mugs and garnish with white chocolate shavings or a peppermint stick. Serves 6.

Apple Skins a la Mode

CHAPTER 5

Breads We Love

FOR A WHILE NOW, I have been on a bread crusade. It seems like everyone I know thinks baking bread is too time-consuming, something that you just don't do anymore. Why make it when you can buy a loaf at the bakery down the block? Now, don't get me wrong. I'm also too busy to bake bread every week. But I am determined to let people know how easy and rewarding it is to make a loaf of bread from scratch every once in a while.

It used to be that everyone knew how to bake yeast bread. Mixing the flour, kneading the dough, and letting it rise were part of daily life. Over the years, we have grown further away from our food sources — and now too many children are growing up thinking bread comes from a plastic bag in the grocery store. Baking something so basic and wholesome is worth the effort, even if you only do it once a year. When you bite into a warm slice of any of the breads in this chapter it will hit deep down, connecting you to a time gone by.

Bake bread when you are home for the afternoon. Contrary to what your mother may have told you, it doesn't take very long to bake bread. You do need to be around the house for several hours, but the work of mixing and kneading can be done in as little as thirty minutes. While the bread rises, you can take a break and go for a walk — or leave dough covered in the refrigerator overnight and punch it down in the morning.

Best Ever Banana Bread: *Page 63*

The World's Simplest Bread Dough: *Page 69*

Bread Shortcuts

☞ Always have all-purpose and whole wheat flour as well as yeast on hand (yeast keeps for several months in the refrigerator or at room temperature).

☞ For fresh muffins and quick breads in the morning, prepare the dry ingredients the night before and store in the refrigerator. In the morning, add the liquids and bake.

☞ Freeze homemade bread and then thaw at room temperature in a sealed plastic bag to avoid moisture loss.

☞ Prepare a batch of Quick Biscuit Mix (see page 64) and store it in a canister in the refrigerator for fresh biscuits in minutes.

Put bread back on the table. In the rush to lower fat and cut down on calories, don't cut back on your bread intake. It is not the thing that holds the sandwich together that racks up the calories, but the fillings — the mayonnaise, dressing, and so on. In fact, nutritionists say it's important to maintain your grain intake at six to eleven daily servings.

Make extra loaves and freeze. When you make the effort to bake bread, you might as well double the recipe. Freeze extra loaves in plastic bags for a welcome treat on a busy day.

Make bread in all shapes and sizes. Shaping yeast bread dough can be as creative as working with clay. Quick breads can't be twisted into the same pretzels and rolls, but you can pour the batter into different size pans and experiment with muffins (mini, regular, or giant).

Pass on the art of bread baking. After about the age of four, any child can help bake bread, though he might not be interested in or able to do every step. That's okay. Just play it by ear and be prepared to pick up the slack.

Quick Breads

Best Ever
Banana Bread

Corn Bread

Thanks to the Native Americans, the early American settlers learned how to grow corn, and a version of this bread was born.

- 1 cup all-purpose flour
- 1 cup cornmeal
- 2 teaspoons baking powder
- ½ teaspoon baking soda
- ¼ cup brown sugar
- ½ cup milk
- ½ cup plain yogurt
- 1 egg, lightly beaten
- ¼ cup butter, melted

Preheat the oven to 425° and grease an 8-inch square baking pan. In a large bowl, mix the flour, cornmeal, baking powder, baking soda, and brown sugar. In a separate bowl, whisk the milk, yogurt, egg, and melted butter together. Gradually add this mixture to the dry ingredients and stir until just combined. Pour into the prepared pan and bake for 15 to 20 minutes. Serves 6 to 8.

Corn Sticks:

Add an additional ¼ cup milk to the batter. Spoon into preheated and greased cast-iron corn stick molds. Makes 21 corn sticks.

Best Ever Banana Bread

Before you haul your overripe bananas to the compost, turn them into banana bread; the riper the banana, the sweeter the bread. Unlike a yeast bread, this quick bread tastes best a day old.

- ½ cup vegetable shortening
- 1¼ cups sugar
- 2 eggs
- 5 overripe bananas
- 2 cups all-purpose flour
- 1 teaspoon salt
- 2 teaspoons baking soda
- 2 tablespoons wheat germ
- 1 cup chopped nuts (optional)

Preheat the oven to 350° and grease two 8½-inch loaf pans. Cream the shortening and sugar in the bowl of an electric mixer. Add the eggs and bananas and blend until the bananas are thoroughly mashed. In a separate bowl, sift the flour, salt, and baking soda and stir in the wheat germ and nuts, if desired. Add the dry ingredients to the banana mixture and blend until just mixed. Pour the batter into the prepared pans, dividing it evenly. Bake for 50 minutes, or until the top springs back when gently pressed. Makes 2 loaves.

Fruit Freeze

Store overripe bananas for another day's baking by peeling and then freezing them in a sealable plastic bag. Defrost for 1 to 1½ hours before mixing into bread batter.

FunFact
The average American eats 52 pounds of bread every year (that's about 41 loaves).

Corn Sticks

Quick Biscuits

Dog Biscuits

You can bake treats for your favorite pet, too. In a large bowl, beat 3 eggs, then mix in ¼ cup soy flour, 1 tablespoon nutritional yeast, 2 tablespoons wheat germ, 2 tablespoons instant dry milk, and 2 cups whole wheat flour. Add 2 tablespoons water or enough to make the dough hold. Knead for 3 minutes, then spread to ½ inch thick. Use a cookie cutter to cut into "bones." Place on an ungreased cookie sheet and bake in a 325° oven for 25 minutes, flip, and bake 25 minutes more. Makes 7 to 10.

Quick Biscuit Mix

Making your own mix means you can have biscuits for dinner at the drop of a hat — and they're worlds better than those made from a store-bought mix.

- 6 cups all-purpose flour
- 3 tablespoons baking powder
- 3 teaspoons salt
- 1½ cups butter or margarine

Sift the flour, baking powder, and salt on waxed paper a few times, then transfer to a medium-size mixing bowl. Cut in the butter or margarine, working the dough until it resembles a coarse meal. Store the mixture in covered Mason jars in the refrigerator for up to 2 months. Makes about 7 cups of mix, enough for 36 biscuits.

Quick Biscuits:

If your oven has a light, your kids can watch the biscuits rise.

- ¼ cup buttermilk, plain yogurt, or sour cream
- 1 cup Quick Biscuit Mix (above)

Preheat the oven to 450°. Add the buttermilk, plain yogurt, or sour cream to the biscuit mix. If the dough is too sticky, add more biscuit mix. Turn the dough out onto a lightly floured surface and knead lightly. Roll out to about ½-inch thickness and cut into 2-inch circles. Press the scraps together, roll, and repeat until all the dough is used. Bake on an ungreased cookie sheet for 12 minutes. Makes 6 biscuits.

Cheese Wedge Biscuits

When our taste-testers bit into these moist biscuits, they all said "Cheese!" The key ingredient is grated Cheddar.

- 2 cups all-purpose flour
- 1 tablespoon baking powder
- ¼ teaspoon salt
- 5 tablespoons butter
- ⅔ cup milk
- ½ cup grated Cheddar cheese

Preheat the oven to 425°. Combine the flour, baking powder, and salt in the bowl of a food processor or electric mixer. Add the butter in chunks and blend until the mixture resembles a coarse meal. Add the milk and mix until just combined. Turn the dough out onto a lightly floured surface and pat into a round, about ⅓ inch thick. Place the round in a 9-inch pie plate and cut into wedges. Cover evenly with the cheese and bake for 15 minutes, or until lightly toasted on the top. If the cheese hasn't browned, broil for 1 minute. Makes 6 large wedges.

How To Warm Biscuits

☞ To reheat biscuits and rolls, place them in a dampened paper bag in a warm oven (set below 200°) for 5 to 10 minutes.

Crazy Cheese Straws

Your kids won't be able to sip through these totally twisty straws, but they can gobble them up at dinner. You can buy the frozen puff pastry in the freezer section of your grocery store.

- 1 sheet frozen puff pastry, about 12 by 14 inches
- 1 egg white
- 2 teaspoons water
- 1½ teaspoons grated Parmesan cheese

Let the frozen puff pastry thaw for about 30 minutes, then lay it on a floured surface. Preheat the oven to 400°. In a small bowl, mix the egg white and water. Use a pastry brush to "paint" the mixture onto one side of the pastry. Sprinkle with the Parmesan cheese and cut the pastry into strips, ½ inch wide and as long as the pastry. Place the strips on an ungreased cookie sheet and gently twist several times (a good job for kids). Press the ends onto the cookie sheet so the strips don't unravel. Bake for 10 minutes, or until golden brown. Makes 15 to 20 straws.

Irish Soda Bread

In Ireland, this bread is better known as Dairy Bread (it's loaded with buttermilk), and it's eaten every day. Raisins or currants are added to our cakelike American version.

- 3 cups all-purpose flour
- 2 cups whole wheat flour
- 2 teaspoons baking soda
- 1 tablespoon baking powder
- 2 tablespoons brown sugar
- 2 to 2¼ cups buttermilk
- ½ cup currants or raisins (optional)

Preheat the oven to 400°. In a large mixing bowl, combine the all-purpose flour, wheat flour, baking soda, baking powder, and brown sugar. Add the buttermilk and stir until the mixture forms a soft dough.

Turn the dough out onto a lightly floured surface and knead just to blend the ingredients. If desired, add currants or raisins to the dough. Divide the dough into two portions and form each into a rounded loaf.

Place on a greased baking sheet and bake for 45 minutes, or until golden brown. Cool on racks for 10 minutes, then serve. Makes 2 loaves.

Crazy Cheese Straws

On St. Patrick's Day

Make an authentic Irish sandwich with corned beef on Irish Soda Bread with steamed cabbage or sauerkraut and Cheddar cheese.

SNAKE ON A STICK

To make this novel campfire treat, mix 2 cups all-purpose flour, 3 tablespoons buttermilk powder, 1½ teaspoons cream of tartar, and ½ teaspoon baking soda in a large bowl. Rub in ¼ cup margarine or butter until it resembles a coarse meal. At the campfire, stir in ¾ cup water. Roll the dough into a long, thin snake and twist it around the peeled end of a green stick. Pinch the dough ends and roast it over a campfire until brown and cooked through. Slip it off the stick and enjoy.

Navajo Fry Bread

These fry breads act like edible plates. Use as a scoop for chili or serve piled with Tex-Mex toppings — refried beans, chili, cheese, tomatoes, olives, onions, sour cream, even salsas.

1 cup all-purpose flour
1 cup white whole wheat flour (see page 70)
1 cup cornmeal
2 teaspoons baking powder
1 teaspoon salt
1 cup water
½ cup milk
1 tablespoon vegetable oil
4 cups peanut or vegetable oil for deep-frying

In a large mixing bowl, stir the all-purpose and white wheat flours, cornmeal, baking powder, and salt. Add the water and milk and stir until a moist dough forms (if your dough is too soft, add more flour). On a lightly floured surface, knead the dough into a mound and return to the bowl. Coat with the tablespoon of vegetable oil and cover the bowl with a damp cloth. Let sit for 15 to 30 minutes.

Meanwhile, fill a deep fryer or soup pot with the oil (it should be at least 3 inches deep). Just before you roll out the dough, turn up the heat on the oil.

Pinch off a tangerine-size ball of dough and roll it into a disk on a well-floured surface. It should be about ⅛ inch thick (the thinner the dough, the crispier the fry bread). Place the round into the oil and fry for 2 minutes, watching carefully for the dough to turn a deep golden brown. Remove the bread with a spatula, drain, gently pat off the excess oil, and cool on a rack covered with paper towels. After the first one, adjust the temperature, thickness of the dough, and frying time. Repeat for the rest of the dough. Makes 6 to 8 large fry breads.

Homemade Tortillas

This delicious recipe is adapted from *The Well-Filled Tortilla* by Victoria Wise and Susanna Hoffman (Workman Publishing Company).

3 to 4 cups all-purpose flour
⅓ cup vegetable oil
1 teaspoon salt
1 cup warm water

In a medium-size bowl, mix the flour and vegetable oil until it crumbles. Dissolve the salt in the warm water and pour it over the flour mixture, then use your fingers to combine the dough (if your dough is too soft, add more flour). Knead the dough on an unfloured surface until elastic, about 4 minutes. Place it back in the bowl, cover with a damp cloth, and let it rest for at least 1 hour. Divide it into 12 balls and roll each one into a thin, 8-inch round (make sure the edges are as thin as the middle). Place one tortilla at a time on an ungreased skillet over medium-high heat and cook each side for 1 to 3 minutes. Makes 12.

Yeast Breads

Teddy Bear Bread, Pretzels, and Crescent Rolls: *Pages 119–120*

The World's Simplest Bread Dough

Last year, I invited my six-year-old nephew, Matty, to pull a stepladder up to the kitchen counter and help me bake bread. We used this unfussy recipe that didn't dirty every bowl in the kitchen, collapse during the inevitable interruptions, or yield to Matty's desire to treat it like a mound of clay. When my brother picked up his son later in the day, Matty had a bag of his own fresh-baked breads to take home. You can use this master recipe, inspired by the King Arthur Flour bread recipe, to shape two traditional loaves or any of the variations on the following pages — crescent rolls, a teddy bear loaf, pretzels, or a braided loaf.

2 cups warm water (for a tender, brown crust use ½ cup warm water and 1½ cups warm milk)
1 tablespoon active dry yeast
1 tablespoon sugar
5½ to 6 cups all-purpose or whole wheat flour, or a combination
2 teaspoons salt

1. The key to activating yeast is finding the right water temperature.

Don't let this intimidate you; just think bathwater. If it feels warm on the wrist, but not hot, it's ready to pour into a bowl.
2. Add the stinky yeast. (Matty plugged his nose for this step.)
3. Measure the sugar into the bowl. Explain that the sugar helps the yeast grow.
4. Whisk until the sugar and yeast are dissolved.
5. Measure 2 cups of the flour into the bowl. Show your kids how to get an exact measure: Spoon the flour into a dry measuring cup and level it off with a knife.
6. Whisk the mixture well, then let it "proof," or sit for 10 minutes. If tiny bubbles appear (8s and 0s, according to Matt) and the batter looks slightly expanded, you're on the right track.
7. Stir in the salt, then add the remaining flour, 1 cup at a time. This

can be quite messy, so if your child is not up to the challenge, take over at this point.
8. Turn the dough onto a lightly floured countertop.
9. To knead, fold the dough in half and push it down and away with the heel of your hand, rotate the dough, and repeat until it is smooth and elastic. (Kneading can take up to 10 minutes.)
10. Place the ball in a bowl greased with vegetable oil and turn to coat.
11. Cover with a damp cloth or plastic wrap and let the dough rise in a draft-free area for 1 to 2 hours, or until it has doubled in size.
12. Punch the dough down (a fun job for kids).
13. Knead it again to remove air bubbles, then shape and bake it according to the directions starting on page 70.
14. Cool on a wire rack, and enjoy.

Braided Loaf

This attractive loaf, which resembles the traditional Jewish bread, challah, gives parents and kids a chance to show off their braiding skills. If you don't have poppy seeds, you can use sesame seeds or skip the seeds altogether.

½ recipe World's Simplest Bread Dough (page 69), through step 13
Butter or margarine
2 tablespoons poppy seeds

Roll the dough into three thick snakes, each about 10 inches long. Lay the strands side by side and loosely braid them (to avoid tearing the dough, braid from the center out to an end; repeat with the other side). Pinch the three strands together at each end, tuck them under, and arrange the loaf on a greased cookie sheet. Cover with plastic wrap or a damp cloth and let it rise in a draft-free area for 30 minutes.

Preheat the oven to 400°. Brush the dough with egg wash and sprinkle with poppy seeds. Bake for 25 minutes, then transfer to a wire rack to cool. Wrap the cooled bread tightly in plastic until ready to eat, or freeze. Makes 1 loaf.

An Egg Wash Shine

Add shine to your loaves of bread by brushing them with an egg wash just before popping them in the oven. To make an egg wash, whisk 1 egg with 1 table-spoon water. Use a pastry brush or a new, clean paint-brush to carefully cover the surface (be delicate — you don't want the risen loaf to fall).

Best Wheat Flour

☛ **King Arthur White Whole Wheat Flour makes a flavorful loaf; if you can't find it in your grocery store, order it from The Baker's Catalogue, 800-827-6836.**

The No-Frills Loaf

Although baking bread dates back some ten thousand years, sliced white bread is a relatively new, American tradition.

½ recipe World's Simplest Bread Dough (page 69), through step 13
Butter or margarine

Roll the dough into a rectangle and fold it into thirds like a letter. Turn the ends under and place the dough, seam side down, in a greased loaf pan. Cover with plastic wrap or damp cloth and let rise again for about 45 minutes.

Preheat the oven to 400° and bake the bread for 30 minutes. Remove the bread from the oven; if the bottom of the loaf sounds hollow when tapped, it's done. Cool in the pan for 10 minutes, then transfer to a wire rack. Rub with butter for a shiny finish and enjoy a warm slice. When cool, wrap the remaining loaf tightly in pastic. Makes 1 loaf.

No-Frills Wheat Bread:

Use all or part wheat flour in step 5 of the World's Simplest Bread Dough.

Crescent Rolls

Once you have formed half your bread dough recipe into a loaf, shape the other half into crescent rolls. You can make the rolls more flavorful by substituting warm milk for the water in the World's Simplest Bread Dough, adding an extra tablespoon of sugar, and mixing in 2 beaten eggs with the salt.

½ recipe World's Simplest Bread
Dough (page 69), through
step 13
Butter or margarine, softened

Roll the dough into a large circle, about ⅛ inch thick. Spread the butter on the circle, then cut it into 8 wedges. Roll the wedges up, starting with the outside of the circle. Pinch the tip of each wedge to seal it and bend the ends to make the crescent shape. Place them on a greased cookie sheet, cover with plastic wrap or a damp cloth, and let them rise for 20 minutes. Bake for 15 minutes in an oven preheated to 400°. Cool on a rack slightly; serve warm. Makes 8 rolls.

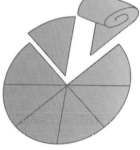

Teddy Bear Bread

When my nephew saw bread shaped like a teddy bear in *My First Cookbook* by Angela Wilkes (Alfred A. Knopf), he was determined to make one, adding his own embellishments such as a cinnamon-sugar belly and "fur" made with scissor snips. Shaping the dough is half the entertainment value for kids (the other half is eating the heads off their creations).

½ recipe World's Simplest Bread
Dough (page 69), through
step 13
Raisins

To make the bear's head, form a ball with a diameter of about 4 inches, place it on a greased cookie sheet, and flatten it slightly. For the bear's body, form a larger ball, about 6 inches in diameter, and place it just below the head. Make 2 small balls for the ears and 4 more for the paws and position them as shown above. Use raisins for eyes and a small ball of dough for a button nose. For a furry bear, snip its body with scissors.

Cover the bear with plastic wrap or a damp cloth and let it rise for 30 minutes. Brush the bear with egg wash (see page 70), then bake for 25 minutes in an oven preheated to 400°. Transfer the bread to a wire rack to cool. Eat it right away or tightly seal it in plastic wrap until ready to serve. Makes 1 bear.

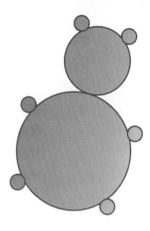

How To Make Honey Butter

For a delicious spread on a loaf of warm bread, mix 2 tablespoons honey with 6 tablespoons softened butter.

The Baker's Barnyard

Bread dough just begs to be patted, rolled, and pinched into little creatures. Once an animal is formed, cover and let rise for 30 minutes. Brush with egg wash (see page 70) and add raisin eyes. Bake for 15 minutes in an oven preheated to 375°.

Pigs: Make a round face with a button nose, pointed ears, and a curlicue tail.

Turtle: Mold a large round shell (use a knife to make crisscrosses for the shell) and a head, tiny tail, and stubby legs.

Sheep: Add wool to an oval body by pushing the dough through a garlic press, then shape legs, a tail, and head.

Rooster: Form a mound of dough into a baseball glove shape and add tiny legs, a long neck, and a beak.

Throw a Pizza Party

If your kids want pizza on the menu at their birthday party *again*, don't get it delivered this time. Let the kids make the pizzas themselves. With a bit of planning and preparation, a pizza party can be a live-ly way to entertain and feed young guests. Supply the dough and a variety of toppings for the artistic chefs to use as their mixed media. Some kids prefer abstract expres-sionism, whereas others are bent on more repre-sentational efforts — faces, clowns, and the like. Whatever the shape, the finished masterpieces are cer-tain to be gobbled up.

Ultimate Pizza Dough

Making your own pizza is half the fun of eating it. You can prepare this dough ahead and store the rolled-out rounds in the freezer (stack them between sheets of waxed paper). On busy week-nights, you'll have pizza in a flash.

- 2 teaspoons active dry yeast
- 1 cup warm water
- 1 teaspoon salt
- 3 cups all-purpose flour (or ½ cup whole wheat, semolina, or rye flour mixed with 2½ cups all-purpose flour)
- 1 to 2 tablespoons virgin olive oil Additional flour or cornmeal for rolling out the dough

In the bowl of a food processor or electric mixer, dissolve the yeast in the water and let stand for 5 minutes. Add the salt, flour, and 1 tablespoon of olive oil and mix until the dough forms a ball; if using a mixer, gradually add flour ½ cup at a time (if the mixture is hard to work, add extra oil). Turn the dough out onto a surface dusted with flour or cornmeal and knead briefly until smooth. Lightly oil a medium-size mixing bowl and turn the dough in the bowl to coat. Cover with a damp dish towel or plastic wrap and let the dough rise in a warm, draft-free area for 1 to 2 hours, or until doubled in size.

Punch down the dough and place it on a surface dusted with flour or corn-meal. Flatten it into a disk and divide it into four or eight equal portions with a knife or spatula. Roll out each portion, gently stretching it with your hands and set on a cookie sheet. Makes 4 12-inch crusts or 8 individual ones.

Ultimate Pizza:

Top the Ultimate Pizza Dough rounds with your favorite toppings (see list at right) and place in a preheated 450° oven. Bake for 10 to 15 minutes, or until the cheese melts and the crusts are golden brown.

Focaccia

The predecessor of pizza, focaccia is an Italian flatbread flavored with olive oil and herbs. It's a great appetizer, side dish, or pizza crust — for pizza just add your favorite toppings before the second rising.

- 1 tablespoon active dry yeast
- 1 teaspoon honey
- 1 cup warm water
- 3⅔ cups all-purpose flour, sifted
- 1 teaspoon salt
- ⅓ cup olive oil, plus extra for brushing
- 3 tablespoons fresh rosemary
- 2 tablespoons cornmeal

In a large bowl, mix the yeast and honey with the water and let it sit for 5 minutes. Stir in 1 cup of the flour, then the salt and the ⅓ cup of olive oil. Add the remaining flour, ½ cup at a time. Knead the moist dough on a lightly floured surface for 8 to 10 minutes. Grease a large bowl with olive oil and turn the dough to coat. Loosely cover the bowl with a dish towel or plastic wrap and let rise until doubled in size, 1 to 2 hours.

Punch the dough down and divide it in half. Pat each half into an oval, then use a rolling pin to roll each one out to ½-inch thickness. Sprinkle with the rosemary and press the herb into the dough. Spread the cornmeal on a cookie sheet and place the dough on it. Cover and let rise for about 20 minutes.

Just before baking, make dimples in the bread by gently pressing your fingertips into the dough 2 inches apart. Brush the circles with the extra olive oil and place in an oven preheated to 375°. Bake for 16 to 18 minutes, or until the bread is golden brown. Makes 2 focacce.

Pizza Toppings

A wide selection of ingredients ensures that your pizzas will be good tasting — and good looking. You can go over this list (enough for four large pizzas) with your family and adjust according to tastes. When the pizzas are assembled, bake according to the Ultimate Pizza directions on page 72.

- 2 cups tomato sauce
- 3 cups grated Mozzarella cheese, sprinkled with a tablespoon of olive oil
- 4 Italian plum tomatoes, sliced
- 4 carrots, sliced
- 1 cup fresh mushrooms, sliced
- 1 cup zucchini, sliced
- 1 large red onion, thinly sliced, soaked in cold water for an hour, then drained
- 1 cup broccoli florets, blanched
- 1 cup spinach, chopped
- 1 8-ounce package pepperoni, sliced
- 1 red and green pepper, thinly sliced
- 1 jar roasted red peppers, diced
- 1 cup grated Parmesan cheese
- ½ cup pitted black olives, sliced
- Chopped fresh basil, parsley, and chives, or dried oregano and basil
- Cayenne pepper flakes

CHAPTER 6

Dinner's Ready

Your job as the family chef can be as demanding as that of a chef in a three-star restaurant. You have to find a winning recipe, shop for the ingredients, and cook for an audience that won't eat anything too soft or too green. And after all that, you still risk having your creation wrapped in a napkin or slipped to the dog. So how do you please those picky diners and make sure they eat a well-balanced meal?

Culinary school probably won't make your job any easier, but the selection of recipes in this chapter, all approved by kids, just might help. Adapting them to suit your family's very particular tastes is the next step. Try giving our recipes a taste-test, then amend away — add an avocado, cut back on the curry — then jot down in the margins of this book what works for you and what doesn't.

Make it fast. You don't want to spend an hour cleaning up after a thirty-minute meal, so choose recipes that can be made in one pan or try a no-cook recipe, such as the Peanut Butter Dip on page 52 or the Rainbow Buffet on page 97.

Make the meal innovative. As *FamilyFun* reader Patricia Vega so aptly puts it, sometimes what the whole family really goes for are the "foods that don't seem like they're supposed to be for dinner." Look for recipe ideas in other chapters in this book — breakfast, lunch, or snacks — and serve them. Or, shake up the standard Monday through Friday fare by giving each meal a theme (see page 76 for inspiration). Try a Mexican Fiesta, page 80, serve a no-fork dinner with foods you can eat with your hands, or cook a meal based

Jazz up the dinner table. Dinner doesn't always have to be served at the table. Eat your supper outside during warmer weather or spread a tablecloth on the family room floor and have an indoor picnic in the winter. If you're staying put, set the table in a new way: use paper plates, fold your napkins into pockets for silverware (see page 15), or take a cue from *FamilyFun* reader Nancy Weber and try a designer table setting (see page 15).

Give the kids options. You can avoid making a different meal for every person at the table by serving dishes with optional mix-ins. Recipes such as the Terrific Taco Filling on page 80, or Chicken Curry on page 86 can be dressed up and customized with toppings and fillings.

Turn off the tube; turn on the answering machine. On the nights that your family can all eat together, eliminate the biggest distractions — the television and telephone — and enjoy each other's company. Go around the table and share one good and one bad thing that happened that day, tell a new joke, or answer the questions in the Table Topics game on page 11.

Serve restaurant foods at home. If your kids like the foods they eat in restaurants, recreate the dishes at home. You'll find several Americanized versions of international foods in this chapter as well as some diner favorites.

Beef Fajitas: *Page 81*

Meats

Back-to-Basics London Broil

Dress up the all-American steak with one of our accompanying sauces. For a true back-to-basics dinner, support your town butcher — you'll often get the best cut of beef while contributing to an important local trade.

> 2 pounds London broil or
> flank steak, 1 inch thick
> Coarse salt and black pepper
> Vegetable oil

Preheat your broiler or prepare the coals for grilling. Oil the broiling pan or grill before laying on the steaks. Rub the meat with the coarse salt and a bit of pepper. Cook 3 inches from the flame for 4 to 6 minutes per side for medium. To serve, slice the meat on the diagonal, following the grain. Serves 4 to 6.

Back-to-Basics London Broil with Dijon-Herb Butter

Dijon-Herb Butter:

In a food processor or by hand, mix 6 tablespoons butter with 2 tablespoons mustard and 1 minced shallot. Add 8 chopped sprigs of parsley and 8 chopped chives. Pat into a log on waxed paper, refrigerate, and slice into rounds. Dot on warm steak.

Lemon Pepper:

Before you cook the steak, coat both sides with store-bought lemon pepper.

Veggie Smother:

Sauté 8 ounces of sliced mushrooms, 1 medium chopped onion, 1 sliced green pepper, and 1 crushed garlic clove in 1 tablespoon of butter or olive oil. Spoon over the warm steak just before serving.

Parsley Pesto:

In a food processor, blend 2 cups fresh parsley, 1 crushed garlic clove, and 2 tablespoons sunflower seeds with ⅓ cup olive oil. Add 3 tablespoons Parmesan cheese and ½ teaspoon salt. Dot on warm steak.

Horseradish Dipping Sauce:

Mix ½ cup sour cream with ¼ cup prepared horseradish and a dash of Worcestershire sauce.

Last-Minute Marinade:

Marinate the steak in Dijon Vinaigrette (page 110), Soy-Honey Dressing (page 110), or any Italian salad dressing for at least 1 hour prior to cooking.

Cube Steak Sandwich

For a quick, inexpensive dinner or lunch, panfry cube steaks for 2 to 3 minutes per side. Place them on bulky rolls and sauté a sliced onion in the pan drippings. Top the steak with the onions and, if desired, Creamy Dreamy Blue Cheese dressing (see page 110).

Homemade Catsup

Blanch 8 large tomatoes in boiling water until the skins split (about ½ to 2 minutes), then plunge into cold water and peel. Slice the tomatoes in half, remove the seeds, and cut into quarters. Place quarters in a large saucepan with 1 cup of water and simmer for 20 minutes, or until soft. Drain any excess liquid and set aside. Puree the tomatoes with 1 chopped onion and 1 garlic clove in a blender or food processor (add reserved liquid, if necessary). Return to the saucepan and add ½ cup white vinegar and 1 tablespoon salt. Cook over medium heat for 5 minutes, stirring constantly. Add ¼ cup brown sugar, 1 teaspoon pepper, and ¼ teaspoon each of cinnamon, ground cloves, and mustard powder. Continue cooking, stirring occasionally, for 1½ hours, or until thick. Transfer to a jar and cool before refrigerating. Makes about 2½ cups.

Mean and Lean Meat Loaf

In diners across America, meat loaf is often part of the blue plate special, so named because the meal was once served on a blue plate divided into three sections for meat, potatoes, and vegetables. This recipe comes from Rosie's Diner in Rockford, Michigan. If you're lucky enough to live near Rosie's, your family can play a round of diner-theme miniature golf at the diner while you wait for your blue plate special.

Meat loaf:

   2 pounds lean ground beef
   2 eggs, beaten
   1 cup rolled oats
  ½ cup chopped onion
  ½ cup catsup
  ¼ cup chopped green pepper
   2 tablespoons steak sauce
   1 teaspoon black pepper
  ½ teaspoon salt
  ½ teaspoon basil
  ½ teaspoon garlic powder

Sauce:

  ½ cup catsup
   3 tablespoons packed brown sugar
   1 teaspoon ground mustard

Preheat your oven to 350° and grease an 8½-inch loaf pan. In a large bowl, combine the ground beef and eggs. Add the oats, onion, catsup, pepper, steak sauce, black pepper, salt, basil, and garlic powder and mix well. Transfer to the loaf pan and smooth the top.

In a small bowl, whisk the catsup, brown sugar, and mustard together, then spread it over the meat loaf before baking. Bake for 1 to 1½ hours, or until the inside reaches 160°. Let the meat loaf sit for 10 minutes before slicing. Serves 4 to 6.

Steak on a Stick

FamilyFun reader Louann Sherbach of Wantagh, New York, has to cook a pound and a half of steak to satisfy her family: Sara, fourteen; twins Matt and Alison, eleven; and Kimberly, nine.

  1½ pounds London broil or flank steak, about ¼ inch thick
  ½ cup soy sauce
  ¼ cup vegetable oil (optional)
  ¼ cup water
  2 tablespoons molasses
  2 teaspoons dry mustard
  1 teaspoon powdered ginger
  ½ teaspoon garlic powder

Cut the steak on the diagonal in ¼-inch slices and place them in a sealable bag. Mix the remaining ingredients in a bowl, then pour into the bag. Seal the bag with no air pockets, shake, and marinate in the refrigerator for at least 4 hours, or freeze until ready to use.

When you're ready to cook, skewer the meat ribbon style with 3 to 4 pieces on a skewer (soaked bamboo skewers work well). Broil or grill the meat, about 3 minutes on each side. Makes 10 to 16 skewers.

Steak on a Stick

Where's the Beef Stir-fry

A little beef goes a long way when it's stir-fried with Chinese cabbage, green beans, or broccoli. You can marinate the beef and prepare the vegetables in advance.

½ pound boneless top round or flank steak, trimmed and sliced on the diagonal into thin, 2-inch-long strips

Marinade:

2 teaspoons cornstarch
2 teaspoons soy sauce
2 teaspoons dry sherry
2 tablespoons sesame seeds, toasted in a skillet until they start to pop (but don't burn)
1 teaspoon sugar

Vegetables:

½ pound Chinese cabbage, trimmed string beans, or broccoli florets
½ red pepper, cut into strips

Sauce:

6 tablespoons chicken broth
2 tablespoons oyster sauce
2 teaspoons cornstarch
1 tablespoon soy sauce
1 tablespoon dry sherry
½ teaspoon sugar
1 crushed garlic clove
1 tablespoon minced fresh ginger

For the pan:

2 tablespoons peanut oil

Mix the marinade ingredients in a shallow dish, toss in the beef, and marinate while you prepare the vegetables. If you are using Chinese cabbage, blanch it for about 3 minutes in boiling water, drain, and cool; slice diagonally into strips. For string beans, blanch 2 minutes, drop into ice water to stop the cooking, drain, and cut in half. For broccoli, blanch florets for 2 minutes, drain, and cool. (At this point, you can

Where's the Beef Stir-fry

cover and refrigerate the vegetables for up to 12 hours. Just bring them to room temperature before proceeding with the recipe.) In a small bowl, combine the sauce ingredients, except the garlic and ginger. Set aside.

Heat 1 tablespoon of the peanut oil in a wok or large nonstick frying pan. When the oil just smokes, add the cabbage, beans, or broccoli and the red pepper and stir-fry for 1 minute; remove to a plate. Add the remaining oil to your pan, heat, then toss in the strips of beef, stirring for 1 minute. Sprinkle on the garlic and ginger and stir for 1 more minute. Return the vegetables to your pan. Restir the sauce and add it to the pan. Stir until the sauce thickens slightly and the ingredients are coated evenly. Remove from the heat and serve with rice. Serves 3 to 4.

AS EASY AS STIR-FRY

☛ For best results, use a nonstick skillet or wok. Coat with oil, cooking spray, broth, wine, vinegar, or water.

☛ Heat oil until it's very hot. Test with a drop of water — if oil snaps, it is ready.

☛ Cut meat into small, uniform pieces before heating the skillet.

☛ Keep food in almost constant motion to avoid overcooking.

Smiling Tostadas

Terrific Taco Filling

You can buy a package of taco shells or make your own by laying corn tortillas on the rack in an oven preheated to 300°. When they have softened, fold them over the oven rack grills so that they hang down, then heat until crisp, about 5 minutes.

½	tablespoon vegetable oil
½	cup chopped onion
1	pound lean ground beef
2	crushed garlic cloves
⅓	cup tomato juice, beef stock, water, or wine
2	tablespoons chili powder
½	teaspoon cumin
	Salt and pepper to taste

Heat the oil in a skillet over medium heat. Add the onion and sauté until translucent. Break up the ground beef with a fork and add it to the skillet. Stir in the garlic and continue stirring until the meat browns; drain out any excess fat. Stir in the tomato juice, chili powder, cumin, and salt and pepper. Continue cooking, stirring occasionally, until the mixture is heated through and the tastes are well combined. Spoon the beef mixture into prepared taco shells and top with your favorite accompaniments: shredded lettuce, olives, avocado, tomatoes, cheese. Makes 2½ to 3 cups.

Chicken Taco Filling:

For a leaner version, substitute ground chicken for the ground beef.

Turkey Taco Filling:

Substitute ground turkey for the beef.

Beef Fajitas

This help-yourself meal, a Texas original, combines sizzling steak, onions, and peppers in a warm tortilla. Using skirt steak is traditional, but if you can't get this from your butcher, substitute flank steak.

- 1   tablespoon vegetable oil
- 2   pounds skirt steak or flank steak
- 4   small onions
- 2   red, green, or yellow peppers
- 8   to 10 flour tortillas
      Salsa Fresca (see page 53)
      Tomatillo Salsa (see recipe below)
      Chunky Guacamole (see page 53)

Heat the oil in a large nonstick frying pan over medium-high heat. Cook the steak on both sides, about 12 minutes for medium, and remove from the pan. Slice the onions and peppers and sauté until soft. Warm your tortillas in a skillet. Thinly slice the steak on the diagonal and arrange on a platter with the vegetables. Serve with salsas, guacamole, and the tortillas. Serves 4 to 6.

Grilled Fajitas:

Peel the onions and cut them in half; slice the peppers in half, too. Rub the vegetables with olive oil and place on your grill. Cook for several minutes, then push them aside. Cook the steak on both sides. Warm the tortillas on the grill. Slice the grilled vegetables and steak and serve with the tortillas.

Chicken Fajitas:

Substitute 2 boneless, skinless chicken breasts for the skirt steak.

Veggie Fajitas:

Substitute mixed vegetables — peppers, onions, carrots, zucchini, and squash — for the skirt steak.

How To Make Smiling Tostadas

☞ These open-faced sandwiches begin with a crispy shell. You can either purchase the shells or briefly fry corn tortillas in 2 tablespoons of oil. Spread the shell with taco filling or refried beans and grated cheese, then arrange shredded lettuce for hair, olive slices for eyes, a carrot slice for a nose, and tomato pieces for lips.

Tomatillo Salsa

Tomatillos, also known as Mexican tomatoes, have a wonderful, mild lemon flavor and make an excellent sauce for any Mexican dish. Husk and rinse 1 pound of fresh tomatillos. In a large saucepan over medium heat, combine the tomatillos, 1 small jalapeño, seeded, veined, and chopped, 1 cup chopped onion, 1 cup water, and 3 to 4 crushed garlic cloves. Bring to a boil, reduce the heat to low, and simmer, covered, for about 15 minutes. In a blender or food processor, puree the juice of 1 lime, ¼ cup Italian parsley, and ¼ cup fresh cilantro. Add the tomatillo mixture, one third at a time, and process until smooth. Cool in the refrigerator. Makes 3½ cups.

Dinner's Ready

Mexican Fiesta

TOOLS OF THE GRILLING TRADE

☛ For best results, use long-handled utensils — fork, spatula, basting brush, and tongs.

☛ Keep a table nearby to hold serving platters, an oven mitt, and marinades and sauces.

☛ Use vegetable spray to coat the racks before grilling to prevent foods from sticking.

☛ For cooking fish and vegetables, invest in a wire-mesh hinged basket.

☛ An instant-read meat thermometer will help you judge the temperature or doneness of meat.

☛ A wire brush makes cleaning the racks after grilling a cinch.

TIPS OF THE GRILLING TRADE

☛ Always heat the rack for 5 minutes over coals before cooking.

☛ Brush on thick or sweet sauces during the last 5 minutes of grilling to prevent burning.

☛ Try not to pierce meat often, as juices will be lost.

☛ For kabobs, soak wooden skewers in water for 30 minutes prior to piercing with meats and vegetables.

Lamb and Vegetable Shish Kabobs

For an authentic Middle Eastern meal, serve these delicious kabobs with Tabbouleh, Cucumber Dipping Sauce (see page 52), couscous, and warm pita bread.

Marinade:
- 1 cup olive oil
- ⅓ cup fresh lemon juice
- 2 crushed garlic cloves
- 1 teaspoon salt
- 1 teaspoon coarse black pepper

Meat:
- 3 pounds lean lamb from the leg or shoulder with the fat removed, cut into 1½- to 2-inch cubes

Vegetables:
- 12 whole cherry tomatoes
- 1 green, yellow, or red pepper, cut into 1½-inch squares
- 1 dozen large mushroom caps
- 1 small eggplant, peeled and cut into 1½-inch cubes
- 1 dozen small white onions, peeled and parboiled for 5 to 10 minutes until just tender

Combine the ingredients for the marinade in a glass mixing bowl. Add the meat and marinate for 2 hours, turning frequently, or overnight in the refrigerator.

Prepare the coals for grilling. Using ten 14-inch skewers, pierce the meat and vegetables; leave about 2 inches of space at the handle and the tip. (If you pack the skewers tightly, you will get rarer meat; leave more space for well done.) When the coals are hot, arrange the kabobs on the grill, about 3 inches from the heat. Brush them with the marinade and turn frequently. Start testing for doneness after about 12 minutes. The kabobs will continue to cook a bit off the flame, so be careful not to overcook them. Serves 6 to 8.

Beef and Vegetable Kabobs:
Substitute cubes of beef for the lamb.

Vegetable Kabobs:
Skip the lamb; use just the vegetables.

Pork Chops with Apples

When *FamilyFun* contributor Becky Okrent needs dinner on the table *fast*, she cooks up this one-skillet dinner.

- 4 medium apples, peeled, cored, and cubed
  Juice of 1 lemon
- ¼ teaspoon nutmeg
- 1 to 2 tablespoons vegetable oil
- 4 pork chops
  Salt and pepper
- ¼ cup apple cider or juice
- 1 tablespoon butter (optional)

Sprinkle the apples with the lemon juice and nutmeg. Warm a 10-inch or larger skillet over medium-high heat and add enough oil to keep the pork from sticking. When the skillet is hot, add the chops and a pinch of salt and pepper. After about 6 minutes, turn the chops to brown the other side. After 5 minutes, push the chops aside and add the apples. Cover the pan and cook for about 2 minutes. Remove the cooked pork chops from the pan to a warmed serving platter (at this point, the center of the pork chops should be white, and the juices should run clear).

Continue cooking the apples until soft, about 3 minutes. Deglaze the pan with the cider or juice by turning up the heat, stirring the juice and apples, and scraping up the browned bits. To make a richer sauce, swirl in 1 tablespoon butter. Remove the pan from the heat and pour the apples and sauce over the pork chops. Serves 4.

Pork Chops with Mint Pesto:

In a food processor, blend 2 cups fresh mint, ⅓ cup olive oil, 1 garlic clove, and ¼ teaspoon salt. Serve atop pan-fried pork chops (follow the method above but skip the apples and sauce).

Dinner's Ready

Baked Ham with Chutney-Mustard Glaze

This succulent ham can be eaten right away or cooked in advance, covered, and refrigerated, and then served as part of a buffet (an ideal main course for a Party on the Move at right).

- 1 5-pound smoked, boneless ham, fully cooked
- ⅔ cup fresh fruit chutney
- ⅓ cup Dijon mustard
- ⅓ cup white wine

Preheat the oven to 375°. Line a roasting pan with foil. Set the ham into the pan, and with a sharp knife, score the top of the meat in a grid pattern (about ¼ inch deep).

Blend the remaining ingredients in a bowl until smooth, adding more wine if necessary for a spreadable consistency. With a brush, evenly spread the glaze over the top and sides of the ham. Bake for 45 minutes to 1 hour, basting several times. Cool completely, if desired, and slice thin before serving. Serves 12.

A Party on the Move

Progressive dinners are popular for a reason: you get to throw a party, but you don't have to do all the cooking (and cleaning up). To plan a party, ask a few neighborhood families to serve a course in their homes. Arrange for the party group to visit one house for appetizers, another for the main course, and a third for dessert. Families can plan their part of the meal around favorite foods and share the recipes with their guests. Or have an international theme or "kids' choice" dishes prepared by young chefs.

Pork Chops with Apples

Poultry

Veggie Roast Chicken

Plain and Simple Roast Chicken

On weeknights, dinner in my household is a rushed affair, so once a month, I try to roast a chicken and make an old-fashioned Sunday dinner. We bring out the cloth napkins and candles and eat slowly, enjoying each other's company. This crispy-skin recipe welcomes your embellishments.

1   4- to 5-pound roasting chicken
    Half a lemon
1   large onion, sliced
2   tablespoons olive oil
1   teaspoon thyme
    ½ teaspoon coarse salt
    ¼ teaspoon pepper

Preheat the oven to 400°. Remove the giblets, thoroughly rinse the chicken, and pat dry. Squeeze the juice from the lemon half over the chicken, then stuff the half into the cavity. Close the cavity with small skewers and tie the legs together with string. Make a bed of onion slices in the bottom of the pan and place the chicken, breast side up, on the onions. Drizzle with the olive oil, sprinkle with the thyme, salt, and pepper and bake for 1¼ to 1½ hours, basting frequently, until the juices from behind the leg run clear. Let rest 5 minutes, then carve. Serves 4 to 6.

Veggie Roast Chicken:
Surround the chicken with peeled carrots and pearl onions, unpeeled new potatoes, and whole mushrooms. Serve with the roasted vegetables on the side.

Orange-Ginger Chicken:
Arrange orange slices on the bird, sprinkle with minced fresh ginger, and pour ½ cup orange juice over the top.

Apple-Hazelnut Chicken:
Place cored apple halves and peeled pearl onions in the roasting pan. Arrange apple slices on the bird and dash with cinnamon. Drizzle apple brandy over the bird for a full flavor. Ten minutes before the chicken is done, add 1 cup hazelnuts to the pan.

Lemon-Rosemary Chicken:
Place lemon slices on the chicken and sprinkle generously with rosemary and a little olive oil.

Stuffed Chicken:
Just before roasting, loosely stuff the chicken with your favorite stuffing or the recipe on page 151. Increase the cooking time by 25 minutes.

Potato Chip Chicken Fingers

These irresistible fingers get their crunch not from deep-frying but from potato chips. Experiment with chip flavors, from barbecue to sour cream and chive.

- 1   whole boneless, skinless chicken breast
- 5   to 6 ounces potato chips, plain, barbecue, or sour cream
- 1   egg
- 2   tablespoons milk

Preheat the oven to 400°. Cut the chicken into finger-size pieces. Fill a large, sealable plastic bag with the potato chips, seal the bag, and crush the chips with the back of a wooden spoon.

In a small bowl, whisk the egg and milk. Dip the chicken pieces into the egg mixture, then into the bag. Shake gently to cover. Place on an ungreased cookie sheet. Bake for 20 minutes, flipping once during the cooking time. Serve with barbecue sauce, salsa, or Honey Mustard Dip (page 42). Serves 4.

Bat Wings

Soy sauce and honey transform ordinary chicken wings into exotic bat wings — a special Halloween treat.

- ½   cup honey
- 1   cup soy sauce
- 1   cup water
- 2   crushed garlic cloves
- 2   dozen chicken wings

Combine the honey, soy sauce, water, and garlic in a large baking dish, reserving ⅔ cup in a bowl for the sauce. Toss in chicken wings and marinate for at least 1 hour. Broil for 10 minutes on each side, allowing the wings to char slightly. Present with sauce. Serves 8.

MOM'S RESTAURANT

FamilyFun **reader Sue Jones, of Altamont, New York, created an "at home" restaurant that has her family jumping for leftovers. She dreamed it up because it didn't make sense for her to prepare a new meal when the refrigerator was already overcrowded. On the other hand, when the response to "What's for dinner?" was "Leftovers!" her family predictably groaned. So Sue inventoried her refrigerator and made a menu for Mom's Restaurant. (She used her computer to write the menu, but a handwritten one will suffice.)**

At dinnertime, she met her family at the entrance to the dining room, apron on, menus in hand, and asked, "How many in your party?" The first response was a giggle. Then they said, "Three." When Sue returned with a notepad, they were ready to place an order.

If your kids really take to this idea, you might suggest they occasionally play waiter and head chef themselves, deciding what kind of restaurant to have (fast food, ethnic, or gourmet), and what to make for an upcoming meal. If they add prices to their menu and you request an itemized bill, the kids will also have to do some quick math.

Dinner's Ready

Cindy's Steak and Chicken Stir-fry

2 to 3 stalks celery, sliced
1 pound frozen chopped broccoli (or use fresh)
½ head of green cabbage, chopped
4 cups cooked rice

Cut the chicken and steak into bite-size pieces and place in a large bowl. Cover with the teriyaki sauce and marinate for at least 6 to 8 hours in the refrigerator. Drain the meat with a slotted spoon before stir-frying to avoid a soupy quality in the final meal.

In a large wok or deep skillet, heat the oil and stir-fry the meat until brown. Add the cut vegetables in order of cooking: carrots, celery, broccoli, then cabbage. Stir until tender but not over-cooked. Serve over rice. Serves 4 to 6.

Chicken Curry

For an authentic Indian meal, I like to serve this dish with chapatis, basmati rice, and little bowls of condiments, such as chopped peanuts or cashew nuts, grated coconut, plain yogurt, and chutney. (Chapatis are available in the frozen food section of health food stores; basmati rice can be found in the rice section of most grocery stores.)

1 tablespoon vegetable oil
1 onion, chopped
1 whole boneless, skinless chicken breast, cut into 2-inch chunks
2 tablespoons butter or margarine
2 tablespoons curry powder
1 crushed garlic clove
1 14-ounce can coconut milk, or ½ cup chicken broth or milk, or 1 cup plain yogurt and ½ cup applesauce
½ cup golden raisins (optional)
½ cup frozen peas (optional)

Heat the vegetable oil in a large frying pan over high heat. Add the onion and chicken and cook for 5 minutes, or until the chicken is browned on all

Cindy's Steak and Chicken Stir-fry

The Miles family of Canon City, Colorado, loves stir-fry and that's just fine with mom Cindy: it's easy to prepare, it tastes good, and it gets her three-year-old son, Paden, to eat his broccoli. Cindy saves time by cutting the meat the day before and marinating it in the refrigerator overnight.

2 to 4 boneless chicken breasts
1 to 1½ pounds round steak
2¼ cups teriyaki barbecue sauce (or your family's favorite barbecue or teriyaki/soy sauce mixture)
2 tablespoons sesame oil
2 to 4 carrots, diced or sliced

FunFact

The name *chopsticks* is our attempt to say the Chinese word *Kuai-za*, meaning quick ones.

Moo Goo Gai Pan

sides. Place the chicken and onion in a bowl. Pour out any leftover oil and use a paper towel to wipe the pan clean.

Melt the butter in the pan over low heat. Add the curry powder and garlic and cook for 3 minutes. Stir in the coconut milk and raisins. Return the chicken to the pan, cover, and simmer for 10 to 12 minutes (be sure the heat is very low or the sauce will curdle). Add the peas in the last 2 minutes of cooking. Serves 4.

Moo Goo Gai Pan

This Chinese dish calls for cooked chicken — and it's a wonderful way to use the remains of a roast chicken. If you don't have leftovers, poach a chicken breast for 20 minutes, then cool and cut into bite-size cubes.

- 2 tablespoons peanut oil
- ½ pound Chinese cabbage or bok choy
- ½ cup button mushrooms, thinly sliced
- 12 snow peas (or more)
- 4 water chestnuts, thinly sliced
- ¼ cup bamboo shoots, thinly sliced
- ¼ cup water
- 1 whole cooked chicken breast, cubed
- 1 teaspoon cornstarch mixed with 3 tablespoons water
    Dash of pepper
- ¼ teaspoon sugar
- 1 to 2 tablespoons soy sauce

Heat the oil in a frying pan or wok over high heat. Just as the oil begins to smoke, add all the vegetables and stir-fry for 30 seconds. Add the ¼ cup water. Cover and cook for 2 minutes. Add the chicken, cornstarch mixture, pepper, sugar, and soy sauce. Stir until the sauce has thickened and the ingredients are coated evenly and cooked throughout. Dish out over rice. Serves 2 to 4.

DINNER WITH FLAIR

When "Oh, Mom, not again," became a frequent chorus at her dinner table, *FamilyFun* reader Rachael Muro created theme dinners. Each family member takes a turn preparing a meal with a theme. Everyone must dress appropriately and bring music or activities to share. The Muros have dined Asian style (with robes and chopsticks), read cowboy poetry at their country and western meal, and dined on Dr. Seuss's *Green Eggs & Ham*.

Turkey Breast Scallopini

Turkey Breast Scallopini

This recipe calls for turkey cutlets, which are boneless, skinless portions of turkey breast. You can use them interchangeably with any recipe that calls for chicken breasts.

- 4   turkey breast cutlets
- ¼   cup grated Parmesan cheese
- ¼   cup bread crumbs
- 3   tablespoons butter
      Juice of half a lemon or orange

Pat the turkey cutlets dry. Mix the cheese and bread crumbs on a plate and coat the cutlets in the mix. Heat 2 tablespoons of the butter in a skillet on medium and add the cutlets. Brown on both sides, about 3 minutes per side, and transfer to a platter. Deglaze the pan by turning the heat to high, adding the lemon juice, and scraping the browned bits into the sauce. Turn off the heat and stir in the remaining butter. Pour the sauce over the turkey and serve immediately. Serves 4.

Turkey Sloppy Joes

FamilyFun contributor Cynthia Caldwell adapted this lean version of the beef classic from her mother's "mean" sloppy joe recipe.

- 1   tablespoon vegetable oil
- 1   medium onion, minced
- 1   green pepper, minced
- 1   pound ground turkey
- ¼   cup tomato paste
- 2   tablespoons chili sauce
- 2   teaspoons Worcestershire sauce
- 2   tablespoons sweet pickle relish
- ¼   teaspoon salt
- ¼   teaspoon pepper
- ¼   to ⅓ cup water
- 4   to 6 bulky rolls

In a large frying pan over medium-high heat, sauté the onion and pepper in the oil for 5 minutes, or until soft. Add the turkey and cook until lightly browned. Add the remaining ingredients, except for the water, and cook until well combined. Add enough water to make the meat "sloppy." Pile onto bulky rolls and serve. Serves 4 to 6.

Fish & Seafood

Salmon Steaks with Quick Dill Sauce

As the Japanese have known for years, fish is a light and healthy dinner option, worthy of being served at least once a week. Whether you're shopping at your local grocer's or a fish market, always look for the freshest fish. It should have a firm, moist flesh and a sweet smell — never a fishy smell, which is a sure sign of aging. Salmon is great with this sauce, but any fresh filet you choose will work.

Quick Dill Sauce:

½	cup sour cream
¼	cup mayonnaise
2	tablespoons milk
1½	teaspoons dill
1	small crushed garlic clove
	Salt and pepper

Fish:

4	6-ounce salmon steaks, 1 inch thick
	Half a lemon

In a small bowl, whisk the sour cream, mayonnaise, and milk until creamy. Add the dill, garlic, and salt and pepper to taste. Stir well; set aside.

Preheat your broiler or prepare the coals for grilling. Rinse the salmon steaks and pat them dry. Squeeze the lemon over the steaks and sprinkle with salt and pepper. Broil or grill the steaks 3 inches from the heat for 8 to 10 minutes, or until the meat has turned from a bright pink to a pale orange. Serves 4 to 6.

Fast Fish Filets

The microwave turns seafood into fast food that is nutritious and delicious.

2	to 3 fish filets, any white fish
	Salt and pepper
	Juice of half a lemon
1½	tablespoons chopped fresh herbs, such as dill, parsley, mint, cilantro, or sage
4	thin lemon slices
	Toppings (see right)

Rinse the filets and pat dry. Salt and pepper both sides and lay them like the spokes of a wheel in a glass pie pan with the thickest portions on the edges. Sprinkle with the lemon juice and herbs and top with the lemon slices. Cover and cook on high for 3 to 6 minutes, or until the fish flakes. Add toppings. Serves 4.

Salmon Steak with Quick Dill Sauce

Fish Filets and...

☛ **Tartar Sauce: Mix ½ cup mayonnaise with 2 to 3 tablespoons relish.**
☛ **Quick Cocktail Sauce: Mix ½ cup ketchup with 2 tablespoons horseradish.**
☛ **Salsa Fresca: See page 53.**
☛ **Quick Dill Sauce: See recipe at left.**
☛ **Teriyaki sauce: Buy at your grocer's.**

Panfried Fish-in-a-Flash

Fish-in-a-Flash Mix

This fish coating works well with almost any filet — scrod, sole, even trout. For extra crunch, use cornmeal instead of the flour.

- ½ cup all-purpose flour
- 2 teaspoons parsley
- 1 teaspoon dried minced onions
- 1 teaspoon garlic powder
- 1 teaspoon basil
- ½ teaspoon salt
- ¼ teaspoon dried lemon peel
- ¼ teaspoon pepper
- Pinch of cayenne pepper

Shake all the ingredients in a large, sealable plastic bag. Makes 1 cup.

Panfried Fish-in-a-Flash:

Gently shake two to three 8-ounce fish filets in the bag of Fish-in-a-Flash Mix. Heat 1 tablespoon butter in a heavy frying pan set on the stove over medium-high heat or on a grill 1 inch above the hot coals. Cook the filets for 6 minutes, flip, and continue cooking until the flesh flakes. Serves 4 to 6.

Citrus Swordfish

This flavorful marinade is ideal for any firm fish (swordfish, tuna, or hake).

- ¼ cup olive oil
- 4 crushed garlic cloves
- 2 teaspoons ground cumin
- ¼ cup chopped fresh Italian parsley or cilantro
- Juice from 2 lemons
- Salt and pepper to taste
- 1 to 2 pounds swordfish

In the bowl of a food processor, combine the oil, garlic, cumin, parsley, and lemon juice. Puree until smooth and add salt and pepper to taste. (You can also do this by hand with a whisk in a large mixing bowl.)

Place the fish in a shallow dish with the sauce and marinate for several hours or overnight. Toss occasionally. Preheat your broiler or prepare the coals for grilling. Broil or grill the fish 3 inches from the flames for 6 to 8 minutes, flip, and continue cooking until it flakes. Serves 4 to 6.

Grilled Shrimp

I haven't met the child who doesn't like shrimp, especially when it's marinated and grilled, as in this recipe. Shrimp can be pricey, so serve it as part of a buffet with rice, vegetables, and salads.

¾　cup olive oil

2　crushed garlic cloves

1　cup dry white wine

1　teaspoon salt

1　teaspoon black pepper

¼　cup finely chopped Italian parsley

2　pounds raw shrimp, peeled and deveined

Combine the oil, garlic, wine, salt, pepper, and parsley in a glass bowl. Add the shrimp, cover, and marinate in the refrigerator for 2 to 3 hours or overnight, turning occasionally.

Prepare your coals for grilling and place the shrimp on the grill, about 2 inches from the heat (a grilling basket makes it easier to turn shrimp on the grill). Grill for about 3 minutes per side, depending on the size of the shrimp. Serves 4 to 6.

Grilled Shrimp

How To Boil Lobsters

Theories on how to boil, steam, or grill lobsters are outnumbered only by the amount of spots on a lobster shell. To prepare either of our methods, look for lobsters that are lively, with wiggly legs, moving claws, and a tail that goes into a curl when you pick it up. At home, store in the coldest part of your refrigerator and cook that day.

Boiling Method

2 tablespoons salt

2 to 4 lobsters, 1¼ pounds each

4 tablespoons butter, melted

1 lemon, cut in quarters, for garnish

Fill a large pot three quarters of the way with fresh water and bring it to a rolling boil. Add salt. Rinse each lobster with cold water, then plunge it head first and upside down into the pot. After the water has returned to a fast boil, reduce the heat and cook, covered, for 12 minutes. Remove each lobster with tongs and serve immediately with melted butter for dipping and lemon wedges. Serves 4.

Stove-top Clambake

Fresh seaweed, about 4 pounds, thoroughly washed of sand

1½ quarts fresh water

4 large potatoes, rolled in foil

2 lobsters, 2 pounds each

4 ears fresh corn, silk removed but husk intact, wrapped in foil

28 to 36 steamer clams, scrubbed

8 tablespoons butter, melted

In a 20-quart pot, place a layer of seaweed. Pour in the water and bring to a boil. In 12-minute increments, add the potatoes and another layer of seaweed, the corn and a layer of seaweed, the lobsters and a layer of seaweed, and finally the clams. Cover the pot during the cooking periods. When the clams have opened fully, serve the medley on large platters with melted butter and pot liquid on the side. Serves 4.

Pasta

Down-home Spaghetti

On Top of Spaghetti

For pasta pronto, top your noodles with one of these savory combos.

☞ Stir-fried vegetables with garlic and herbs

☞ Tuna, capers, and a little cream

☞ Fresh tomatoes, olive oil, red wine vinegar, basil, and Mozzarella cheese

☞ Italian salad dressing

☞ Chopped scallions, peas or broccoli, olive oil, and lemon zest

☞ Can of stewed tomatoes, chopped olives, oregano, and black pepper

☞ Can of chopped clams sautéed with butter and garlic

☞ Strips of chicken breast sautéed in olive oil with black pepper and parsley

☞ Soy sauce and ginger

☞ Salsa and red or black beans

Down-home Spaghetti Sauce

There are a number of good sauces on the market, but if you have the time, it is easy, gratifying, and less expensive to make your own. This recipe requires a long, slow simmer, but little chopping and stirring. It is adaptable (you can add chopped peppers or other vegetables), but if your kids are the kind who search for and toss out any add-ins, the sauce is equally good without the extras.

2 tablespoons olive oil

1 cup chopped onion

2 ribs celery, thinly sliced

1 to 2 carrots, chopped

1 pound ground beef, ground turkey, or ground sweet Italian sausage, or a mixture (optional)

⅓ cup white or red wine

2 28-ounce cans Italian plum tomatoes, whole or crushed

1 teaspoon oregano

1 teaspoon basil

Salt and pepper to taste

In a large skillet or pot, sauté the olive oil and onion over medium heat until the onion is soft. Add the celery and carrots and cook 8 to 10 minutes (lower the heat, if necessary, to prevent the vegetables from browning). For a meat sauce, crumble the ground meat into the pan; cook, stirring, until the meat loses its pink color.

Turn the heat to high, add the wine, and cook, stirring, until the wine evaporates. Add the tomatoes and their juice (if you are using whole tomatoes, break them up in the pan). When the mixture begins to bubble, reduce the heat to low and simmer for 1½ hours, stirring occasionally. Finally, mix in the oregano, basil, and salt and pepper, and remove from the heat. Serve immediately, save for 1 to 2 days in the refrigerator, or cool, then freeze. Makes 2½ quarts.

Lasagna a la Mom

If you're tight on time, make this dish with uncooked noodles (add an extra cup of sauce to the bottom of the pan). No one will ever know the difference.

- 2 cups low-fat ricotta cheese
- ½ cup grated Parmesan cheese
- 1 egg, lightly beaten
- ¼ cup chopped fresh parsley
  Salt and pepper to taste
  Dash of nutmeg
- 2 tablespoons butter
- 2½ cups spaghetti sauce (see Down-home Spaghetti Sauce, at left)
- ½ pound lasagna noodles, cooked according to package directions
- ½ pound Mozzarella, grated

Mix the ricotta and Parmesan cheeses, egg, and parsley. Add the salt, pepper, and nutmeg. Butter a 13- by 9- by 2-inch baking pan and dot sparingly with a bit of the tomato sauce. Place a layer of noodles over the bottom of the pan, overlapping as little as possible. Spread half of the ricotta mixture over the noodles, then the tomato sauce, then the Mozzarella. Repeat layering, finishing with a layer of noodles, the remaining sauce, and a sprinkle of Parmesan. At this point the lasagna may be refrigerated, frozen, or baked. Bake in a preheated 375° oven for 20 minutes, or until hot and bubbling. Remove from the oven and settle for 10 minutes before slicing. Serves 6.

Spinach Lasagna:

Defrost and drain a 10-ounce package of frozen spinach and spread it over the ricotta layers.

Turkey Sausage Lasagna:

Cook ½ pound ground turkey sausage and layer it on top of each of the ricotta layers.

Spaghetti Carbonara

The smell of bacon frying in the pan is enough to heighten any kids' curiosity about this Italian carbonara.

- 1 pound dried spaghetti
- 1 pound bacon, cut in 1-inch pieces
- ½ cup chopped onion
- 2 eggs, lightly beaten
- ½ cup grated Parmesan or Romano cheese
  Salt and pepper to taste
- 2 tablespoons heavy cream

Prepare the spaghetti according to package directions. While the pasta is cooking, sauté the bacon in a large skillet until crisp. Drain on paper towels and reserve 3 teaspoons of fat from the pan. Add the onion and sauté until soft; set aside.

Drain the cooked pasta and return it to the pot over very low heat. Toss in the bacon fat and bacon, onion, eggs, cheese, salt, pepper, and cream. Cook until all the ingredients are well blended and heated through. Serves 4 to 6.

SLURPING SPAGHETTI

How can your kids avoid getting tomato sauce everywhere when they eat spaghetti? According to Ms. Demeanor, the trick is to twirl just three or four strands with your fork, which should spin into the perfect mouthful. You can put a spoon underneath the fork to get the spaghetti under control. The goal is to pick up any loose ends before you bring the pasta up to your mouth.

Lasagna a la Mom

Bow Ties with Veggie Cutouts

The trick to our pasta dish is in the vegetables, which are cut into stars, hearts, and flowers with tiny cookie cutters, also known as aspic cutters (available at kitchen supply stores).

Bow Ties with Veggie Cutouts

2   to 3 cups vegetable cutouts (carrots, zucchini, yellow squash, red and green peppers)
1   pound bow tie pasta, cooked according to package directions
2   tablespoons olive oil
⅓   cup ground almonds
⅓   cup milk
3   crushed garlic cloves
½   teaspoon salt
    Black pepper
    Parmesan cheese

To make the cutouts, slice the vegetables into ⅛- or ¼-inch thicknesses and cut into shapes with tiny cutters (with thick-skinned vegetables, cut from the fleshy side); set aside.

While the pasta is cooking, prepare the sauce. Heat 1 tablespoon of the olive oil in a frying pan over medium heat. Sauté the cutouts for 3 to 4 minutes. Remove the vegetables, add the remaining olive oil and the almonds, stirring until lightly browned. Return the cutouts to the pan and add the milk, garlic, and salt. Cook for 1 to 2 minutes. Drain the pasta, toss in the pan, and stir to coat. Serve with pepper and Parmesan. Serves 4 to 6.

Ziti with Ricotta and Spinach

This straightforward pasta casserole, which is brimming with spinach, ricotta, and tomato sauce, is worth doubling and freezing half for a busy weeknight. You can enhance the flavor with halved cherry tomatoes, grated Mozzarella, fresh basil, pine nuts, or bread crumbs.

2   pounds fresh or 10 ounces frozen spinach, chopped
1   pound ricotta cheese
3   eggs, well beaten
⅔   cup grated Parmesan cheese
⅓   cup chopped fresh parsley
    Salt and pepper to taste
3   cups spaghetti sauce (see Down-home Spaghetti Sauce, page 92)
1   pound ziti or penne, cooked according to package directions

Steam the spinach until it wilts or heats through. Drain any excess moisture. In a large bowl, combine the spinach with the ricotta, eggs, Parmesan, parsley, salt, pepper, and 2½ cups of the sauce. Whip the mixture until it becomes fluffy, then add the cooked pasta. Spread the remaining tomato sauce on the bottom of a 13- by 9- by 2-inch baking dish and cover with the pasta mixture. Bake in a preheated 375° oven for 20 minutes, or until heated through. Serves 8.

Tortellini with Pesto

My niece and nephew insist on having this dish at least once a week, and my brother sends the leftovers to school with them for lunch. This, I'd say, is a true sign of the times — a generation being brought up on foods I'd never heard of until I hit my twenties.

- 2 cups fresh basil, rinsed and patted dry
- ¼ cup pine nuts, sunflower seeds, or walnuts
- 2 crushed garlic cloves
- ¾ cup olive oil
- ½ cup grated Parmesan cheese
  Salt and pepper to taste
- 2 pounds fresh or frozen cheese tortellini, cooked according to package directions

Put the basil, nuts, and garlic in the bowl of a food processor or blender and process until the leaves are all chopped up. With the motor running, pour in the oil and process or blend until smooth. Stir in the cheese and salt and pepper. Scoop this pesto into a large serving bowl and add the drained tortellini. Toss well with tongs. Serves 4 to 6 with leftovers for lunch.

We're Going Greek Pasta Salad

"The cheese is yum" was the review of four-year-old taste-tester Rafael Marchand Jaeger. An ethnic creation from the Paull-Baird family, *FamilyFun* readers, this recipe combines the distinctive flavors of feta cheese and olives with child-pleasing pasta spirals. The result is a modern variation on old-world cuisine. For a complete Mediterranean meal, serve with warm pita bread and Hummus (see page 36) or Cucumber Dipping Sauce (see page 52).

Dinner's Ready

- 1 pound regular or tricolored pasta spirals, cooked according to package directions
- 2 crushed garlic cloves
- 2 tablespoons olive oil
- 1 small eggplant, peeled and cubed
- 1 large tomato, chopped
- 2 celery stalks, diced
- 12 Greek or black olives, pitted
  Salt and pepper to taste
- 8 ounces feta cheese

In a large saucepan, sauté the garlic in the oil for about 2 minutes. Add the eggplant and sauté for another 5 minutes. Cover and continue cooking on medium-low heat for 10 minutes, then add the tomato, celery, olives, and salt and pepper. Sauté, uncovered, for 5 more minutes. Toss with the pasta and feta cheese and mix well. Serve immediately. Serves 6 to 8.

Pasta Jewelry

The art of pasta jewelry is no longer limited to macaroni — today's kids can thread wheels, bow ties, and more. Paint pasta in a rainbow of colors with acrylics and thread on ribbon or kite string for bracelets and necklaces.

We're Going Greek Pasta Salad

Angel Hair with
Tiny Tomato Sauce

Macaroni and Cheese and....

Simple additions turn mac and cheese from ordinary to extraordinary.

- ☞ **Steamed frozen peas**
- ☞ **A sprinkle of bread crumbs**
- ☞ **Cooked chicken pieces**
- ☞ **Sautéed ground beef and steamed string beans**
- ☞ **White tuna**
- ☞ **Red kidney beans**
- ☞ **Steamed broccoli florets**
- ☞ **Chopped olives**
- ☞ **Chopped tomatoes**
- ☞ **Pepperoni slices**
- ☞ **Chopped fresh basil**
- ☞ **Feta or Romano cheese**
- ☞ **Pesto (see page 95)**

Angel Hair with Tiny Tomato Sauce

Too hot to cook? Try this no-cook sauce that's made with garden-fresh tomatoes. If you grow your own cherry tomatoes, ask the kids to do the picking for the sauce.

½ pound angel hair pasta, cooked according to package directions
1 pint cherry tomatoes, sliced in half
½ cup olive oil
¼ cup fresh basil leaves, thinly sliced
1 tablespoon butter
1 cup fresh bread crumbs
Salt and pepper to taste
Parmesan cheese

In a large bowl, mix the tomatoes with the olive oil and basil. In a medium-size frying pan, melt the butter, toss in the bread crumbs, and sauté briefly; set aside. Toss the cooked pasta in the bowl with the tomato mixture until evenly combined, then add the salt and pepper. Garnish with the bread crumbs and cheese. Serves 3 to 4.

Wagon Wheel Mac & Cheese

We jazzed up this dish, which is much better homemade than out of the box, by using wagon wheel pasta. Feel free to use any shape you like — bow ties, spirals, whatever is available.

½ pound wagon wheel pasta
3 tablespoons butter
3 tablespoons flour
1 teaspoon dry mustard
3½ cups milk
1½ cups grated Cheddar cheese
1 teaspoon salt
½ teaspoon white pepper
¾ cup bread crumbs
½ teaspoon oregano
½ teaspoon basil
½ teaspoon vegetable oil

Preheat the oven to 350°. Cook the pasta for *half* of the recommended cooking time. Rinse under cold water, drain, and set aside. Meanwhile, in a saucepan melt the butter. Add the flour and dry mustard and cook over low heat for 2 to 3 minutes, continuously stirring. Slowly add the milk, whisking constantly to avoid lumps. Continue cooking until thickened, but do not boil the sauce. Take the sauce off the heat and whisk in the cheese. Add the salt and pepper, then mix in the pasta until coated. Pour into a greased baking dish. In a small bowl, mix the bread crumbs, herbs, and oil. Sprinkle over the macaroni and cheese and bake for 20 minutes, or until bubbly. Serves 4.

Vegetarian

Rainbow Buffet

A novel meal that looks stunning and tastes better, the rainbow buffet evolved four years ago when *FamilyFun* reader Jenny Mulligan of Seattle noticed her kids ate heartily when their meals were colorful and they could dispense with utensils. Her kids, Michael, eight, and Jamey, five, get into choosing and arranging the color-coordinated ingredients of this all-in-one meal that combines the salad, main course, and dessert. Make the rainbow as big or as small as you want and pick from a variety of edible colors:

Red: Cherry tomatoes, apple slices, strawberries, peppers, radishes

Orange: Cheddar cheese cubes, melon balls, baby carrots, peach slices

Yellow: Cheese cubes, banana slices, pear slices, peppers, hard-boiled egg slices

Green: Green grapes, pea pods, Celery, kiwi, peppers, broccoli

Blue/purple: Blueberries, plums, red grapes

Brown: Raisins, bread (rolls, bagels, breadsticks, muffins)

Juice of a lemon (optional)

Help your youngsters select at least two foods from each color, making sure that all the food groups are represented. Let the kids rinse, trim, and arrange them on a large, chilled platter in a rainbow or a color wheel. To prevent the apples, pears, and bananas from browning, sprinkle with lemon juice. Serves 4 to 6.

Rainbow Buffet

Ratatouille

This French Mediterranean stew is meant to be served over rice.

1   large eggplant, cubed
¼   to ⅓ cup olive oil
1   onion, thinly sliced
1   red or green pepper, chopped
2   to 4 crushed garlic cloves
4   small zucchini, chopped
4   tomatoes, chopped
    Salt and pepper to taste
¼   cup chopped fresh basil
    Parmesan cheese

Salt the eggplant, drain in a colander for 1 hour, and pat dry. Heat half the oil in a large saucepan and briefly sauté the eggplant until brown, then add the onion and pepper. Next, add the garlic, zucchini, and tomatoes. Cook until a soft stew has formed, about 15 to 30 minutes. Add the salt, pepper, and basil. Sprinkle with the cheese and serve. You can freeze leftovers. Serves 4.

Meatless Meals in a Flash

Hummus (page 36), pita bread, and tabbouleh with tomatoes and peas

Tortellini with Pesto (page 95), garden salad, and garlic bread

Turtle Bean Burritos (page 99) and Mexican Rice (page 113)

Veggie burgers and Oven-Baked French Fries (page 116)

Mini Veggie Potpies with Hats

As vegetarians, the Rohms of West Linn, Oregon, are always on the look-out for interesting new meals. They struck gold with this recipe, which uses a creamy cashew sauce to delicately blend the vegetables. Andrea says her kids — Nicholas, ten, Elena, seven, and Michael, five — especially like putting the pastry shell "hat" on the pies. Substitute fresh vegetables in season and try a variety of them, such as cubed zucchini and yellow squash.

> 1   small onion, chopped
> 1   tablespoon vegetable oil
> 1   1-pound package frozen mixed
>   vegetables, such as peas, carrots,
>   green beans, and lima beans
> 1   10-ounce box frozen corn
> ½   red pepper, diced (optional)
> 2   10-ounce packages frozen puff
>   pastry shells

Sauce:

> 2   cups water
> ½   cup cashew nuts
> 1   tablespoon poultry seasonings
> 2   tablespoons flour
> 2   teaspoons onion powder
> ½   teaspoon garlic powder
> 1   teaspoon brewer's yeast (optional)

In a large skillet, sauté the onion in the oil until transparent. Add all the vegetables and cook until heated through. Set the pan aside and cover.

Bake the pastry shells according to the package directions while you prepare the sauce. In a blender or food processor, blend 1 cup of the water with the cashews until creamy. Add the remaining water and ingredients, process until smooth, and pour the liquid into a heavy saucepan. Cook on medium-low heat, stirring constantly, until the sauce thickens, about 15 to 18 minutes.

Add the sauce to the vegetable medley, mix thoroughly, and spoon into hollowed-out pastry shells. Use the crispy shell tops as "hats" for the vegetables. Serve immediately. Serves 6.

Celebrate Vegetarian Awareness Month

If you're family isn't already vegetarian, try going meatless for a day in the month of October. Serve up grain cereals for breakfast and make veggie sandwiches for lunch. For dinner, order a meatless entrée at a Mexican, Chinese, or Indian restaurant (three ethnic cuisines with excellent vegetarian dishes).

Draw Your Dinner

While your kids are waiting for dinner, keep them entertained with this instant art project. Let your child know what is on the menu and set out crayons, markers, and a few sheets of place-mat-size paper. While you are cooking, your child can draw up his or her version of the meal, including the food, plates, napkins, cups, and silverware. The result is a colorful place mat for everyone around the table. (Don't be surprised if your broccoli has been replaced with an ice-cream sundae.)

Turtle Bean Burritos

There are a variety of excellent canned beans and refried beans on the market for filling tortillas. Pinto and kidney beans are most commonly used in the canned varieties, but when *FamilyFun* contributor Becky Okrent makes burritos at home, she likes to serve black beans (particularly for their other name — turtle beans). For a speedier version, use three 15-ounce cans of black beans, rinsed, and add an extra cup of water for cooking.

Beans:

2¼	cups dried black beans
4	crushed garlic cloves
1	onion, chopped
1	jalapeño pepper, seeded, veined, and chopped
8	cups water
4	cups vegetable stock or water
¼	teaspoon ground cloves
¼	teaspoon mild chili powder
2	teaspoons salt
8	to 10 flour tortillas

Fillings:

1	cup chopped tomato
1	cup shredded lettuce
1	cup grated cheese
	Salsa

Rinse the beans, sorting through them to remove any stones. In a large pan, cover the beans with water and let them soak while you prepare the garlic, onion, and jalapeño.

Drain the water, rinse the beans again, and pour in the 8 cups of water. Place all the remaining bean ingredients except the salt into the pan with the beans and cook over medium heat, simmering for about 2 hours, until the beans are tender. (To test a bean for doneness, try blowing on it; if the black skin lifts off, the beans are cooked.)

Drain the beans, reserving the liquid, and then pour them into a serving bowl. Toss with the salt.

Wrap a stack of tortillas in foil or spread them directly on the racks in a 400° oven and bake for about 3 minutes. Or, heat them, one at a time, on an ungreased skillet for 15 seconds per side.

Set out the fillings in bowls on the table. Fill the warm tortillas with the beans and the fillings of your choice and fold burrito style (see at right). The leftover turtle beans can be stored in the refrigerator; keep the reserved liquid separate for reheating the beans. Makes about 8 cups.

Kitchen Sort

A sorting and pouring project, this Montessori school classic is good for three-year-olds, who know not to put small things in their mouth. Set up your child on the kitchen floor or at a table with some big mixing bowls and empty egg cartons, plus scoops or plastic pitchers, and a bag of fifteen-bean soup (aka a variety of dried beans). Let her sit there, pouring and sorting while you fix dinner. Over time, as she gets good at the big bowls and scoops, give her smaller ones, plus an ice-cube tray, smaller spoons, and various kinds of macaroni. For advanced sorting, let her try salad tongs and a pile of cotton balls; then tweezers and a half cup of uncooked rice. While you are cooking nearby, occasionally ask questions about the colors, shapes, and textures.

Burrito Folding 101

1. Fill a tortilla with favorite toppings and turn in the sides.

2. Fold up the bottom edge.

3. Then turn the top edge down.

CHAPTER 7

Side Dishes & Salads

MASHED POTATOES and peas were the only side dishes I liked as a child. The potatoes could hold a swimming pool of gravy, and garden-fresh peas tasted as sweet as candy. But mine is a family of vegetable-lovers, and we were raised eating carrots, corn, and beans from our garden, freshly picked in the summer and frozen, then steamed in the winter.

When I refused to eat anything but my mashed potatoes and peas, my grandmother would quietly sit at the table, hands folded, napkin in lap, waiting for me to finish, as if it would be impolite to let a child sit at the table alone. Eventually, I caught on that she wasn't going to excuse herself until all my turnips disappeared. One day in sixth grade, I decided to break the silence. So I said, "Grandma, the only reason why you like vegetables is because your taste buds are all worn down." Exasperated and no doubt a bit offended, she finally left me to cope with the turnips alone.

Getting kids to eat the required five servings of vegetables a day has tried many an adult's patience. Kids come up with a host of creative excuses — some as rude as my comment to my grandmother. But there are a few tips we could learn from her generation (like growing our own vegetables) and a few new approaches we might want to consider (beginning with the premise that forcing kids to eat their vegetables rarely changes their attitude toward food). The following ideas should be a start:

Eat fresh produce in season. For the best-tasting, and often the least expensive, vegetables, shop with the season in mind. Look for seasonal produce at your grocer's

Waldorf Salad: *Page 109*

Vegetables Kids Love

Serve vegetables you know your kids will eat — and introduce a new one once a week for variety.

- ☞ Raw, peeled baby carrots or carrot sticks
- ☞ Snow peas (see page 107)
- ☞ Broccoli Trees (see page 104)
- ☞ Sliced cucumbers
- ☞ Corn on the cob (see page 106)

or shop at a farmers' market, where your kids can meet the people who grow the vegetables. Pick up your family's favorites and some never-seen-before varieties, from white eggplants to purple potatoes, to prepare at home. If you want to receive a weekly supply of vegetables, join a food bank. Stock up and freeze the abundant supplies — out-of-season, frozen vegetables actually taste better than fresh ones shipped too far.

Grow your own. Planting a garden gives kids a chance to see for them-

selves where food actually comes from. Generally, they have the greatest success with the large-seeded vegetables (peas, squash, and watermelon) because they are easy to handle, and with the early risers (radishes and cucumbers) because they hold the kids' interest. If your children participate in the whole process — planting through harvesting — they will be more likely to sample the goods.

Serve raw vegetables instead of cooked. Cooked vegetables have a stronger flavor to kids than they do to adults, so try serving raw vegetables for a change. Carrot sticks, cucumber slices, and a spinach salad may go down the hatch easier than their cooked counterparts. You might also offer a dip for their veggies (see pages 52 and 53).

Make a meal of side dishes. For a satisfying, light dinner, serve two or more side dishes from this chapter. Or for fun, set up a salad or baked potato bar on your kitchen table with a host of creative toppings set out in small bowls. Then let everyone build their own baked potato or salad dinner.

Serve fruits instead of vegetables. If your child balks at string beans or peas, serve him apples, pears, or strawberries. Although they taste sweeter, fruits are often just as nutritious.

Vegetables

Asparagus with Sesame-Orange Dipping Sauce

Although asparagus is available from January to June, the biggest, freshest supply hits the markets in early spring (March and April). This dish can be served warm or cold, depending on your family's preference.

> 1 pound asparagus, trimmed
> ½ teaspoon salt
>
> Sauce:
> 2 tablespoons orange juice
> 1 teaspoon orange rind, finely grated
> ¼ cup olive oil
> 1 teaspoon sesame oil
> Sea salt to taste
> Freshly ground pepper to taste

Find a saucepan wide enough to hold the asparagus spears lengthwise and set it over medium-high heat. Fill about three quarters with water, add the salt, and bring to a boil. Plunge the spears into the boiling water, return to a boil, and cook until the spears are just tender when pierced with a fork, about 2 to 6 minutes depending on thickness (do not overcook). Rinse under cold running water to stop cooking and then drain on a clean kitchen towel.

To prepare the sauce, whisk together the orange juice, orange rind, olive oil, sesame oil, and coarse salt and pepper until they are well blended. Arrange the asparagus on a large serving platter with dipping sauce on the side. Serves 4.

Asparagus with Sesame-Orange Dipping Sauce

Sesame Broccoli

When cooked in the microwave oven, broccoli keeps its bright green color and crispiness. For even more crunch, I add sesame seeds.

> 2 tablespoons sesame seeds
> 1 head broccoli, cut into florets with the tough stems removed
> 2 tablespoons water
> Salt and pepper to taste

Spread the sesame seeds on a paper towel. Microwave on high for 3 to 4 minutes, or until the seeds turn light brown. Set aside. Place the broccoli in a microwave-safe casserole with the stems pointing out. Add the water, cover tightly, and cook on high for about 4 minutes. Uncover and let stand for 2 minutes before draining and tossing with the sesame seeds and seasoning. Serves 4.

Veggie Toppers

Give your vegetables extra flavor with a sprinkle of the following:

- Toasted chopped nuts, such as almonds, walnuts, and peanuts
- Crumbled bacon
- Toasted sesame seeds
- Bread crumbs
- Chopped fresh herbs (see Herb Flavorings on page 105)
- Grated Parmesan or Cheddar cheese
- Chopped hard-boiled egg

Carrot Coins

Oven-Roasted String Beans

When it's too cold to grill, I roast my vegetables for a great smoky flavor.

- 2 pounds green and/or yellow string beans, washed and trimmed
- 1 tablespoon olive oil
  Salt

Toss the beans with oil and spread them out on a cookie sheet. Sprinkle with salt. Roast in a 450° preheated oven for 10 minutes. Serves 8.

Oven-Roasted Asparagus:

Substitute 2 pounds asparagus for the beans and roast for 8 minutes. Serves 8.

Broccoli Trees

Watch the vegetables disappear as your kids create and eat a forest of broccoli. Prepare a dip by combining ¼ cup light sour cream, ⅓ cup mayonnaise, ½ teaspoon sugar, 1 tablespoon lemon juice, and 1 tablespoon chopped fresh basil leaves. To make the trees, cut 3 cups broccoli florets and peel 4 carrots. Cut each carrot widthwise and then lengthwise into 4 pieces. Assemble on a plate by laying 3 carrot pieces for a trunk with the broccoli florets as the leaves. Spread dip under the trunks for the forest floor. Makes 5 trees.

PLANTING CARROTS FOR SNOWMEN

The Shilling family of Fayetteville, West Virginia, started an annual tradition by accident. The first year their son planted carrots, they never got around to harvesting them all. After the first snowman of the season was built, a dash to the refrigerator brought a moan: "No carrots for the nose, Mom." Then mom, Terri, remembered the ones left in the ground, and sure enough, she dug down through the snow and frozen ground and pulled up beautiful carrots. Now, every spring the Shillings plant a special area of carrots to be saved for snowmen's noses.

Carrot Coins

Cynthia Caldwell, a regular *FamilyFun* contributor, learned to make these when she was a Girl Scout. She has passed her love of carrot coins on to her daughter, Isabelle.

- 3 to 4 carrots
- ½ cup water
- 2 tablespoons brown sugar
- 1 tablespoon butter
- 1 teaspoon cider vinegar
  Salt and pepper to taste

Peel and slice the carrots into thin rounds or coins. Place them in a medium-size frying pan with the water. Cover and cook over medium-high heat for 6 to 7 minutes, or until the water has nearly evaporated and the carrots are soft. Uncover and add the sugar, butter, and cider vinegar. Turn up the heat and sauté, stirring for 2 to 3 minutes. A copper-colored glaze will form over the carrots. Season with salt and pepper and serve. Serves 3 to 5.

Flower Power Carrots:

For a special occasion, cut slightly wider carrots into coins. Using an aspic cutter (tiny cookie cutter), cut each coin into a flower.

Grilled Vegetables

If you want your kids to eat all their veggies, try grilling. Grilled green beans taste as good as french fries, and red onions turn as sugary as a dessert. The easiest way to grill large amounts is to use grilling baskets, which make turning vegetables hassle-free. A spatula and patience will suffice as well. Wash and prepare all the vegetables and then toss them with olive oil (leaving the water on them ensures that not too much oil will stick). Prepare the hot coals and set the grill about 3 inches from the heat. The cooking times are flexible — just be sure to turn, turn, turn.

Grilled Vegetables

Green and Yellow String Beans:

Trim the beans; rinse and toss with olive oil, salt, and pepper. Grill for 8 minutes, or until crisp but brown.

Red, Yellow, and Green Peppers:

Wash, seed, and slice the peppers into quarters. Toss or rub with oil and cook for 8 minutes.

Baby Carrots:

Wash the carrots, toss with oil, and grill for about 8 minutes.

New Potatoes:

If you don't grow your own, look for a selection of red or yellow fingerlings at a farmers' market. Scrub them, cut into halves, and toss with oil, salt, pepper, and rosemary. Grill for 10 to 15 minutes, or until browned.

Red Onions:

Peel the outer skin and rub with olive oil. Grill for 15 minutes, or until tender. Use this same method for small leeks and white and yellow onions. If they're large, halve them, and grill with the cut side down.

Eggplant:

Slice lengthwise into 1-inch-thick slices and sprinkle with salt. Let sit for a half hour. Pat dry, then rub with oil and grill until tender, about 15 minutes.

Summer Squash:

Select the smallest varieties available and grill them whole or halved. If whole, cook until tender; if halved, cook until browned, about 6 minutes.

Tomatoes:

Place whole, washed tomatoes on the grill (cherry tomatoes taste wonderful). Cook until they are charred on the outside, about 6 minutes.

Beets:

Trim the bottoms and leave about 1 inch of the greens' stems. Rub the beets with oil and grill for 15 minutes, or until tender.

Herb Flavorings

Basil: Beans, peas, peppers, potatoes, spinach, squash, and tomatoes

Dill: Beans, cabbage, cucumbers, potatoes, and squash

Oregano: Beans, eggplant, mushrooms, potatoes, squash, and tomatoes

Rosemary: Cabbage, tomatoes, cauliflower, potatoes, and squash

Sage: Asparagus, beans, corn, carrots, and peas

Tarragon: Asparagus, beans, beets, broccoli, cabbage, cauliflower, cucumbers, mushrooms, peas, squash, and tomatoes

Thyme: Artichokes, beans, broccoli, carrots, corn, leeks, onions, peas, potatoes, and tomatoes

Butternut squash, which keeps well through the winter, has a nutty flavor that melds well with herbs and spices. "This scalloped pie warms us twice," says *FamilyFun* contributor Vivi Mannuzza. "Once as it bakes and again as we devour it." You can increase or decrease the butter and flavorings to suit your family's taste.

- 2 tablespoons butter
- 1 3- to 4-pound butternut squash
- 1 onion, thinly sliced
- ¼ teaspoon each of thyme, sage, rosemary, marjoram, oregano, basil, garlic powder, salt, and ground black pepper
- 1 to 2 cups fresh bread crumbs

Preheat the oven to 375°. Lightly butter a 9- by 13-inch baking pan and set the remaining butter aside. Split the squash in half lengthwise, scrape out the insides, and crosscut slices about ⅛ inch thick. Trim off the hard skin.

Layer the squash and onion slices (this part is a fun job for kids). Sprinkle each layer with the herbs and spices, and dot with the remaining butter. Top with the bread crumbs.

Cover with foil and bake for 30 to 40 minutes, or until tender when a fork is inserted. Uncover and bake for another 5 minutes, or until the bread crumbs are toasted. Serves 6 to 8.

How To Boil Corn

Once picked, corn quickly begins to convert its sugar to starch. So for a peak taste experience, put water on to boil just before you pick the corn. If you don't have your own corn patch, try for recently picked corn from a farm stand. Plunge the corn into boiling water (purists suggest adding a few tablespoons of milk) right before you're ready to sit down. Cook for 3 minutes after the water returns to a boil. Drain and serve.

Roasted Corn on the Cob

Corn never tastes better than when it's still on the cob, and cooking it doesn't get much easier than when you roast it in its husk on the grill.

- 1 dozen ears unhusked corn
- 1 stick butter
  Salt and pepper

Without removing the husks or silk, soak the corn in water for 15 minutes. Remove from the water and place ears directly on the grill or coals. Rotate them with a pair of tongs while grilling so that all the sides are evenly cooked. The corn should be ready in 8 to 16 minutes, depending on how hot the fire is. Remove from the grill and peel carefully because the ears will be very hot. The husks and silks should come off easily. Spread butter on the corn and season with salt and pepper. Serves 12.

Stir-Fried Snow Peas

Chinese flavorings — soy sauce, ginger, and garlic — make any vegetable more appetizing to kids. Put your kids to work stripping the stems off the snow peas.

- 2 teaspoons sesame oil
- ½ to 1 teaspoon fresh minced ginger
- 1 pound fresh snow peas, rinsed and stems removed
- 1 8-ounce can water chestnuts, sliced
- 1 tablespoon soy sauce

In a frying pan or wok, warm the sesame oil over medium-high heat. Add the ginger, snow peas, water chestnuts, and soy sauce, and stir-fry for about 3 to 5 minutes, or until the peas turn bright green. Serves 4 to 6.

Candy Corn

With this recipe, you can magically turn ordinary corn into candy corn. The trick is a tablespoon of sugar. The novelty may be enough to get your kids to eat their corn.

- 1 10-ounce package frozen corn
- 3 tablespoons butter
- 1 to 2 tablespoons brown sugar
- ¼ cup diced, sweet red pepper (optional)
- 2 scallions, chopped (optional)

Cook the frozen corn according to package directions. Melt the butter in a saucepan over medium-low heat, add the brown sugar, and stir until smooth (be careful the mixture doesn't burn). Drain the corn and add it to the brown sugar mixture with the red pepper and scallions. Cook for 2 minutes, stirring constantly. Serve hot or cold. Serves 4.

Side Dishes & Salads

Spaghetti Squash

Dragging a fork down the middle of a spaghetti squash transforms the squash to a mess of playful strings. This yellow squash can be found in your local grocery store during the fall and winter.

- 1 medium spaghetti squash
  Salt and pepper to taste
- 2 tablespoons butter
  Parmesan cheese

Preheat the oven to 375°. Cut the squash in half lengthwise, sprinkle the halves lightly with salt and pepper, and place in an ovenproof glass pan. Add about ½ inch of water. Cover with foil and bake for about 1 hour, or until the squash is cooked through.

To serve, add 1 tablespoon of the butter to each half and scrape the stringy flesh with a fork to make "spaghetti." Garnish with the cheese. Serves 6 to 8.

Garlic Spaghetti Squash:

Sprinkle the cooked squash with sautéed garlic and bread crumbs.

Candy Corn

Salads

Cucumbers with Yogurt-Dill Dressing

A generation ago, most parents made this refreshing dish with sour cream. This version, made with low-fat yogurt, is lighter and equally delightful.

3 to 5 cucumbers, thinly sliced
  Salt
1½ cups low-fat yogurt, drained of excess liquid
1 cup chopped fresh dill
¼ teaspoon ground cumin
  Chopped fresh mint (optional)
  Black or white pepper to taste

Lightly salt the sliced cucumbers and drain in a colander. Mix the yogurt, dill, and cumin in a serving bowl, then toss in the cucumbers. Refrigerate until ready to serve. Garnish with mint and pepper. Serves 8 to 10.

Tomatoes with Basil and Mozzarella

It's almost impossible to find tasty tomatoes out of season, so when they're at their seasonal best, this dish can be served as often as you like. I prefer to use fresh Mozzarella, which is packed in water and available in the deli section of most grocers.

6 or more large ripe tomatoes, sliced fairly thick
1 pound whole or part skim milk Mozzarella, sliced the same thickness as the tomatoes
  Handful of fresh basil leaves rinsed, patted dry, and minced
¼ cup olive oil
  Salt and pepper to taste

Alternate the tomato and Mozzarella slices on a large serving platter. Sprinkle with the basil and drizzle with the olive oil. Prepare in advance, then season with salt and pepper just before serving. Serves 8 to 10.

Tomatoes with Basil and Mozzarella, Couscous with Peas, Cucumbers with Yogurt-Dill Dressing: *Page 108, 112*

One-Bean Salad

Tossed in a light vinaigrette, this dish is for kids (and adults) who pick out the good beans in three-bean salads. For the chickpeas (garbanzos), you can substitute any bean you prefer — kidney, black, or pinto.

 2 19-ounce cans of garbanzo beans, rinsed and drained
 2 scallions, chopped
 1 red onion, diced
 1 tomato, chopped
 1 crushed garlic clove
 ¼ cup red wine vinegar
 ¾ cup olive oil
 ½ cup chopped fresh parsley
 ¼ teaspoon salt
 ⅛ teaspoon black pepper

In a large bowl, combine all the ingredients and stir well. Cover and refrigerate before serving. Serves 6 to 8.

One-Bean Salad

Festive Corn Salad

Serve this bright yellow and green salad with tacos, fajitas, or any Mexican dish. For a bite, add minced jalapeño.

 2 15-ounce cans whole corn kernels
 1 green pepper, finely chopped
 1 red onion, chopped
 1 tomato, chopped
    Half a bunch of parsley, chopped
 ¼ cup cider vinegar
 2 tablespoons olive oil
    Salt and pepper to taste

In a medium bowl, mix the corn, pepper, onion, tomato, and parsley. Toss with the vinegar and oil, then sprinkle on the salt and pepper. Serve immediately or refrigerate until ready to serve. Serves 8 to 10.

Waldorf Salad

This salad dresses up a plate nicely. Use fresh ingredients and toss well to coat the apples and prevent them from browning.

 2 to 3 cups chopped apple
 1 cup Cheddar cheese chunks
 1 cup green or red grapes
 ½ cup diced celery
 ½ cup walnut pieces
 ½ cup raisins
 ⅓ cup mayonnaise
 1 tablespoon fresh lemon juice

In a large bowl, toss all the ingredients and stir well to coat with the mayonnaise and lemon juice. Refrigerate until ready to serve. Serves 6 to 8.

Polar Picnics

With winters as cold as they are in Wisconsin, *FamilyFun* reader Patti Barnes of West Bend has found it hard to think of indoor activities to keep her kids happy. Last winter, she and her three-year-old son, Danny, hit on a solution — an indoor picnic. Patti put a red-checkered, vinyl tablecloth over her carpeting in the living room. She filled a basket with summer foods — salads, fruit, chips, and other goodies. Then they put on music and had a feast. As Patti says, "As long as kids think it's a party, they make their own fun."

Salad Dressings

Honey-Poppy Seed Dressing

Creamy Dreamy Blue Cheese

Once you learn how easy it is to make this dressing, you'll never buy it again. It is best prepared a day in advance.

- ½ cup sour cream
- ¼ cup mayonnaise
- 2 tablespoons milk
- 1 tablespoon lemon juice
  Salt and black pepper to taste
- ¼ cup crumbled blue cheese

Using a fork, mix the sour cream, mayonnaise, milk, and lemon until smooth. Add the salt, pepper, and blue cheese. Refrigerate. Makes about 1¼ cups.

Soy-Honey Dressing

A versatile mixture, this can be used as a salad dressing, marinade, or dip.

- 4 tablespoons light soy sauce
- 3 tablespoons water
- 3 tablespoons honey
- 1 tablespoon sesame oil
- 2 tablespoons rice wine vinegar
- 1 tablespoon dry or cooking sherry
- 1 tablespoon crushed garlic
- 1 teaspoon minced fresh ginger
- 2 scallions, white part only, chopped

Combine all the ingredients and store in the refrigerator. Makes 1 cup.

Dijon Vinaigrette

Kids can do all the measuring and mixing for this classic dressing.

- ⅓ cup red wine vinegar
- ½ cup olive oil
- ½ cup vegetable oil
- ⅛ teaspoon coarse black pepper
- 1 crushed garlic clove
- ½ teaspoon thyme
- 2 teaspoons Dijon mustard
- ¼ teaspoon salt

Combine all the ingredients in a clean jar with a tight-fitting lid. Shake well. Makes 1⅓ cups.

Honey-Poppy Seed Dressing

A sweet dressing with a crunch, this is the hit of my household.

- 1 cup oil
- ⅓ cup vinegar
- 2 tablespoons water
- 2 tablespoons honey
- 1 to 2 tablespoons poppy seeds

Blend the oil, vinegar, water, and honey in a blender until creamy, then stir in the poppy seeds. Store in the refrigerator. Makes 1½ cups.

Pineapple Boats

The key to this fruit salad is in the presentation. Be sure to buy a fresh pineapple (the bottom should be slightly yellow and a leaf should pull out easily).

- 1 pineapple, cut in half lengthwise
   Juice from half a lemon
- 1½ cups seedless grapes
- 2 kiwis, peeled and sliced
- 2 11-ounce cans mandarin oranges
- 12 strawberries, hulled and sliced
- 1 sliced banana (optional)
- ½ cup chopped walnuts (optional)

Remove the core of the pineapple halves, carve out the remaining fruit, cut it in bite-size chunks, and place them in a large bowl. Squeeze the lemon over the shells and chunks to prevent browning. To the bowl, add the grapes, kiwis, oranges without the juice, strawberries, banana, and walnuts. Toss well, then spoon into the pineapple shells. Chill covered until serving time. Serves 6 to 8.

Carrot Stick Salad

This uncomplicated salad, which comes from *FamilyFun* contributor Emily Todd, combines several foods kids like: carrots, pineapple chunks, and raisins. Although the result might seem like dressed-up carrot sticks to adults, kids recognize its true worth. To julienne the carrots, cut them with a sharp knife into matchstick-thin strips (a job for patient adults).

- 1 pound carrots, julienned
- 1 8¼-ounce can pineapple chunks in syrup (about 1 cup)
- 1 cup raisins
- ¾ cup walnuts (optional)

In a medium-size bowl, toss together the carrots, pineapple, and raisins. Add the walnuts, if desired. Cover and refrigerate until you're ready to serve. Serves 6.

Fabulous Fruit Sauce

FamilyFun **contributor Mollie Katzen makes a quick raspberry sauce to drizzle over fruit, and her kids love it. To make it, puree 1½ cups fresh or frozen raspberries and 2 tablespoons orange juice concentrate (if you are using fresh or unsweetened berries, add 2 to 3 tablespoons sugar or honey as well). Pour the mixture into a strainer placed over a bowl. Stir with a spoon, pressing the smooth liquid through. Taste and adjust as necessary, adding more sugar, or lemon or lime juice to your liking.**

Rices & Grains

Couscous with Peas

Couscous with Peas

Originating in North Africa, this fine, grainlike cereal cooks even faster than rice or potatoes. You can serve it plain, embellish it with peas and onion as it is here, or experiment with just about any fresh herb or chopped vegetable.

1 onion, diced
1 crushed garlic clove
1 tablespoon olive oil
1 cup frozen peas
1 tablespoon minced fresh dill
Salt and pepper to taste
1½ cups vegetable or chicken stock
1 cup couscous

Sauté the onion and garlic in the oil in a saucepan over medium heat until translucent, about 5 minutes. Stir in the peas, dill, salt, pepper, and stock and bring to a boil. Add the couscous, cover, and return to a boil. Remove from the heat and let the mixture sit for 5 minutes, or until the liquid is absorbed. This can sit, covered, for about 10 more minutes or may be served immediately. Fluff with a fork before serving. Serves 4.

White Long-Grain Rice

White Short-Grain Rice

Brown Rice

Wild Rice

How To Cook Rice

Cooked just right, plain rice makes a wonderful, healthy side dish. Enhance the flavor by using broth or sprinkling it with herbs and spices. Directions are for 3 to 4 cups cooked rice.

Long-Grain: Boil 2 cups water, add 1 cup rice, stir, cover, and simmer for 15 to 20 minutes.

Short-Grain: Boil 1½ cups water, add 1 cup rice, stir, cover, and simmer for 15 to 20 minutes.

Brown Rice: Boil 2½ cups water, add 1 cup rice, stir, cover, and simmer for 30 minutes.

Wild Rice: Boil 4 cups water, add 1 cup rice, stir, cover, and simmer for 35 to 40 minutes.

FunFact
Fifty percent of all the world's rice is eaten within 8 miles of where it is grown.

Mexican Rice

A meal wouldn't be Mexican without a side of rice and beans, whether inside or alongside a tortilla. This seasoned rice is flavored with everything Mexican — cumin, jalapeño, garlic, and more. To save time preparing it, use a food processor to chop the onion, garlic, and pepper.

- 1 tablespoon vegetable oil
- 1½ cups white rice
- 1 16-ounce can Italian plum tomatoes, peeled and chopped, with their juice
- 2 onions, chopped
- 2 crushed garlic cloves
- 1 jalapeño pepper, seeded, veined, and chopped
- ½ teaspoon cumin
- 2 cups chicken stock, tomato juice, or water
- 1 cup frozen corn kernels (optional)
- 1 cup frozen peas (optional)
- ½ cup chopped fresh or frozen carrots (optional)
  Fresh parsley or cilantro (optional)

Heat the oil in a large saucepan and add the rice. Stir for about 3 minutes. Add the tomatoes, onion, garlic, pepper, cumin, and the stock, tomato juice, or water, as well as a combination or all of the corn, peas, and carrots.

Bring to a boil and simmer, covered, until the liquid is absorbed and the rice is tender, about 15 minutes. Garnish with chopped fresh parsley or cilantro. Serves 6 to 8.

Seasoned Rice Mix

Seasoned Rice Mixes

FamilyFun contributor Susan Purdy says these quick rice mixes make wonderful gifts from the kitchen. Store in widemouthed jars or take-out cartons.

Herb Rice:
- 1 cup uncooked long-grain white rice
- 2 beef or vegetable bouillon cubes
- 1 teaspoon green onion flakes
- ½ teaspoon each: rosemary, marjoram or oregano, and thyme leaves
- ½ teaspoon salt or celery salt

Curried Rice:
- 1 cup uncooked long-grain white rice
- 2 chicken or vegetable bouillon cubes
- ½ to 1 teaspoon curry powder
- 1 teaspoon dried minced onion
- ½ teaspoon ground cumin
- ½ teaspoon parsley flakes
- ½ teaspoon salt or celery salt

In a large mixing bowl, stir all the ingredients for either rice and pour into a sealable container.

Seasoned Rice:

In a large saucepan combine either the Herb or Curried Rice mixture with 2 cups cold water. Bring to a boil. Reduce the heat to low, stir once, and cover. Simmer for 14 to 20 minutes, or until the liquid is absorbed. Serves 4.

Kids Dig Rice

At nursery school, the favorite activity of *FamilyFun* reader Janet Buckley's four-year-old son is playing at the rice table, so she decided to create one for home use. After sealing the cracks of a large cardboard box with colorful hockey tape and decorating it with stickers, they filled the box with ten pounds of uncooked, inexpensive rice and added small pasta (orzo and tubettini), which they had painted with watercolors. With spoons, cups, and scoops, Sean pours and measures the rice, hides things in it, and builds hills and valleys.

Potatoes

Potato Pals

If your kids are wandering around the kitchen antsy for dinner, let them dress up a crowd of potato people. Begin with a plain potato and slice off the bottom. Using toothpicks or pushpins, attach cutout paper eyes, noses, mouths, or clothing. Other kitchen items — raisins, pasta, straws, peanuts, and muffin cup liners — can become ears, buttons, hair, or hats. After dinner, host a potato fashion show.

Red Potatoes with Garlic and Rosemary

The garlic in this side dish is cooked in its skin, so that it comes out sweet and creamy. To eat, just hold a clove by its "tail" and pull out the insides.

- 2 pounds of small, new red potatoes, scrubbed and halved
- 10 cloves of garlic, left in their skins, excess paper removed
  - Sea salt to taste
  - Black pepper to taste
- 1 tablespoon chopped fresh rosemary or 1 teaspoon dried

Preheat the oven to 350°. Lightly oil a large roasting pan or baking dish and arrange the potatoes and garlic in one layer. Sprinkle with the salt, pepper, and rosemary. Cover tightly with foil and bake for 1 hour, or until the potatoes are soft when poked with a fork. Serves about 6.

Classic Mashed Potatoes

Hand-mashed and flavored to perfection, homemade mashed potatoes are my favorite comfort food. They may seem like a lot of work, but a little peeling and mashing are certainly worth the effort. Serve them as they are or embellish them with toppings.

- 4 to 5 large potatoes, peeled
- ½ to 1 cup milk
- 2 tablespoons butter
  - Salt and pepper to taste
  - Pinch of nutmeg (optional)

Cover the potatoes with cold water and bring to a boil. Cook for 20 minutes, or until tender. (Be careful to watch the pot; potatoes have a tendency to boil over.)

While the spuds are cooking, slowly heat the milk and butter. When the potatoes are done, drain them and add half the hot milk mixture. Mash the potatoes with a handheld potato masher or an electric mixer. Keep adding the hot milk until you reach the proper consistency (which, of course, varies from family to family). Season with salt, pepper, and nutmeg, if desired. Serves 4 to 6.

Spuds with Jewels:

In a frying pan, heat 1 teaspoon of vegetable oil and briefly sauté 1 diced red pepper (add hot peppers such as green jalapeño for fire). Stir in ½ teaspoon basil. Immediately pour on top of mashed potatoes.

Green Potatoes:

Use an electric mixer to blend 1 to 2 cups chopped cooked spinach into mashed potatoes until they turn green.

Red Coats:

Use purple, red, or new potatoes with their skins on.

The Cheddar Broccoli:

Mix grated Cheddar cheese with 1 cup chopped, steamed broccoli florets and fold into the mashed spuds.

Prague Potatoes:

Panfry 4 strips of bacon until crisp. Remove from the pan and add 1 diced onion, cooking until translucent. Crumble the bacon into the onion. Top mashed potatoes with bacon, onion, and drippings, using about 1½ teaspoons or less of fat per serving.

Golden Broil:

Spread prepared mashed potatoes in an oven-to-table baking dish. Drizzle ½ cup heavy cream over the top and sprinkle with Parmesan cheese. Broil until the top turns golden.

Breakfast for Dinner:

Serve mashed potatoes in a large bowl topped with 3 to 4 chopped hard-boiled eggs and chopped fresh parsley and chives.

Tatties 'n' Neeps:

For the Scots' way of using up leftover mashed potatoes, mix equal amounts of mashed potatoes and mashed turnips.

Colcannon:

Mix mashed potatoes with 1½ cups shredded, cooked, and drained cabbage or kale.

Bangers and Mash:

Try this English recipe: serve plain mashed potatoes with broiled or pan-seared sausages ("bangers") on the side.

Fenced-in Spuds:

Surround a mound of mashed potatoes with a "fence" of steamed green beans and carrot sticks.

Toppings for Mashed Spuds:

- Chopped black olives and scallions
- Sautéed mushrooms
- Crosscut leeks cooked in butter until soft
- Herbed bread crumbs
- Toasted sesame seeds
- Salsa
- Cheddar or Parmesan cheese
- Crumbled cooked bacon
- Sautéed onion with red or green peppers
- Chopped basil and fresh tomatoes
- Cumin and/or chili powder

Red Coats

The Cheddar Broccoli

Prague Potatoes

Green Potatoes

Spuds with Jewels

Potato Salad Vinaigrette

Unlike most potato salads, which are coated with mayonnaise (an unwelcome picnic condiment), this version has a light oil and vinegar dressing. Be sure to pour the dressing over the potatoes while they are still warm, so it can be thoroughly absorbed. Potato salad always seems to taste better after the flavors have mingled, so you may want to mix up this one a day in advance.

1½	pounds small, new red potatoes, washed and quartered
¼	cup vegetable oil
¼	cup red wine vinegar
	Salt and pepper to taste
½	pound bacon, cooked until crisp, drained, and crumbled
3	eggs, hard-boiled and chopped
1	onion, grated
1	bunch scallions, chopped
2	tablespoons sweet pickle relish

Bring a pot of salted water to a boil and add the potatoes. Cook until just tender, about 15 minutes. Be careful not to overcook — potatoes can become mushy.

Drain the water and transfer the potatoes to a large bowl. Using a fork and knife, roughly cut the potatoes into bite-size pieces. In a small bowl, whisk the oil and vinegar and add the salt and pepper. Pour the mixture over the potatoes and toss.

Let the potato salad sit for 30 minutes, then add the bacon, eggs, onion, scallions, and relish, tossing gently until the ingredients are well combined. Refrigerate covered. Serves about 6.

Flavored French Fries

In France, they're called *pomme frites*. **But the term "french fry" has nothing to do with France. It refers to a method, called frenching, or cutting the potatoes into narrow strips. Bake your next bag of frozen fries with a little flavor:**

☛ **Cheese Fries: Melt grated cheese over fries.**

☛ **Herb Fries: Sprinkle herbs over fries before baking.**

☛ **Italian Fries: Melt Mozzarella cheese over baked fries and dip in spaghetti sauce.**

☛ **Thanksgiving Fries: Serve your fries with gravy.**

Oven-Baked French Fries

These fries are healthier than their fast-food counterparts. For a lower-fat version, use olive-oil-flavored cooking spray instead of the peanut oil.

1	medium-size potato per person, such as all-purpose, Yukon Gold, or red
2	teaspoons peanut oil
	Salt to taste

Preheat your oven to 425°. Peel the potato and slice it into squared fries, about ¼ inch thick. Dry off any excess starch with paper towels.

In a baking dish, toss the potatoes with the oil to coat. Bake for 15 to 20 minutes, turning at least once. Salt the fries and serve while hot. Serves 1 person per potato.

Tater Boats

The basic baked spud seems more adventurous when it's tricked out with a ship's rigging. To save time, bake a few potatoes ahead or use frozen skins, then let kids stuff and decorate them with carrot stick masts and red or yellow pepper sails.

1   medium baked potato
⅛   cup grated Cheddar cheese
2   to 3 tablespoons milk
½   tablespoon butter or margarine
    Salt and pepper to taste
    Extra grated Cheddar cheese,
        carrot sticks, red or yellow
        pepper, and peas or corn

Cut the baked potato in half lengthwise. Leaving a ¼-inch layer of potato along the skins, scoop the insides into a bowl. Mash in the cheese, milk, butter, salt, and pepper, then spoon the mixture back into the potato skins.

Warm the potatoes for 2 minutes on high in the microwave. Decorate the halves with the extra cheese, then add carrot stick masts, pepper sails, and a deck of peas or corn. Makes 2 boats.

Baked Sweet Potatoes with Orange Sauce

Spice up the sweetest of potatoes with orange juice and the flavors of fall — ginger, nutmeg, allspice, and walnuts. You can find sweet potatoes in most grocery stores year-round, but the best arrive in September and October.

3   sweet potatoes (about ½ pound
        each), scrubbed and pierced
        with a fork
¾   cup fresh orange juice
3   tablespoons brown sugar
½   teaspoon grated ginger
⅛   teaspoon nutmeg
¼   teaspoon allspice
2   tablespoons chopped walnuts
        (optional)

Preheat the oven to 400°. Place the potatoes on foil to catch the drippings and bake for 30 minutes, or until tender on the outside. Meanwhile, mix the juice, brown sugar, and spices in a bowl and set aside. Remove the sweet potatoes and cool slightly. Reduce the oven temperature to 375°. When the potatoes are cool enough to handle, peel and cut into 1-inch chunks. Place them in a casserole dish and top with the sauce. Bake for 25 to 30 minutes, spooning the liquid over the potatoes two to three times. Garnish with the nuts. Serves 4 to 6.

Tater Boats

How To Make Potato Prints

While you're cooking potatoes, set up a potato print craft for your child. Cut a potato in half, then have your child draw simple designs on the flat surfaces of the two halves with a ballpoint pen. When each image is ready, an adult can cut down about ½ inch around the shapes with an X-Acto knife, then remove the excess.

Pour acrylic paint into a pie plate. Dry the potatoes with a paper towel, then let your child press them into the paint, making sure that the shapes are well coated. Try a few test prints on scrap paper (pressing down with firm, even pressure will make the clearest print). Now your child can stamp away, decorating paper, cards, gift wrap, or fabric.

CHAPTER 8

Can I Have Dessert?

E VER SINCE she was a kid, *FamilyFun* contributor Barbara Albright has always liked having dessert first — especially if it's a cookie, brownie, or piece of cake. But it wasn't until this former editor-in-chief of *Chocolatier* watched her daughter, Samantha, take her first taste of chocolate that she witnessed the truly magical effect of sweets.

From the earliest age, sweets make us happy. We are born with a natural love for sugar — it's the first flavor a baby responds to (yes, it's in a mother's milk). Growing up, it's the sweet stuff that we remember — a chocolate birthday cake, a trip to the candy store, or waiting for the ice-cream truck.

It's for this reason that Barbara doesn't mind having sweets around the house, from the giant chocolate chip cookies she developed for this chapter to the brownies she made for her latest cookbook. She believes that if you serve it in moderation, your kids won't crave it. She's also intent on developing their palates: "I want my kids to be discerning and to know what a really good cookie is supposed to taste like."

To help your family bake the kind of quality desserts Barbara is talking about, try the recipes that follow, keeping these guidelines in mind as you bake.

Don't forbid sweets. Children who aren't allowed to eat candy and other sweets are more likely to overeat goodies when adults aren't around. Also, if you make a big deal about desserts and consider them

Monster Pops: *Page 121*

Keep flour, sugar, and butter on hand for dessert making. Instead of picking up packaged sweets at the store, buy flour, sugar, baking powder, chocolate chips, and other baking essentials. Making cookies or brownies from scratch is more rewarding than opening a store-bought version, and your home-baked goodies will taste much better.

Encourage your kids to bake. Baking a sweet can actually hook kids on cooking — it all starts when they lick the batter or frost the cake. First try the Giant Chocolate Chip Cookies on page 121, then test any other recipe in this chapter.

When baking desserts, measure flour carefully. Unlike cooking, baking is a science, and for best results, you want to measure precisely. Spoon flour into a dry measuring cup and level it off with a dinner knife. You also should level off your teaspoons of baking soda and powder. (Another tip: Be sure to use fresh baking powder.)

Keep your ingredients at room temperature. For best results, take your eggs out of the refrigerator a few hours before you plan to use them for a recipe.

Invest in an oven thermometer. Although your oven dial may say 375°, you should double-check the temperature by keeping a thermometer in your oven. This will help you get evenly baked cookies or cakes.

Quick Desserts

Fresh Fruit in season

Chilly Yogurt Sandwiches (see page 56)

Strawberries dipped in melted chocolate chips

Instant pudding or gelatin

Cinnamon graham crackers

Frozen yogurt

a "special treat," your kids may crave them when they're older.

Balance sweets with a nutritional diet. It's okay to eat desserts as long as they are figured into the overall diet for the day. If your child starts the day with a sugar cereal and has a cupcake after school, consider skipping dessert or offering fresh fruit.

Serve small portions: Generally, one cookie or a small piece of pie or cake is enough to feed a child for dessert. If you set an example of moderate eating, your kids are apt to follow your lead.

120

Giant Chocolate Chip Cookies

When Ruth Wakefield added chopped chocolate to her basic butter cookie recipe at the Toll House Inn, chocolate chip became the most popular cookie in America. Here, we've updated Ruth's 1930s recipe to a '90s extravaganza. The goodies that go in them are up to you (chocolate chips, crushed toffee bars, butterscotch chips, or M&M's). The size they take is your decision, too — you can make them as small as a dime or as big as your hands.

- 2¼ cups all-purpose flour
- ¾ teaspoon baking powder
- ½ teaspoon salt
- 1 cup unsalted butter, softened
- ¾ cup sugar
- ½ cup packed light brown sugar
- 2 eggs
- 2 teaspoons vanilla extract
- 2 cups semisweet chocolate chips

In a large bowl, mix the flour, baking powder, and salt. In a separate bowl, cream the butter and sugars, then add the eggs, one at a time, mixing well after each addition. Stir in the vanilla extract, then gradually stir in the flour mixture until combined. Add the chips and stir again. For chewy cookies, refrigerate the dough for 2 hours or overnight.

Preheat the oven to 300°. Using a ⅓-cup measuring cup, drop the dough onto a baking sheet, leaving 3 inches between mounds.

Bake for 30 to 35 minutes, or until light brown. Cool for 5 minutes, then transfer to a wire rack and cool completely. Makes 15 giant cookies.

Monster M&M's:
Substitute M&M's for the 2 cups of chocolate chips.

Monster Chip & Nut:
Stir in 1 cup chopped walnuts, pecans, or other nuts with the chips.

Monster Pops:
Before baking the cookies, insert a Popsicle stick into the dough.

Monster Stir-ins:
Try other chips, such as peanut butter, butterscotch, or white chocolate.

Mini Cookies:
Use mini chips or M&M's. Measure out rounded teaspoons of dough, leaving 1½ inches between cookies. Bake for 17 to 20 minutes. Makes 85.

Can I Have Dessert?

Sugar Cookies

This foolproof recipe will unleash the cookie monster in anyone. Creative cooks can cut the dough with any size cookie cutter, color it red, white, and blue, flavor it with chocolate, almond, and lemon, or use the baked cookies as an empty canvas for a frosting design.

1	cup butter, softened
¾	cup sugar
1	large egg
1	teaspoon vanilla extract
2¾	cups all-purpose flour
1	teaspoon baking soda
1	teaspoon cream of tartar

In a large bowl, cream the butter and sugar until fluffy. Add the egg and beat well, then mix in the vanilla extract. In a separate bowl, combine the flour, baking soda, and cream of tartar. Add the flour mixture to the butter mixture, one third at a time, until thoroughly combined.

Divide the dough into two equal portions and flatten each into a disk. Cover each disk in plastic wrap and refrigerate for 2 to 3 hours, or until the dough is firm enough to work with. If it becomes too firm, soften at room temperature for about 5 minutes.

Preheat the oven to 350°. On a lightly floured board, roll out the dough until it is about ¼ inch thick. Cut out cookies with cutters or by hand.

Using a metal spatula, carefully transfer the cookies to a baking sheet, leaving about 2 inches between them. Bake for 8 to 10 minutes, or until lightly browned around the edges.

Remove the cookie sheet from the oven, place it on a wire rack, and cool for 2 to 3 minutes. Using a metal spatula, transfer the cookies to the rack and cool completely. Repeat this procedure with the remaining chilled dough. Form any extra dough scraps into a disk, chill if necessary before rerolling, then continue until all the dough has been used. Baked cookies can be stored in an airtight container in the freezer for up to 1 month before frosting and decorating and for up to 3 days at room temperature. Makes about 3 dozen cookies, depending on their size.

Pinwheel cookies

Colored Sugar Cookies:

To make colored sugar cookies, mix and knead liquid or paste food coloring, drop by drop, into the basic sugar cookie dough until it reaches the desired hue.

Chocolate Cookie Dough:

After the last third of flour has been incorporated in the dough, mix in 2 ounces of melted and slightly cooled unsweetened chocolate.

Almond Cookie Dough:

Stir 1 teaspoon of almond extract into the dough right after the last third of flour has been incorporated.

Lemon Cookie Dough:

After the last third of flour has been added to the dough, stir in 2 teaspoons of grated lemon peel.

Appliquéd Stars

Cookie Necklace

Easier Cookie Baking

Appliquéd Stars:

For this multicolored cookie, you'll need three different dough colors and two or three similarly shaped cutters in differing sizes. Cut a large star (or another shape) out of one color of cookie dough and place it on a baking sheet. Using a smaller star cutter, cut out the center of the first star and remove it. Use the smaller cutter to cut out a star from a contrasting color and insert it into the center of the big star. Repeat with a third color of dough and the smallest cutter, if desired. Gently pinch the seams between the doughs so they won't separate during baking. Bake for 10 to 12 minutes.

Pinwheel Cookies:

Roll out chocolate and sugar doughs separately between sheets of plastic wrap into 12- by 8-inch rectangles. Remove the top sheet of wrap from one dough rectangle. Remove both sheets from the second rectangle and place that dough on top of the first. Starting with one of the 12-inch sides, roll up the doughs, jelly roll fashion. (Do not roll the plastic wrap up in between the dough, but wrap it around the outside of the roll.) Refrigerate or freeze for

1 hour, or until firm. Remove the plastic wrap, cut the roll into ¼-inch-thick slices, and place them on baking sheets. Bake for 10 minutes, or until the cookies are just lightly browned.

Cookie Necklaces:

Use letter-shaped cutters or cardboard templates to create names and words from the dough. Punch a hole in the top of each letter with a drinking straw. After baking the cookies for 10 minutes, cool and decorate. String them together on a piece of thin licorice.

Alphabet Cookies:

These edible letters can be used as spelling aids, word game pieces, or treats. Roll the dough into three cylinders (about 1 inch in diameter), cover, and refrigerate for 1 hour. Slice the logs into ¼-inch-thick rounds. Bake for about 10 minutes. When cool, use icing to inscribe a letter on each one. The most commonly used letters in the English language are *A*, *E*, *I*, *S*, and *T*, so make extras of these. The least commonly used are *Q*, *X*, and *Z*, so one of each should suffice.

Easier Cookie Baking

☛ Cut from the edge of the dough to the center, removing the cookies as you go.

☛ Position the oven rack in the center of the oven. If you use two racks, switch the positions of the baking sheets halfway through baking.

☛ Bake similar-size cookies together on one baking sheet so they are done at the same time.

☛ Don't run your hot baking sheets under cold water — the abrupt temperature change can cause them to warp.

Alphabet Cookies

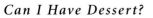

Cakes

Chocolate Celebration Cake

Chocolate Celebration Cake

When frosted with Chocolate Ganache (see page 126), this cake is a celebration of the richest chocolate flavor around.

Cubcakes

5	ounces unsweetened chocolate, coarsely chopped
2	cups all-purpose flour
2½	teaspoons baking powder
¼	teaspoon salt
¾	cup unsalted butter, softened
1½	cups sugar
2	teaspoons vanilla extract
3	large eggs, at room temperature
1¼	cups milk

Preheat the oven to 350°. Lightly butter two 9-inch round cake pans. Line the bottoms of the pans with circles of baking parchment or waxed paper. Dust the sides of the pans with flour and tap out the excess. In a microwave-safe bowl, melt the chocolate on high for 1 to 2 minutes, or until melted, stirring halfway through cooking. Set the chocolate aside to cool to room temperature for 10 minutes.

In a large bowl, stir the flour, baking powder, and salt. In another large bowl, using a handheld electric mixer, beat the butter and sugar until combined. Beat in the melted chocolate and vanilla extract. One at a time, add the eggs, beating well after each addition. Add the flour mixture and milk in thirds, beating until just combined. Scrape the batter into the prepared pans and spread evenly. Bake for 25 to 30 minutes, or until a toothpick inserted in the center of each layer comes out clean. Transfer the pans to a wire rack. Cool 10 minutes. Carefully invert the cake layers onto the rack and cool completely.

Place one layer on a serving plate. Spread frosting over the cake and top with the second cake layer. Frost the outside of the cake, then the top. Store in the refrigerator. Serves 12.

Cubcakes:

To make pawprint cupcakes, bake the Chocolate Celebration Cake in two 12-cup muffin tins for 20 minutes. Frost the cupcakes with All-Purpose Buttercream (see page 126) or store-bought icing (for a furry paw, mix the frosting with grated coconut first). Top each cupcake with a small mint patty. Then place three Junior Mints or chocolate chips around the patty for claw marks. Beware — cubcakes walk away fast. Makes 24.

Devilish Devil's Food Cake

Sinfully rich, delicious chocolate gives this cake its name.

- ½ cup butter
- 1 cup sugar
- 2 eggs, at room temperature
- 2 ounces unsweetened chocolate, melted and cooled
- 1 teaspoon vanilla extract
- 1 cup milk
- 1¾ cups all-purpose flour
- 1½ teaspoons baking soda
- ½ teaspoon salt

Preheat the oven to 350°. Grease two 8-inch cake pans or one 13- by 9- by 2-inch pan. Cream the butter and sugar in a large mixing bowl, then beat in the eggs, one at a time. Add the cooled, melted chocolate and vanilla extract and mix well, then stir in the milk.

In a separate bowl, combine the flour, baking soda, and salt. Gradually add the flour mixture to the butter mixture and stir until just combined. Pour the batter into the prepared pans and bake the rounds for 25 to 30 minutes, or the baking pan for 40 to 45 minutes. Cool in the pans for 10 minutes, then turn onto a wire rack and cool completely. Serves 10.

Caterpillar Cake:

Bake the Devilish Devil's Food Cake in two 12-cup muffin tins lined with paper liners for 20 minutes. Mix up a batch of All-Purpose Buttercream (see page 126) or about 2 cups of store-bought white frosting and tint it with green or orange food coloring. Frost the cupcakes and arrange them in a curving, crawling pattern on top of a large cutting board or a piece of cardboard covered with foil. For a fuzzy look, tint the coconut with food coloring and sprinkle it over the cupcakes. Snip shoestring licorice into short lengths to form the antennae and legs. For eyes, try licorice candies or jelly beans.

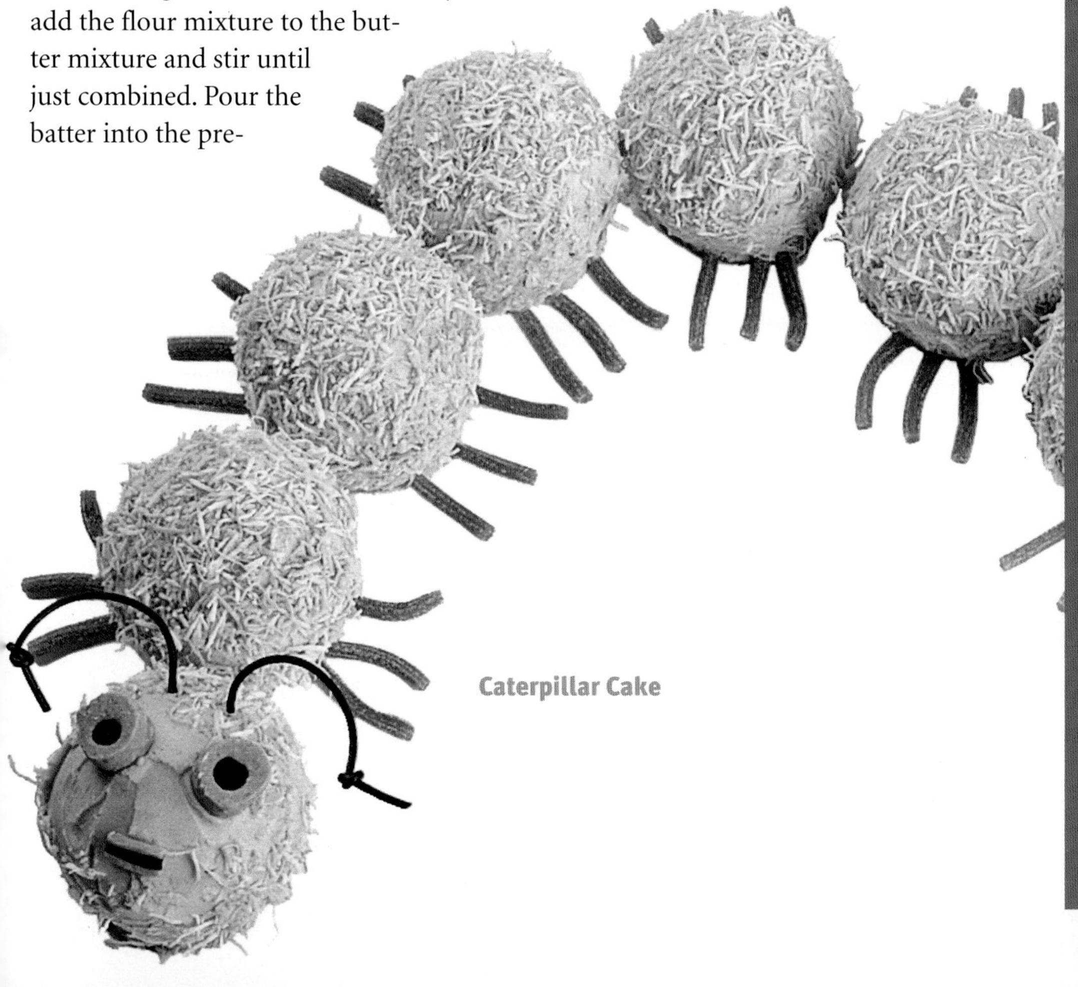

Caterpillar Cake

All-Purpose Buttercream (see page 126)

THE CHOCOLATE FAMILY

Unsweetened Chocolate: 
After cocoa beans are processed and roasted, they are ground to form this smooth, pure form of chocolate.

Bittersweet, Semisweet, and Sweet Chocolate: 
Depending on the manufacturer, these dark chocolates have varying amounts of sugar and flavorings, such as vanilla, added.

Milk Chocolate: 
This favorite is made of chocolate, milk solids, sugar, and flavorings, such as vanilla. It is sensitive to heat, so be careful when melting it.

White Chocolate: 
True white chocolate contains cocoa butter and is ivory colored. It also contains milk solids, sugar, and flavorings, such as vanilla. The more common white confectionery coatings use vegetable fat in place of cocoa butter.

Chocolate Chips: 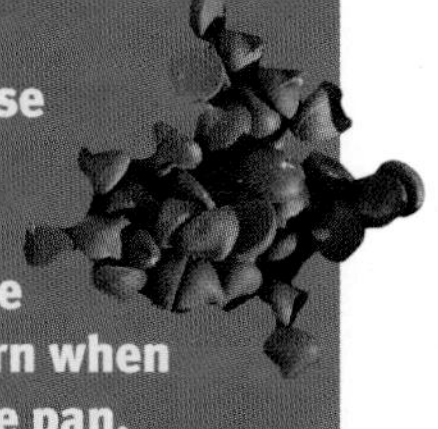
The addition of stabilizers helps chips hold their shape when baked. Because they contain milk solids, milk chocolate chips may burn when they touch the pan.

Cocoa Powder: 
This easy-to-use form of chocolate is made from plain chocolate that has nearly all of the cocoa butter pressed out of it.

Frosting

The Frosting on the Cake

Follow these steps to smooth frosting:
- ☛ Let the cake cool thoroughly.
- ☛ For a flat-top cake, slice off the bumpy top and invert.
- ☛ Brush off crumbs before frosting.
- ☛ For a clean platter, place waxed paper under the edges of the cake before frosting, then remove.
- ☛ Frost with a thin layer of icing to seal in remaining crumbs before applying the final coat.
- ☛ For a smooth finish, keep a glass of hot water nearby to dip your spreader in.

All-Purpose Buttercream

This basic icing recipe can be spread on cakes and cookies or applied as decorative piping with a pastry bag. If you plan to use it for piping, make it a little stiffer by adding less milk.

- 3½ cups sifted confectioners' sugar
- 1 cup unsalted butter, softened
- 1 teaspoon vanilla extract
- 2 to 4 tablespoons milk

In the bowl of an electric mixer, beat the sugar, butter, and vanilla extract on low speed. Add in the milk bit by bit until the mixture has reached a spreadable consistency. Makes about 3 cups.

Chocolate Icing

FamilyFun contributor Becky Okrent recommends using the back of a spoon to spread this simple, shiny icing.

- 12 ounces semisweet chocolate chips
- 2 cups sour cream
- 4 tablespoons confectioners' sugar

In a heatproof dish, microwave the chips on high for 1 minute, or until melted, stirring halfway through cooking time. When the chips are melted, stir in the sour cream a few tablespoons at a time, until smooth and shiny, then stir in the sugar. Refrigerate for ½ hour, or until thick enough to spread. Makes 3 cups.

Cream Cheese Icing

This tangy icing complements carrot cake, banana cake, and pound cake.

- 8 ounces cream cheese, at room temperature
- 4 tablespoons unsalted butter, at room temperature
- 2 cups confectioners' sugar, sifted
- 1 teaspoon lemon juice

In a processor, mixer, or by hand, beat all of the ingredients together until smooth. Makes 1¾ cups.

Chocolate Ganache

Ganache frosting, flavored here with raspberry, is a mixture of chocolate and heavy cream. With more than a pound of bittersweet chocolate, it's for chocolate aficionados only.

- 18 ounces bittersweet chocolate, finely chopped
- 1½ cups heavy cream
- ⅓ cup seedless raspberry jam
- ¼ cup unsalted butter, cut into ½-inch cubes
- Pinch of salt
- 1½ teaspoons vanilla extract

Place the chocolate in a large bowl. In a saucepan, bring the cream, raspberry jam, butter, and salt just to a boil. Pour over the chocolate and let it stand for 1 minute. Whisk until smooth, then mix in the vanilla extract.

Cover with plastic wrap and let the frosting thicken overnight at room temperature, or refrigerate it for no longer than 1½ hours. Makes about 2 cups.

Better-Than-Basic Yellow Cake

Although it certainly is easier to reach for a cake mix, all the ingredients for this moist yellow cake are in your pantry. Try it — it's worth the effort.

    4   eggs, separated
    2¾   cups all-purpose flour
    1½   teaspoons baking powder
    ½   teaspoon salt
    1   cup butter, softened
    2   cups sugar
    2   teaspoons vanilla extract
    1   cup milk

Lightly grease and dust with flour two 9-inch round cake pans, or one 13- by 9- by 2-inch pan. Preheat the oven to 350°. Using an electric mixer, beat the egg whites until stiff, but not too dry, and set aside. Sift the flour along with the baking powder and salt.

In a large bowl, cream the butter, gradually pouring in the sugar, beating until the mixture is fluffy. Beat in the egg yolks, one at a time. Add the vanilla extract and continue to beat.

Using a spatula or wooden spoon, add the flour mixture to the butter mixture in three additions, alternating with the milk. Fold the egg whites gently and thoroughly into the batter.

Pour the batter into the baking pan(s), spreading it out with a spatula. Bake the rounds for 35 to 40 minutes and the rectangle for 40 to 50 minutes, or until a toothpick inserted in the middle comes out clean. Cool in the pan for 5 minutes before inverting onto a wire rack to cool completely. Serves 10.

Hopscotch Cake:

Follow the Better-Than-Basic directions for a 13- by 9- by 2-inch cake. Once cooled, cut the cake into eight equal rectangular pieces. Arrange the pieces on a board or serving tray in the classic hopscotch pattern (see diagram at right). Use about 2 cups of frosting to ice the cake. Decorate each rectangle with snipped licorice strings, shredded coconut, colored crystal sugars, or rainbow sprinkles. Make numbers with candies, raisins, peanuts, or pieces of fruit leather. Then let your kids take turns standing a short way from the cake and tossing a piece of candy or cereal onto it. The "tosser" gets to eat the slice of cake on which his marker lands.

Hopscotch Cake

How To Grease Cake Pans

☞ **For an easy flip out of the pan, grease your cake pans (bottom and sides) with shortening — not butter — and then dust with flour.**

Carrot Cake

"Cake made of *carrots*?" your five-year-old may ask. Don't worry — the moist, sweet results will soothe his fears. He'll never know it's healthier (at least a little) than your standard white or chocolate cake. Frost with Cream Cheese Icing (see page 126).

2	cups grated carrot
	Juice of 1 lemon
½	teaspoon lemon zest
½	cup raisins
½	cup chopped walnuts
2	cups packed light brown sugar
3	eggs, lightly beaten
1	teaspoon vanilla extract
½	cup buttermilk
½	cup vegetable oil
¼	cup honey
2	cups all-purpose flour (or 1 cup each of white and whole wheat)
1	teaspoon cinnamon
1	teaspoon baking soda
½	teaspoon salt
½	teaspoon baking powder

Preheat the oven to 350°. Grease and lightly flour two 8-inch round cake pans. Sprinkle the carrots with the lemon juice and stir in the zest; add the raisins and walnuts and set aside.

In an electric mixer or food processor, cream the sugar, eggs, vanilla extract, buttermilk, oil, and honey. Sift together the remaining dry ingredients and gradually add them to the creamed mixture, stirring just until smooth. Stir the carrot mixture evenly into the batter and pour into prepared pans.

Bake for 35 minutes, or until the top feels firm to the touch. Wait for the rounds to cool before removing them from the pans. Serves 8 to 10.

Dino Carrot Cake:

The itinerary for a great dinosaur birthday party? Make this purple dinosaur cake, hold a cavekids costume contest, and play pin the horn on the triceratops. Before frosting the cooled carrot cake rounds with Cream Cheese Icing (see page 126), cut both into dinosaurs (see diagram at left). Use candy corn for the dinosaur's ridged back and sharp teeth, sliced marshmallows for spots, gumdrops for toes, and Life Savers for an eye. Makes a pair of dinosaurs or a two-layer dino cake.

Dino Carrot Cake

128

Cheesecake

As a child, my brother requested cheesecake every birthday, which I thought was strange until I, too, acquired a taste for the deliciously creamy cake. It is surprisingly simple to make; for easy cutting, make it a day ahead and slice it with a sharp, wet knife.

Crust:
- ⅔ cup all-purpose flour
- 2 tablespoons sugar
- 5 tablespoons unsalted butter, cold
- ½ teaspoon lemon or orange zest
- 2 egg yolks
- ½ teaspoon vanilla extract
- 1 tablespoon heavy cream

Filling:
- 3 8-ounce packages cream cheese, softened
- 1 cup sugar
- 2 tablespoons all-purpose flour
- 2 teaspoons lemon or orange zest
- ¼ teaspoon vanilla extract
- 3 eggs
- 1 egg yolk
- 3 tablespoons heavy cream

Preheat the oven to 350°. In a food processor or electric mixer, blend the flour, sugar, and butter until the mixture resembles a coarse meal. Add the zest, egg yolks, vanilla extract, and heavy cream and blend until the dough combines. Press the mixture into the bottom of an 8-inch springform pan. Bake for 20 minutes, or until lightly toasted.

For the filling, whip the cream cheese in the food processor or mixer until fluffy. Add the sugar, flour, zest, vanilla extract, eggs, egg yolk, and heavy cream. Blend thoroughly. Wrap the bottom and outsides of the pan tightly with tinfoil and pour the filling over the baked crust. Set the pan in a larger baking dish, fill with water to just below the top of the foil. Bake for

Cheesecake with Blueberry Sauce

10 minutes at 400°, then lower the heat to 250° and continue baking for 1 hour, or until the center is set. Cool completely before serving. Serves 8 to 10.

Blueberry Sauce:

When the cheesecake is cool, drizzle each slice with a spoonful of this sauce. Bring 1 cup blueberries, ¼ cup sugar, and 1 tablespoon orange juice just to a boil in a saucepan. Reduce the heat and simmer, covered, for 15 minutes, stirring occasionally. Mash the berries with a fork or puree them in a blender or food processor. Makes 1 cup.

Strawberry Swirl Cheesecake:

Pour the cheesecake into the baked crust. Puree 8 strawberries and dot the liquid over the top of the batter. Using a small rubber spatula, gently swirl the puree into the batter. Proceed with the baking directions.

FunFact
At the turn of the nineteenth century, Jewish immigrants made cheesecake with a smooth, cream cheese filling, and the "New York" cheesecake was born.

Pie Ornaments

For a decorative top crust, use cookie cutters or a knife to cut leftover dough into leaves, stars, bows, or other festive shapes. Glaze the uncooked top crust with eggwash (see page 70), add the shapes, then bake (if the crust browns too quickly, cover with tinfoil).

Real Pumpkin Pie

For years, I made my pumpkin pies from canned pureed pumpkin, and they always tasted fine. But one year, I grew more pumpkins than I needed for jack-o'-lanterns and was determined to turn one into pie. I enlisted the help of an eleven-year-old friend, and making pie became a rewarding afternoon project. Now we always make our pies from real pumpkins.

    1   unbaked single pie crust (see page 133)
    1   small pumpkin
    3   eggs
    ½   cup sugar
    ¼   cup brown sugar
    2   teaspoons cinnamon
    1   teaspoon ginger
    ½   teaspoon cloves
    ½   teaspoon salt
    1   12-ounce can of evaporated milk

Roll out the pie dough and line a 9- or 10-inch pie pan. Cut the pumpkin in half, remove the seeds, and place the halves face down on a greased cookie sheet. Bake at 350° for 40 minutes, or until tender. Cool, then scoop out the meat, and mash or puree it.

Beat the eggs and sugars. Blend in 2 cups of the puree and the rest of the ingredients. Pour into the pie crust. Bake at 450° for 10 minutes, then reduce to 350°. Bake for another 50 minutes, or until the pie sets. Cool, then slice. Serves 6 to 8.

Pecan Pie

When approaching any holiday dinner, *FamilyFun* contributor Becky Okrent has been known to mutter "Save room for pie!" She prefers to make this rich dessert in a 12-inch tart pan with a removable bottom to show it off.

    1   unbaked single pie crust (see page 133)
    4   eggs, lightly beaten
    ¾   cup packed dark brown sugar
    ½   cup dark corn syrup
    ½   cup maple syrup or 4 tablespoons molasses
    6   tablespoons unsalted butter, melted
    2   teaspoons vanilla extract
    2½   cups coarsely chopped pecans
    ½   cup pecan halves

Roll out the dough and line a 12-inch tart pan or 10-inch pie pan. In a large mixing bowl, blend the eggs, brown sugar, corn syrup, maple syrup, butter, and vanilla extract. Stir in the chopped nuts, then pour the filling into the tart shell. Sprinkle with the pecan halves. Bake at 325° for 30 minutes, or until the center has set. Serves 10.

Pecan Pie

Pies

My First Apple Pie

Every kid deserves the chance to make an apple pie — and a child can easily learn with a little help from a patient adult.

- 1   unbaked single pie crust (see page 133)
- 5   cups apple slices
- ½   cup sugar
- 1   tablespoon all-purpose flour
- 2   teaspoons apple pie spice (or ¼ teaspoon each nutmeg and allspice and ½ teaspoon cinnamon)
      Juice of half a lemon
- 2   tablespoons butter

Preheat the oven to 400°. Roll out half the pie crust dough and line an 8-inch pie plate. Trim the edges allowing a slight overhang. Place the apple slices in a large bowl. Add the sugar, flour, apple pie spice, and lemon juice and toss until well combined. Spoon the mixture into the unbaked pie crust and dot with the butter.

Roll out the remaining pie dough into a ⅛-inch thickness. Fold the top crust in half, set it over the fruit, and unfold. Crimp the edges with your fingers or press the tines of a fork around the edges to seal. Cut slits in the crust in a decorative pattern. Bake the pie for 40 minutes, or until bubbly and golden brown. Serves 6.

Apple Crumb Pie:

Skip the top crust and add this crowning touch. In a medium bowl, mix ⅔ cup all-purpose flour, ½ cup sugar, ½ teaspoon cinnamon, and ½ teaspoon salt. With a pastry cutter or your fingers, blend in 5 tablespoons butter

My First Apple Pie

until the texture resembles a coarse meal. Sprinkle over the apples and bake for 40 minutes. If the topping browns too quickly, lightly cover it with tinfoil.

Cranberry-Apple Pie:

In a saucepan, cook 1½ cups chopped cranberries with 1 cup sugar, ½ teaspoon lemon zest, 2 tablespoons tapioca, and ⅓ cup cranberry juice until slightly thickened. Mix with the apples and continue with the directions.

Raisin & Nut Apple Pie:

Mix the apples with ½ cup raisins and ½ cup chopped walnuts before baking.

Pie Shortcuts

Use a ready-made pie crust or frozen unbaked crusts instead of homemade.

Roll out and freeze your own pie crusts in your pie plates for 1 to 2 weeks.

Cut the apples a day ahead and mix them with lemon juice to prevent browning.

Strawberry-Rhubarb Pie

Strawberry-Rhubarb Pie

You can make the most of delectable strawberries and rhubarb by baking them in a pie. The bright red color, not to mention the taste, pleases any crowd.

- 1 unbaked single pie crust (see page 133)
- 4 cups sliced strawberries
- 2 cups ½-inch pieces rhubarb
- ¾ cup sugar
- ¼ cup all-purpose flour
- 1 teaspoon orange zest
- 1 tablespoon butter
- 1 egg, beaten

Preheat the oven to 400°. In a large bowl, mix the strawberries and rhubarb with the sugar, flour, and orange zest. Roll out half of the pie crust dough into a ⅛-inch thickness and line the bottom of 9-inch pie pan. Add the filling and dot with the butter.

Roll out the remaining pie dough and use a pastry wheel or knife to slice it into ¾-inch-wide strips. Weave the strips over the filling and crimp the edges. Brush the crust with the beaten egg. Bake for 45 minutes, or until the filling bubbles and the crust turns golden brown. If the crust browns too quickly, cover it with foil. Serves 6 to 8.

Blueberry Lattice Pie

Sweet, plump, and fresh off the bush, blueberries require no peeling, pitting, or slicing before they are added to pie. During the off-season, use frozen berries (see at left) instead.

- 1 unbaked single pie crust (see page 133)
- 5 cups blueberries, washed and stems removed
- ⅔ cup sugar
- ¼ cup all-purpose flour
- 1 tablespoon lemon juice
- 1 teaspoon lemon zest
  Pinch of salt
- 2 tablespoons butter
- 1 egg, beaten

In a large bowl, mix the blueberries with the sugar, flour, lemon juice, zest, and salt. Let the filling sit for at least a ½ hour.

Preheat the oven to 425°. Roll out half of the pie crust dough into a ⅛-inch thickness and line the bottom of a 9-inch pie pan. Snip the edges evenly, allowing a slight overhang. Fill the pie shell with the blueberry mixture and dot with the butter.

Roll out the remaining pie dough and use a pastry wheel or knife to slice it into ¾-inch-wide strips. Weave the strips over the filling and crimp the edges. Brush the crust with the beaten egg. Bake for 35 minutes, or until the filling bubbles and the crust turns golden brown. If the crust browns too quickly, cover it with foil. Serves 6 to 8.

Pie Crusts

Create a lattice crust with a pastry wheel or knife. Cut rolled dough into ½-inch-wide strips and weave over pie filling.

Processor Pie Crust

With good reflexes, you can use a food processor to make pie dough. The trick here is to press the pulse button for mere seconds.

- 3 cups all-purpose flour
- 2 tablespoons sugar
- ¼ teaspoon salt
- 1½ cups cold, unsweetened butter, cut into chunks
- 4 tablespoons ice water or fruit juice

Place the flour, sugar, and salt in the bowl of a food processor and process for 5 seconds. Scatter the butter pieces over the flour, then pulse until the mixture resembles a coarse meal. Sprinkle with the water and process until the dough starts to come together (but not until it forms a ball). Carefully take out the blade, and press the mixture together to pick up all the bits of dough. Divide the dough in half, flatten into disks, wrap in plastic wrap, and refrigerate for at least 30 minutes before rolling and baking. Makes enough for 2 single crusts, or 1 double crust.

Cream Cheese Crust

A batch of this no-fail pie crust goes a long way. Use any leftover dough for pie ornaments (see page 130).

- 4 cups all-purpose flour
- 1½ cups cold, unsalted butter, cut into bits
- 1 8-ounce package cream cheese, cut into bits

In a large bowl, mix all the ingredients with your fingers or a pastry cutter until it forms a ball. Divide the ball in half and flatten each half into a disk, wrap, and refrigerate for at least 30 minutes. When you're ready to bake, roll out the dough on a lightly floured surface or between sheets of waxed paper, working the dough from the center outward until you have a circle large enough to line your pie pan. Makes 2 single crusts, or 1 double crust.

Chocolate Cookie Crumb Crust

Finally, a job the kids will love to do — smash cookies with a rolling pin.

- 1½ cups crumbs from plain chocolate cookies (use a processor or rolling pin)
- 2 tablespoons confectioners' sugar
- 6 tablespoons unsalted butter, melted

Mix the cookie crumbs, sugar, and butter in a bowl until thoroughly combined. Distribute the mixture evenly around a pie pan. Press it against the pan, the bottom first and then the sides. Bake at 350° for 10 minutes and cool before filling. Makes 1 single crust.

Graham Cracker Crust:

Use graham cracker crumbs instead of the chocolate cookie crumbs.

Gingersnap Crust:

Substitute crushed gingersnaps for the chocolate cookie crumbs.

One quick way to decorate your crust edge is to press the tines of a fork around the edge.

Crimp your crust by pinching the thumb and index finger of your right hand against your left index finger.

Banana Cream Pie

Your family has no doubt figured out that the banana is great when topping cereal or smeared with peanut butter. Now see what they think when it's layered with creamy pudding in a pie. To save time, use instant vanilla pudding.

1   baked Graham Cracker Crust (see page 133)

Filling:

1   cup sugar
⅓   cup cornstarch
3   cups milk
2   eggs, beaten
1   teaspoon vanilla extract
3   tablespoons unsalted butter
2   large ripe bananas
    Whipped cream
    Dried banana chips (optional)

Prepare the Graham Cracker Crust in a 10-inch pie pan. To make the filling, blend the sugar, cornstarch, milk, and eggs in a large saucepan. Stirring constantly over medium-high heat, bring the mixture to a boil for about 15 minutes. Continue stirring until the filling is thick and coats the back of a wooden spoon. Remove from the heat and stir in the vanilla extract and butter. Cover the pudding with plastic wrap so that a skin doesn't form and let the mixture cool for 30 minutes.

Restir and pour half of the pudding into the baked pie crust. Swirl the pie plate so the sides of the crusts are coated with the cream. Slice the bananas evenly over the cream. Pour the remaining pudding over the bananas, then refrigerate until ready to serve. Spread whipped cream over the pie and garnish with banana chips, if desired. Serves 8 to 10.

Banana Trivia

According to an old wives' tale, the inside of a banana peel makes a great shoeshine for patent leather shoes. (We haven't tested this, so you're on your own with this one!)

The earliest dessert recipe ever written was a banana recipe — a mushy mixture of bananas, almonds, and honey.

If your kids have a tough time falling asleep, give them a banana. Like a cup of warm milk, a banana is a sleep enhancer.

The average American eats 26 pounds of bananas a year, making it our most consumed fruit.

There are more than 200 varieties of bananas in the world.

The biggest banana split ever made was 4.55 miles long!

Bananas are botanically classified as a berry.

Chocolate Cream Pie with Oreo Crust

Each year, Americans consume more than 10.5 pounds of chocolate per person in the form of candy, ice cream, cakes, and brownies. You can get your fill with this pie, but be sure to cut small slices — the chocolate flavor is intense.

Crust:
- 1½ cups finely crushed Oreo cookies (crush 15 in a food processor or blender)
- 3 tablespoons butter, melted

Filling:
- 1 cup sugar
- ⅓ cup cornstarch
- ⅛ teaspoon salt
- 4 large egg yolks, lightly beaten
- 3½ cups milk
- 1½ teaspoons vanilla extract
- 6 ounces bittersweet chocolate, finely chopped
- 2 ounces unsweetened chocolate, finely chopped

To make the crust, generously butter a 9-inch glass pie plate. In a large bowl, stir the cookie crumbs and the melted butter. Using your fingertips, firmly and evenly press the mixture into the bottom and sides of the pie plate.

In a large saucepan, combine the sugar, cornstarch, and salt. Whisk in the egg yolks until combined. Gradually mix in the milk. Whisking constantly, cook over medium heat for about 10 minutes, or until the mixture thickens and comes to a boil. Remove the pan from the heat and mix in the vanilla extract and chocolates, whisking until smooth. Immediately pour the mixture through a medium-fine strainer

into the prepared pie crust. Cover the surface of the pie with a piece of plastic wrap to prevent a skin from forming. Cool at room temperature, then refrigerate for several hours or overnight.

Mud Pie

When your kids tire of making real mud pies, serve them slices of edible mud. *FamilyFun* contributor Cynthia Caldwell suggests using Haagen-Dazs ice cream.

- 1 baked Chocolate Cookie Crumb Crust (see page 133)
- 6 cups or 3 pints chocolate ice cream, softened
- 1 cup ready-made fudge topping
- 4 cups whipped cream
- ¾ cup crushed chocolate cookies or chocolate graham crackers

Fill your baked, cooled pie shell halfway with half of the chocolate ice cream and freeze for 30 minutes. Spread the fudge topping over the ice cream and freeze for another 15 minutes. Top with the remaining ice cream, the whipped cream, and cookie crumbs. Then freeze for at least 3 hours. Serves 8 to 10.

Pudding Parfaits

For individual pudding parfaits, spoon alternating layers of Chocolate Cream Pie filling (see at left) and crushed Oreo cookies into stemmed glasses. Top with whipped cream and crushed cookies.

Mud Pie

CHAPTER 9

Home for the Holidays

O F ALL the recipes we run in *FamilyFun* magazine, our holiday ones are treasured the most. Last year, swarms of readers counted down the days before Christmas with a cookie Advent calendar; a year before, the Jell-O eyeballs for Halloween were *the* hit with trick-or-treaters; and this year, the Village People place markers showed up on Thanksgiving tables across America. Why are these holiday recipes and ideas so popular?

For most of the year, families' lives are too overscheduled for indulgence. But during the holidays, we take the time to celebrate, to make special meals, and to bake something incredibly, delightfully sweet. We do it because we have vacation time (hopefully) but, more importantly, because our parents did it for us when we were kids.

Just like eating chocolate on Valentine's Day, jelly beans on Easter, and turkey on Thanksgiving, the recipes in this chapter have become rituals with *FamilyFun* readers. We hope your family, too, will try them once, then look forward to them again next year.

Involve your kids in the holiday preparation. Invite your kids to help you cut the holiday cookie dough with cookie cutters or stuff the turkey on Thanksgiving. They will feel a great sense of pride, having contributed to the holiday meal.

Plan ahead. To relieve some of the holiday pressure, prepare cookie dough and pie crusts when you have spare time, then wrap in sealable plastic bags or freezer paper and

Lucky Red Shake: Page 139

dressed up with themed napkins and centerpieces. Sprinkle confetti on a New Year's Day buffet table, set up a red, white, and blue flower arrangement for the Fourth of July on your picnic table, or make the Village People place markers, page 151, for your Thanksgiving spread.

Look in your grandparents' recipe box. In this chapter, you will find new recipes to add to your holiday repertoire, but be sure to serve your children the traditional foods from your ethnic or religious heritage as well. These foods teach kids about their family history and are a special way to connect one generation to the next.

Celebrate once a month. *FamilyFun* contributor Cynthia Caldwell says it's important to serve a fancy dinner every month or so to celebrate a holiday or birthday (a special event, such as a good report card or winning soccer season, is reason enough, too). Pull out the cloth napkins, china, silverware, and candles, dress up a little, and carve the turkey or roast at the table. Your kids will enjoy the meals and become more comfortable with polite table manners.

Plan Ahead for the Holidays

Make holiday punches (page 139).

Prepare Sugar Cookie dough (page 122) and freeze for up to a week.

Roll out pie crusts (page 133), line pie plates with them, and freeze in pie plates for 1 to 2 weeks.

freeze. During the holiday rush, just defrost and proceed with the recipes.

Be prepared. Stock up on food coloring (red and green for Christmas, orange and black for Halloween, and so on) to add to cookies, frosting, and drinks. Also, pick up cookie cutters and, if you feel like splurging, baking pans (a heart shape for Valentine's Day, a bunny for Easter, a turkey for Thanksgiving).

Make the dinner table special. Any holiday dinner can be appropriately

New Years

Lucky Red Shake

New Year's Eve has all the fixings for a true kid's celebration — the chance to toss confetti, sport silly hats, and stay up late. Toast to the new year with frosted mugs of this ruby-red drink, a lucky color according to Chinese legend.

1 cup strawberry soda
2 strawberries, stemmed and sliced
1 scoop strawberry ice cream

Pour the soda into a mug; add the ice cream and the strawberries. Serves 1.

Chocolate Resolution

Raise a glass of foamy chocolate, a parting gift to parents who swear they will diet in the new year. Garnish the shake with a homemade sparkler: Cut fringe out of a piece of tinfoil, twist one end, and stuff it into the tip of a bendy straw.

2 scoops chocolate ice cream
3 tablespoons chocolate syrup
½ cup milk

Mix all the ingredients in a blender until smooth. Serves 1.

Cloud Nine

When your family makes toasts with this heavenly shake, you'll have sweet dreams for the new year. Splash it up with a frozen grape kabob.

2 scoops vanilla frozen yogurt
1 banana
½ cup white grape juice

Mix the ingredients in a blender until smooth. Serves 1.

Celebration Sticks

FamilyFun reader Sarah Rosemarino, age eight, of North Canton, Ohio, dipped pretzels into a bowl of leftover melted chocolate, and her festive treat was born.

1 cup chocolate chips
12 8-inch pretzel rods
    Colored sprinkles

Melt the chocolate in the top of a double boiler. Dunk the pretzels halfway into the chocolate, then roll in a bowl of sprinkles. Dry on waxed paper. Makes 12.

Ring in the New Year

Whether you want to celebrate the new year with a family party or a sleep-over bash for your kids, here are some ideas to start the year right:

☞ **Clockface Cake:** Frost a round cake with white icing and use decorating gel to draw clock hands striking midnight.

☞ **Resolution Letters:** Write letters to yourselves, seal them in envelopes, and promise not to open them until the next New Year's Eve.

☞ **Fresh New Year:** Open all your doors and windows (for just a minute if it's cold out) and let the new year breeze into your home.

☞ **Good Luck:** Serve Hoppin' John or black-eyed peas, a traditional New Year's good luck charm in the South.

Valentine's Day

CAKE-DECORATING TIPS

Fancy frosting designs are easy to create using a pastry bag and decorating tips. You can buy starter kits at grocery, kitchen supply, and party stores. The most versatile tips are the writing, star, and leaf ones. Before decorating your cake, kids should practice on waxed paper. Use the writing tip's plain line for letters, stems, squiggles, dots, and outlines. Make stars with the star tip by holding the tip straight down near the cake and squeezing until the star forms. For a neat finish, stop the pressure before pulling away. The leaf tip makes a ribbon with a ridge down the center. Squeeze out the icing to form the bottom edge, then relax the pressure and pull the tip away to make a rippling leaf.

Saint Valentine's Sweetheart Cake

Legend has it that ever since Saint Valentine drew a picture of a heart and wrote inside it "From your Valentine" back in 270 A.D., hearts have been a symbol of love. If this saint was still around, his message would be even sweeter written on a heart-shaped cake. In his honor, hand some cake-decorating supplies over to your kids and help them write sweet messages in icing. Here's to love, cakes, and all that good stuff.

- 1 unbaked cake (see recipes on pages 124 to 127) or cake mix
- 3 cups All-Purpose Buttercream (see page 126)

Pour the cake batter into a heart-shaped cake pan (available at kitchen supply stores), or into an 8-inch round pan plus an 8-inch-square pan. Bake according to directions; cool completely. If you used the second cake pan option, cut the round cake in half. On a serving platter, set each semicircle against adjoining sides of the square to form the top of the heart. Frost with the icing, reserving a portion for decorating. Divide the leftover icing into bowls and tint each one a color, then decorate the cake. Serves 10 to 12.

Saint Valentine's Sweetheart Cakes

Chocolate Valentines

Which do kids love more: Giving surprises or getting them? I'm not sure, but I do know they'll have fun making these sweet pops — whether they gobble them up or give them away.

> 1 3- to 4-ounce high-quality dark or white chocolate bar
> Lollipop or Popsicle sticks
> Shredded coconut, chopped nuts, or sprinkles (optional)

Place the chocolate in a sturdy sealable plastic bag. Microwave 1 minute on high until just barely melted, or melt the bag of chocolate in simmering water (with white chocolate, use only the water method).

Cover a cookie sheet with waxed paper and lay down a lollipop or Popsicle stick. Snip a small hole in a corner of the plastic bag. With the slightly cooled chocolate, draw a heart shape around the top part of the stick and then fill it in. If your kids have trouble making the heart shape, just have them form a circle. Make more lollipops until the chocolate is used up. You can decorate the still-warm lollipops with shredded coconut, nuts, or sprinkles. Place the cookie sheet in the refrigerator or freezer to harden. Wrap the cooled pops in plastic and tie a red bow around the sticks. Makes 3 to 4.

Edible Valentine's Day Cards:

Children can paint messages on these chocolate "cards" with a colorful icing. As described above, melt white chocolate (so the messages will show up more clearly). On a cookie sheet covered with waxed paper, squeeze the chocolate into a 3- by 5-inch rectangle or a large heart. Smooth the surface with a knife dipped in warm water and refrigerate or freeze until hardened. Meanwhile, whisk 1 egg white and 1½ cups sifted confectioners' sugar to make the "paint." Divide into bowls and add food coloring to each bowl to make red, purple, green, blue, or any other colors. When the chocolate has hardened, flip it over and use a small clean paintbrush to write messages or draw simple pictures on the chocolate card.

Heart Cookie Pops

Heart Cookie Pops

Once frosted and decorated, these big conversation heart cookies on sticks say "I love you" with more gusto than those tiny candy conversation hearts. If your time is tight, use store-bought cookie dough instead of homemade.

> **Sugar Cookie dough (see recipe on page 122)**
> **Popsicle sticks, soaked in water**

When the cookie dough has thoroughly chilled, preheat the oven to 350°. On a lightly floured board, roll out the dough until it is about ⅛ inch thick. With a cookie cutter, cut out heart shapes. Place one heart on a greased cookie sheet. Lay a Popsicle stick in the center of the heart and place another heart directly on top of the first. Pinch the sides together so that the two pieces become one. Bake for 10 to 12 minutes, or until the edges are slightly browned. When the cookies are cool, let the kids decorate them with icing, cinnamon hearts, sprinkles, or messages. Makes about 24 cookie pops, depending on their size.

Easter

Braided Easter Bread

1½ teaspoons salt

6 soft-boiled, dyed eggs (nontoxic dyes only, see at left)

Egg wash (see page 70)

In a large mixing bowl, dissolve the yeast in the water. Meanwhile, melt the butter in a saucepan, turn off the heat, and add the milk. Pour the mixture into the bowl with the yeast. Add the sugar and eggs and stir well. Mix in 1 cup of the flour and then the salt. Continue mixing in the flour, 1 cup at a time, until a soft dough has formed. Turn the dough onto a floured surface, adding flour if the dough is too sticky to handle. Knead until it becomes elastic. Place in a lightly oiled bowl, cover, and set in a warm, draft-free area until doubled in size (about 1 hour).

Punch down the dough. Divide it into three equal parts and roll each piece into a 25-inch-long strand. Lay the strands side by side and loosely braid them (to avoid tearing the dough, braid from the middle out to each end). Place the braid in a wreath shape on a greased cookie sheet; tuck the ends under. Sink the eggs into the dough, between braided strands. Cover and let rise until double in size, about 30 minutes. Brush the egg wash over the dough. Bake in a preheated 350° oven for 25 minutes, or until golden brown. Serves 6 to 8.

Homemade Egg Dye

To mix up a batch of nontoxic dye for dipping white eggs, place ½ cup hot tap water, 2 teaspoons vinegar, and 6 drops food coloring into a small bowl and stir well. Your kids can mix together a few different food colors to produce purple, turquoise, or other hues.

Braided Easter Bread

Wake your family on Easter morning to a basket from the Easter Bunny and a delicious breakfast bread from you. If the braided loaf is a hit this year, turn it into an annual tradition.

2 tablespoons active dry yeast

½ cup warm water

½ cup butter

¾ cup milk

½ cup sugar

2 eggs, lightly beaten

5 to 6 cups all-purpose flour

Bunny Cake

Every Easter when I was a kid, my sister and I made this rabbit-face cake and decorated it with licorice whiskers and coconut fur.

1 unbaked cake (see recipes on pages 124 to 127) or cake mix

3 cups All-Purpose Buttercream (see page 126)

Pink crystal sugars

1 cup shredded coconut

Bunny Cake

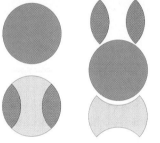

Jelly beans, gumdrops, and black
licorice
Decorating gel

Bake the cake in two 8-inch round cake pans. Cool thoroughly. Lay one round on a platter or cookie sheet covered with tinfoil. Cut the other round into three pieces (see diagram), positioning the two petal shapes above the face for the bunny's ears, and placing the remaining cake below the face for the bunny's bow tie.

Frost with the icing, then sprinkle a line of pink crystal sugars down the center of each ear. Cover the face and ears with the shredded coconut. Place 2 jelly beans for the eyes, a black gumdrop for a nose, a red gumdrop for a tongue, and black licorice for the lips and eyebrows. To decorate the bow tie,

squirt on the decorating gel to resemble polka dots. Serves 10 to 12.

Edible Easter Baskets

This Easter, don't put all your jelly beans in one basket. Put them on top of cupcakes and make edible decorations for the dinner table.

 12   cupcakes
 1½   cups All-Purpose Buttercream (see page 126) or white frosting
 12   pipe cleaners
  1   cup shredded coconut
       Green food coloring
       Jelly beans

Frost the cupcakes with the icing. Bend a pipe cleaner into an arch and push the ends into the sides of each cupcake. Make green coconut grass by adding a few drops of the food coloring to the coconut. Then, rest jelly bean eggs on top of the grass. Tie a ribbon bow on the pipe cleaner handle at a jaunty angle. Put one cupcake basket by each place setting or give them as gifts. Serves 12.

Edible Easter Baskets

Jelly Bean Bingo

Playing bingo has never been this sweet. Across the top row of each bingo card, affix the same sequence of stickers, then randomly color the remaining squares with jelly bean–colored markers. To play, the caller draws 1 sticker and 1 jelly bean and announces them. If a frog sticker and a pink jelly bean are chosen, a player with a pink square in the frog column can cover it with a pink jelly bean. The first to complete a line horizontally, vertically, or diagonally wins all his jelly beans.

143

Mother's & Father's Day

A Hat for Mother

Mom deserves royal treatment on Mother's Day, so here's a cake her littlest fans can make with help from Dad or a big sibling.

    1   18-ounce package yellow cake mix
    4   eggs
    ¾   cup vegetable oil
    ¾   cup apricot nectar
    3   teaspoons almond extract
    1   recipe Lemon Icing (see below)
         Gumdrops

A Hat for Mother

Preheat the oven to 325° and grease and lightly flour two pans: a rimmed, 12-inch round pizza or cake pan and a 1½-quart metal or ovenproof baking bowl. Combine all the ingredients except the icing, then beat in an electric mixer at medium speed for 4 minutes. Divide the batter between the pan and bowl; bake the pan for 20 to 25 minutes and the bowl for 45 to 50 (both are ready when a toothpick inserted in the center comes out clean). Let the cakes rest for 5 minutes before removing from the pans. Cool completely.

Center the bowl-shaped cake over the flat one. Ice the cake and finish with a hat ribbon and gumdrop "flowers" (see at left). Serves 10 to 12.

Lemon Icing

This buttercream frosting is flavored with lemon, but raspberry, mint, and vanilla are just as delicious.

    ½   cup unsalted butter
    4   cups confectioners' sugar
    2   teaspoons lemon extract,
            or zest and juice of
    1   lemon
            Pinch of salt
    4 to 6 tablespoons heavy cream

Cream the butter, then gradually beat in 1 cup of the sugar. Mix in the lemon extract and salt. Add the remaining sugar and just enough cream to create a spreadable icing. Makes 3 cups.

A Shirt for Dad

FamilyFun contributor Phyllis Fiorotta says you don't have to be a baker or tailor to create this shirt cake for Father's Day.

- Cardboard shirt box, at least 9 by 13 inches
- 1 unbaked cake (see recipes on pages 196 to 199) or cake mix
- 3 cups All-Purpose Buttercream (see page 198) or white frosting
- Food coloring

Line the shirt box with tissue paper. Prepare the cake batter according to directions. Bake in a 9- by 13-inch cake pan, remove from the pan, cool, and place on waxed paper. Cover with a larger piece of waxed paper and flip the cake over and into the box (the cake bottom should face up).

Reserving a small portion for the tie, tint the frosting a pastel color with a couple drops of food coloring. Frost the cake with the pastel icing. Tint the reserved icing a bright color and spread it into a tie shape on the cake. Cut a collar and two cuffs out of white paper. The collar is a strip, rolled into a ring and taped, with a small V cut out of the center. The cuffs are rectangles with candy cuff links. Just before serving, trim away the waxed paper and add the collar and cuffs. Serves 10 to 12.

A Shirt for Dad

Queen for a Day

On Mother's Day, make Mom feel like a queen by laying down the red carpet and giving her the royal treatment.

A Royal Brunch: **Insist that Her Highness sleep late. Meanwhile, the king and his court jesters can *quietly* create a festive brunch including Pineapple Boats (see page 111), Royal Ham 'n' Eggs (see page 20), and Banana Bread (see page 63).**

The Palace Dining Room: **Prepare a throne by padding a table chair with a pillow. Decorate the table with fresh flowers, cloth napkins, and full table settings (two sizes of forks and spoons). Add colorful construction paper place mats.**

King for a Day

On Father's Day, there's nothing grander for Dad than being treated like a king.

A Royal Barbecue: **Let Dad lounge the afternoon away in his favorite outdoor chair while Mom and the kids prepare a regal feast of shish kabob (see page 82), Cheese Wedge Biscuits (see page 64), and Roasted Corn on the Cob (see page 106). Graffiti Tablecloth: To humor the king, his court jesters can cover the picnic table with a white paper tablecloth personalized with messages to Dad.**

Gold Coins: **Offer Dad the riches of his kingdom with homemade coins. Cut circles from yellow construction paper and draw a self-portrait on each coin. Then add a value: a chore that the king can redeem whenever he cashes the coin in.**

Fourth of July

Fourth of July Picnic

Fourth of July Picnic

★ ★ ★ ★

On July 4th, feasts have always been the order of the day. This year, feed a crowd of friends with a potluck. Divide the guest list into groups, assigning salads to one, desserts to another, and beverages to the third. Each family can bring its own chicken to grill.

Barbecued Chicken

Potato Salad Vinaigrette (page 116)

Roasted Corn on the Cob (page 106)

Red, White, and Blueberry Strawberry Shortcake (page 287)

Barbecued Chicken

In summer, the language of barbecue is spoken everywhere. There's something about cooking and eating outdoors that seems to make food taste even better. Here's an easy-to-spread sauce to keep grillside for those who want a little tang with their chicken.

1	yellow onion, minced
2	crushed garlic cloves
2	tablespoons butter
2	tablespoons water
¼	cup brown sugar
1	cup catsup
2	tablespoons white vinegar
1	tablespoon Dijon mustard
2	tablespoons Worcestershire sauce
1	teaspoon grated orange rind
¼	cup orange juice
10	chicken pieces (breasts, thighs, or legs)

Sauté the onion and garlic in the butter until translucent. Add the water and brown sugar and simmer for 1 minute. Add the catsup, vinegar, mustard, Worcestershire sauce, and orange rind, stirring constantly. Pour in the orange juice and stir until blended. Simmer over very low heat for 15 to 20 minutes, stirring occasionally.

Brush the sauce on the chicken pieces several times while grilling. Makes 2 cups of sauce, enough to coat 4 chicken breasts and 6 legs or thighs.

Fruit Salad

None of the watermelon goes to waste with this decorative salad. The rind becomes a basket full of melon stars and sweet grapes.

1	medium-size watermelon
1	cantaloupe
1	honeydew melon
2	pounds seedless grapes

To make the basket, rinse the outer rind of the watermelon. Lay it on its side and slice off the end, about one quarter of the melon. Scoop out the flesh of the entire watermelon and reserve it. Using the tip of a vegetable peeler or lemon zester, inscribe large stars on the rind's outer surface.

Next, cut the cantaloupe in half, scoop out the seeds, and use a melon baller to remove the flesh from one of the halves. Use the second half to make melon stars: Cut the half into 1-inch slices and, using a star-shaped cookie cutter, cut out the melon. Repeat this process with the honeydew melon.

Remove the seeds from the scooped out watermelon and cut stars out of it. Wash the grapes and remove their stems. Fill the watermelon basket with the fruit. Create festive fruit kabobs with any leftovers. Serves 10 to 12.

Red, White & Blueberry Freeze Pops

Sweet, cool, and relatively healthy, these fruity, frozen pops are great pick-me-ups after a Fourth of July parade.

10   5-ounce plastic or paper cups
1   quart raspberry juice
10   Popsicle sticks
2   cups cold water
1   pint frozen vanilla yogurt
¾   cup fresh or frozen blueberries

Assemble the cups on a cookie tray. Pour 1 inch of the raspberry juice into each cup, then place the tray in the freezer. When the juice is partially frozen, set a Popsicle stick in the center of each cup and let the juice freeze solid. Next, blend 1 cup of the water and 4 large scoops of the frozen yogurt until smooth. Pour 1 inch of the yogurt mix on top of the frozen juice layer in each cup and freeze again. Once the yogurt layer sets, blend the second cup of water, the blueberries, and a large scoop of the frozen yogurt. Spoon the blueberry mix into the cups and freeze overnight. To serve, slide the pop out of the cup. Makes 10 pops.

Old-Fashioned Lemonade

After helping cut the lemons, you may want to turn this recipe over to the kids, who tend to be the lemon squeezing experts.

5   to 6 large lemons
1   cup sugar
2   quarts cold water

Slice the lemons in half and squeeze each of them into a large measuring cup (this should yield about 1½ cups of juice). Remove any seeds.

In a large pitcher or Mason jar, combine the juice and the sugar. Stir in the cold water and serve over ice. (For a nice touch, place mint leaves in the ice cube trays before freezing.) Makes about 10 cups.

> **FunFact**
> A 2-mile long picnic table bordered the Fourth of July parade in Ontario, California, in the 1940s.

Strawberry Sparklers

Turn fresh strawberries into a festive and refreshing Fourth of July treat with this quick trick. Melt 12 ounces of white chocolate chips in a microwave according to the package directions (make sure the container and the strawberries are dry; even a little moisture will alter the texture of the candy). One at a time, dip strawberries halfway into the melted chocolate and then one quarter of the way into blue sugar or edible glitter (sold at many party stores). Makes 35 to 45 Strawberry Sparklers.

Frozen Witches

with the fruit. Carve a small face in each orange (triangle shapes for eyes? circles on the sides for ears? a diamond for a nose? a mouth with a solitary tooth?). Fill the orange with the fruit salad and replace its top. As a finishing touch, garnish each top with mint leaves for stems. Make as many as you like.

Frozen Witches

Throw a fiendish party the neighborhood kids will never forget. They'll screech with delight over these bewitched desserts, but the real pleasure will be your family's — the little witches are a kick to decorate. For best results, assemble ahead of time and freeze.

Tube of chocolate decorating gel
8 chocolate sugar cones
8 thin, round chocolate wafers
1 pint pistachio ice cream
Black shoestring licorice
Chocolate chips
Candy corn

To avoid witch meltdowns, make these desserts in batches of four. For each witch hat, squeeze a ring of the decorating gel around the edge of a cone and attach the cone to a chocolate wafer "rim," then set it aside. Using an ice-cream scoop, drop "heads" of the ice cream onto a cookie sheet lined with waxed paper. Arrange cut licorice pieces into hair and a mouth. Add chocolate chip eyes and a candy corn nose. Top each ice-cream head with a cone hat (flatten the ice cream slightly so the hat doesn't fall off). Freeze for at least 2 hours, or until the hats are set in place. Makes 8.

Jack-O'-Lantern Fruit Salad

This Halloween, carve jack-o'-lanterns out of oranges instead of pumpkins. Fill them with fruit salad, and serve as snack, appetizer, or dessert.

Assorted fruit, such as melon, strawberries, apples, and kiwis
Oranges (1 per person)
Mint leaves

Chop the assorted fruits and mix them in a large bowl (you will need about ½ cup per orange). To carve a pumpkin cup, slice off the top of an orange (as you would a jack-o'-lantern). Using a knife to loosen the edges, scoop out the inside of the orange with a spoon. Toss the juice in

Haunted Graham Cracker House

If you can't turn your house into a diabolical mansion for Halloween, then use graham crackers to create an equally scary one with a rickety porch, a Keep Out sign, and a graveyard. Increase the recipe and you can make a complete ghost town.

The Paste:

- 2 egg whites
- 3 cups confectioners' sugar
- 1 teaspoon black cake-decorating paste (available at party and kitchen supply stores)

The Structure:

- 1 empty cereal or cracker box
  Graham crackers
  Black and orange candies, such as black shoestring and twisted licorice, candy corn, orange candy sticks, Tic Tacs, M&M's, and Necco wafers
  Marshmallows
  Crushed chocolate cookies

In the bowl of an electric mixer, blend the egg whites with the confectioners' sugar and the black paste until smooth. Cover the bowl with a damp cloth to keep the paste from hardening and set it aside.

Arrange the empty cereal or cracker box upright on a piece of foil-covered cardboard (you can tape it down to secure it). Use the paste to glue the graham crackers onto the sides of the box. Tape the top flaps of the box together to form a pitched roof, then cover them with graham crackers.

Next, fill in the cracks by squeezing the paste through a pastry bag with a plain tip (you also can use a plastic bag with a small hole cut from the corner). Draw crooked windows and board them up with graham cracker scraps.

Home for the Holidays

Cover the roof with candy corn and M&M's. You can add a porch by gluing a graham cracker horizontally to the side of the house; support it with licorice or candy sticks. For a backyard graveyard, flatten the marshmallows, snip off the sides with scissors, then use paste to stand them up in the courtyard. As a finishing touch, add a crooked walkway of Necco wafers and ice a Keep Out sign on a graham cracker. Finally, sprinkle crushed chocolate cookies to make the yard.

Fun! Turnips were the first jack-o'-lanterns, carved by the Celts in ancient Ireland. In America, the Irish used pumpkins.

Haunted Graham Cracker House

Roasted Turkey

What the Pilgrims Ate

Lobster Duck Clams
Leeks Watercress Pumpkin
Goose Corn bread Eel
Venison Plums Dried berries
Corn Popcorn Oysters
Green vegetables
Cranberries

Turkey Potpies

Looking for a fun way to polish off Thanksgiving leftovers? Set them up buffet style, starting with the turkey tray. Add bowls of peas, green beans, carrots, corn, and the gravy bowl. Hand out individual-size, pastry-lined pie tins and let your kids customize their potpies. Adventurous diners might want to try adding cranberry sauce, mashed potatoes, stuffing, or herbs. Add the top crusts, crimp the edges, poke vent holes in the tops, and bake at 425° for 20 to 30 minutes, or until lightly browned.

Roasted Turkey

Preparing a holiday turkey can give any cook jitters. With a few of *FamilyFun*'s pointers on your side, though, it needn't be such a daunting task.

1   12- to 15-pound turkey (neck, giblets, and excess fat removed)
    Salt and pepper
6   to 8 cups Country Herb Stuffing (see page 151)
    Double thickness of cheesecloth
⅓   to ½ cup melted butter

Preheat the oven to 325°. Rinse the turkey inside and out with cold water and pat dry. Lightly salt and pepper the cavities. Loosely fill the neck and body cavities with the stuffing. Using a thin metal skewer or needle and thread, skewer or sew the openings shut. Tie the legs together with kitchen twine and fold the wings back and under the body of the turkey.

Place the turkey breast side up on a roasting rack in a roasting pan. Next, soak the cheesecloth in water and squeeze it dry. Saturate it in the melted butter and drape it over the turkey. Pour 1 cup of water in the bottom of the pan and bake the turkey for about 15 to 20 minutes per pound. The cheesecloth will help keep the meat moist, but you also should baste the bird once every hour or so.

Forty-five minutes before the turkey is done, remove the cheesecloth and let the turkey brown. If the legs and breast are browning too quickly, cover them with foil. The turkey is cooked when an instant-read meat thermometer inserted into the thickest part of the thigh registers between 180° and 185°. Remove the turkey to a serving platter. Cover it loosely with foil and let it rest for 20 to 30 minutes before carving. Serves 8 to 10 with enough for leftovers.

Country Herb Stuffing

Most families want more stuffing than can fit into the bird, so this recipe makes enough extras to bake in a side dish. For safety reasons, cook the bird immediately after stuffing it.

    2   tablespoons butter
    1   onion, diced
    4   celery ribs, diced
    2   tart apples, peeled, cored, and
            finely diced
    1   loaf Italian bread, cubed and
            dried in a 350° oven
    ½   loaf whole wheat or oatmeal
            bread, cubed and dried in a
            350° oven
    2   to 3 tablespoons poultry
            seasoning
        Salt to taste
    3   to 5 cups turkey or chicken stock

In a medium skillet, melt the butter and sauté the onions and celery until soft. Add the apples and sauté for about 5 minutes. Lightly toss the bread cubes with the apple-onion mixture, seasonings, and salt. Bring the stock to a simmer and pour it over the seasoned bread cubes. Stuffing moistness is a personal preference, so adjust to your family's taste and then refrigerate until ready to stuff the bird. Makes about 10 cups.

Pumpkin Ice-Cream Pie

Pumpkin Ice-Cream Pie

FamilyFun contributor Drew Kristofik, of Westport, Connecticut, says her family eats this from Halloween through Thanksgiving, pausing occasionally for the odd fruit, vegetable, and protein meal. Her kids like to decorate the pie with a pumpkin seed face.

    1   quart vanilla ice cream or frozen
            yogurt (allow to get soupy
            before adding to the mix)
    1   cup plain canned pumpkin
    ¼   cup sugar
    ¼   teaspoon cinnamon
    ¼   teaspoon ginger
    1   Graham Cracker Crust (see
            page 133)

You can add the ingredients in any order you like and it still comes out great. Throw everything (except the crust, of course) into a large bowl and stir. When the filling is mixed, which in Drew's house means everyone has had several turns with the spoon, pour it into the prepared crust and set it in a level place in the freezer to harden overnight. Serves 8 to 10.

Village People

Spice up the Thanksgiving table with these handcrafted place markers. Make Native American and Pilgrim figures with toilet paper tubes and construction paper. Draw facial features, make hair, and add headbands and feathers for Native Americans as well as collars and hats for the Pilgrims.

Luscious Latkes

Hanukkah isn't Hanukkah without a steaming plate of latkes. These potato pancakes are fried in oil to commemorate the two-thousand-year-old Hanukkah story of the jar of oil that miraculously burned for eight days in a Jerusalem temple.

4	large potatoes, peeled
1	onion
2	large eggs
1½	teaspoons salt
¼	teaspoon white pepper
2	tablespoons all-purpose flour or matzo meal
¾	teaspoon baking powder
	About 1 cup peanut or vegetable oil

Coarsely grate the potatoes and onion in a food processor or with the large holes of a grater. Place in a colander, then press to squeeze out as much liquid as possible. In a large bowl, combine the potato mixture with the eggs, salt, pepper, flour or matzo meal, and baking powder.

In a large skillet, heat about 1 inch of the oil. When the oil is bubbling, gently drop about 2 tablespoons of the potato batter into the pan (it should hold a round shape). Gently flatten each latke with the back of a spoon. Fry over medium heat for 3 to 4 minutes on each side, or until golden brown and crisp (use two spatulas when flipping latkes so the oil doesn't splatter). Drain cooked latkes on paper towels and set them aside in a warm oven. Add more oil to the pan as needed for frying the rest of the pancakes. Serve hot with applesauce, sour cream, jam, or sugar. Makes about 18 latkes.

Homemade Applesauce

Sweet, tart, homemade applesauce is a perfect complement for a plateful of piping hot latkes. Because the apple skins are left on during cooking, this sauce comes out a rosy pink.

12	medium apples
1	cup water
½	cup sugar
1	tablespoon lemon juice
½	teaspoon cinnamon

Wash, quarter, and core the apples. Place them in a large cooking pot and add the water. Over medium heat, cook the apples until they are nearly soft. Add the sugar, lemon juice, and cinnamon. Cook for a few minutes longer, then press the apples through a medium sieve and let cool. Serve warm or cold. Makes about 4 cups.

Hanukkah Doughnuts

These holeless, jelly-filled doughnuts, also known as sufganiyot, are a popular Hanukkah food in Israel. Like latkes, they are deep-fried in oil to celebrate the Hanukkah miracle. This recipe is adapted from Faye Levy's *International Jewish Cookbook* (Warner Books).

> ¾   cup lukewarm water
> 2   packages active dry yeast
> ¼   cup sugar
> 4   cups all-purpose flour
> 2   large eggs
> 2   large egg yolks
> 7   tablespoons butter, at room
>   temperature
> 1   teaspoon vanilla extract
> 2   teaspoons salt
> ¼   cup apricot or strawberry jam
>   Vegetable oil (at least 5 cups)
>   Confectioners' sugar

Pour ½ cup of the water into a small bowl. Add the yeast and 1 teaspoon of the sugar. Let stand for 10 minutes.

Spoon the flour into a large mixing bowl. Make a well in the center and add the remaining sugar and water, plus the eggs, yolks, butter, vanilla extract, and salt. Mix until the ingredients are blended. Add the dissolved yeast and mix again until a dough forms.

Knead on a lightly floured surface for about 10 minutes to form a smooth ball (if the dough is sticky, add extra flour). Place in a lightly oiled bowl, turn to coat, and cover with a damp cloth. Let the dough rise in a warm place for 1 to 1½ hours, or until doubled in size.

On a lightly floured surface, roll out half the dough to a ¼-inch thickness. Using a 2½- to 3-inch cutter, cut the dough into 28 rounds. Put ½ to 1 teaspoon of the jam in the center of half the rounds. Lightly brush the rim of each round with water, then set a plain round on top. With floured fingers, firmly press the edges together to seal. Transfer this "sandwich" to a floured tray. If it has stretched out to an oval, plump it gently back into a round shape. Continue with the remaining dough. Cover with a slightly damp cloth and let them rise for 30 minutes.

In a large skillet or deep fryer, heat the oil to 350° (measure the temperature with a candy thermometer). Carefully slide in 4 doughnuts or enough to fill the pan without crowding. Fry the doughnuts for 3 minutes on each side, or until golden brown. Drain on paper towels. Repeat with the remaining half of the dough.

Cool (the jam is very hot), garnish with the confectioners' sugar, then serve. Makes about 28 doughnuts.

OH DREIDEL, DREIDEL, DREIDEL

The dreidel game is a form of an old German gambling game. The stakes are low with players betting their fortune in chocolates with a spin of the top. If *Nun* comes up after a spin, that player gets nothing from the communal pot. *Gimel* means the player takes the whole pot. If *Heh* turns up, the player takes half of what's in the pot. *Shin* means the player must add to the pot. The game is over when one player has won all the "chips."

Christmas

Tasty Tags

FamilyFun contributor Heidi King came up with a sweet way to label her holiday gifts — she bakes tags out of cookie dough and inscribes them with icing. To make one, cut rectangles or another shape out of Sugar Cookie dough (see page 122). If desired, poke a small hole (it will close up a bit when baked) for attaching the "tag." Bake the cookies according to the directions and cool. Using tinted All-Purpose Buttercream (see page 126), spread each tag with one color, then, with a pastry tip, add names and designs in a contrasting color. When the icing is dry, thread a thin ribbon through the hole. Seal each cookie in plastic wrap, then attach the tag to the gift.

Frosted Snowmen

FamilyFun contributor Susan Milord made a troop of these friendly snowman cupcakes for a Christmas party centerpiece. If your kids aren't coconut fans, you can eliminate the extra layer.

- 12 regular-size cupcakes (with liners)
- 12 miniature cupcakes (no liners)
- 2 to 3 cups All-Purpose Buttercream (see page 126) or white frosting
  Shredded coconut
  Candy corn or orange gumdrops
  Chocolate chips
  Strips of ribbon or fabric

To assemble the snowmen, frost the tops of the regular-size cupcakes with the icing and set aside. Frost the tops and sides of the miniature cupcakes, then roll them in the coconut. Center the miniature cupcakes on top of the larger ones and sprinkle with coconut.

To decorate the faces, use the candy corns or slivers of the gumdrops for noses, and chocolate chips for eyes and mouths. Tie the decorative strips of ribbon or fabric around the smaller cupcakes like scarves. Makes 12.

Stained-Glass Cookies

Reminiscent of cathedral windows, these cookies make beautiful gifts for neighbors, grandparents, and friends.

Sugar Cookie dough (see recipe on page 122)
Colored hard candies

While the cookie dough is chilling, sort the hard candies by color. Place each batch in a heavy-duty plastic bag and seal. Crush the candies into small chunks with a mallet or rolling pin and set aside. Cover a baking sheet with foil. Roll out the dough and cut out tree-shaped cookies, then use small cutters, such as aspic cutters, to cut out stars or other shapes within each tree. Place the cookies on the baking sheet and fill the cutout holes with the crushed candy so it is even with the cookies' surface. Do not overfill. Bake the cookies at 350° for 10 to 12 minutes. When they are cool, carefully remove them from the foil. Makes about 3 dozen cookies, depending on their size.

Christmas Stockings

These merry cookies make sweet stocking presents or late-night treats for Santa.

Sugar Cookie dough (see recipe on page 122)

All-Purpose Buttercream (see page 126)

Colored sprinkles

Candies

Roll out the dough to about a ¼-inch thickness. Cut out a sock shape using a cookie cutter or a pattern made of cardboard. If you want to hang the stockings, use the end of a drinking straw to cut a hole through the cuff of the sock, but not too close to the edge. Bake the cookies at 350° for 10 to 12 minutes. When completely cooled, decorate the stockings with frosting, sprinkles, and candies. For the recipient's name, pipe out frosting. Makes about 3 dozen, depending on their size.

Cookie Advent Calendar

After we ran the directions for making this cookie Advent calendar in *FamilyFun* magazine, a host of our readers counted down the days before Christmas one cookie at a time.

To make the calendar, take a piece of colorful felt, about 30 inches by 15 inches, and turn one of the shorter edges over 2 inches (to form the top casing). Rough-stitch it to the back of the calendar, leaving room in the fold to run a ¼-inch-thick dowel for hanging.

To number the days, use store-bought cookies or bake a batch of your favorites, such as Sugar Cookies (see page 122) or Gingerbread Cookies (see page 156). You'll need 25 cookies plus a few extra for hungry helpers. If you bake your own, let them cool thoroughly.

Using a tube of colored frosting, number the cookies from 1 to 25. When the frosting dries, wrap each cookie in plastic wrap, twisting the plastic at the top part of the cookie. Arrange them on the calendar, evenly spaced, for placement. Make a small mark with a pen, centered ½ inch above each cookie. Then, set the cookies aside.

Next, secure ribbons to the calendar face. Thread a large-eyed darning needle with a piece of ribbon (or colorful yarn), about 10 inches long and ⅛ inch wide. Make a small stitch at one mark on the calendar. Pull the ribbon through the felt so that both ends of the ribbon are on the face of the calendar. Set the cookies back in place and tie the ribbon in a bow around the twisted plastic wrap at the top of each cookie. To hang your Advent calendar, slide the dowel into the casing. Tie the ends of a 2-foot-long piece of ribbon to the dowel tips, then hang it within reach of your little elves.

Gingerbread Cookies

three or four equal portions and flatten each into a disk. Cover in plastic wrap and refrigerate for 2 hours, or until firm enough to roll.

Preheat the oven to 350°. Roll and cut out the dough, then transfer the cookies to greased baking sheets. Bake for 10 minutes, or until brown around the edges. Remove the baking sheet to a wire rack; cool for 5 minutes. Transfer the cookies to racks and cool thoroughly. Cookies can be stored in an airtight container in the freezer for 1 month and up to 3 days at room temperature before they are decorated with frosting. Makes about 4 dozen cookies.

Popcorn Snowmen

These marshmallow treats disappear faster than a parking spot on the day before Christmas.

15	cups popped popcorn
½	cup butter or margarine
2	10-ounce packages marshmallows
	Thin pretzel sticks, raisins, candy corn, mini jawbreakers, red hots, gumdrops, and fruit leather
	Royal Icing (see page 157)

Pour the popcorn into a large bowl; set aside. Melt the butter in a nonstick saucepan over medium-low heat. Add the marshmallows, stirring constantly until melted. Pour over the popcorn and stir to coat. When cool enough to touch, rub margarine on your hands and form popcorn balls.

Stack three popcorn balls for a snowman. Using Royal Icing for glue, add pretzel stick arms, raisin eyes, and a candy corn nose. Arrange mini jawbreakers into a broad grin. For buttons, use gumdrops or red hots. For scarves, cut rectangles out of fruit leather and fringe the ends. Makes about 5 snowmen.

Gingerbread Cookies

With this standard holiday recipe, you can whip up sturdy gingerbread canvases to ice and decorate. The baked cookies are light and delicious.

4½	cups all-purpose flour
1	tablespoon cinnamon
1½	teaspoons ginger
½	teaspoon ground cloves
½	teaspoon nutmeg
1	teaspoon baking soda
½	teaspoon salt
¾	cup molasses
½	cup firmly packed brown sugar
½	cup butter, softened
2	large eggs, at room temperature

In a large bowl, combine the flour, cinnamon, ginger, cloves, nutmeg, baking soda, and salt. In another large bowl, beat the molasses, brown sugar, butter, and eggs. One third at a time, beat in the flour mixture until thoroughly mixed. Divide the dough into

Ice-Cream Cone Ornament

Assembling this ornament, always a hit with ice-cream fans, is simple enough for pint-size attention spans. Glue a ribbon loop into a sugar cone for hanging the ornament. Run glue along the top edge and stuff a ball of fiberfill into the cone. Add ribbon and glitter "sprinkles" and a red pom-pom "cherry." Hang for all to see.

156

Graham Cracker Village

What to do with your restless brood on a snowbound day? Let them raise the roof, of course, by building a confectionery village.

The Royal Icing:

- 2 egg whites
- 3 cups confectioners' sugar
- ¼ teaspoon cream of tartar

The Structure:

- Pint-size milk cartons (thoroughly washed out and dried)
- Graham crackers
- Nonpareils, Necco wafers, slivered almonds, or peanut halves
- Assorted candy, such as caramels, marshmallows, red hots, gumdrops, candy fruit slices, fruit leather, licorice, gum slices, hard candies, Life Savers, mini jawbreakers, lollipops, or rock candy sticks
- Sugar or shredded coconut

To make the icing for gluing the houses together, beat the egg whites with the sugar and cream of tartar in an electric mixer until creamy and smooth. Spoon half into a pastry bag fitted with a writing tip or a sealable plastic bag with a hole cut in one corner. Reserve the rest of the icing in the bowl, covered with a damp cloth to prevent it from hardening.

Arrange the milk cartons upright on a piece of foil-covered cardboard (you can tape them down to secure them). Use the icing to glue graham crackers to the sides of each carton. Frost two roof crackers to the top of each carton, then apply shingles of nonpareils, Necco wafers, slivered almonds, or peanut halves. Pipe icing along the roof ridge and cap with another row of candy. Use caramels or a marshmallow covered with red hots for a chimney.

For windowpanes, apply gumdrops, candy fruit slices, or fruit leather and trim with piped icing. Make doors out of decorated graham crackers. To create a wreath, attach a shoestring licorice bow to a green Life Saver. "String" colorful holiday lights by decorating roof edges with rows of mini jawbreakers.

For landscaping, plant spearmint gumdrop shrubs. Lay cobblestone walkways of nonpareils or Necco wafers. You can even build a snowman — use toothpicks to skewer marshmallows. For lampposts, top peppermint sticks with yellow gumdrops. Fix them along the village street with frosting. Use whip licorice and mini jawbreakers to string holiday lights between the lampposts. Once all the details are set, let it snow with a generous sprinkling of sugar or shredded coconut.

Kwanzaa Cookies

From December 26th to January 1st, your family can celebrate the African American holiday Kwanzaa by baking Kwanzaa flag cookies. Roll Sugar Cookie dough (page 122) to 1/8 inch thickness and cut it into rectangles. Sandwich a Popsicle stick flagpole between 2 rectangles. Bake as directed, then cool. Decorate with colored frosting to match the picture.

Graham Cracker Village

Homemade Party Hats,
page 172

FamilyFun
Parties

By Deanna F. Cook
and the experts at FamilyFun **magazine**

EDITIONS

New York

Contents

Wizard Cupcak page

Cool-off Party, page 231

Ladybug Party Invite, page 202

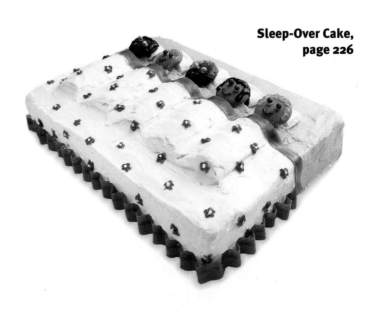

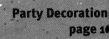

Party Decoration
page 16

Chapter One

Planning a Party

Invitations ★ Decorations
Food ★ Games ★ Crafts ★ Activities
Etiquette ★ Favors & Prizes

DOGGIE!" was my daughter Ella's first word — and first true passion in life. At 12 months, she would pant like a dog, put out a paw, and crawl after her four-legged friends, much to the surprise of her not-so-dog-inclined mom. So for her first birthday, my husband and I threw her a simplified version of the puppy party on page 196. She screeched with delight at the cardboard doghouse and devoured the Dalmatian cake with peppermint patty spots. I knew on that day we had a party animal on our hands, and that this was the first of many parties we would throw for her — and with her.

Parties, after all, are a part of a happy childhood. And despite the work and cost of planning them, they're a heck of a lot of fun for parents, too. Getting together with friends for birthdays, holidays, or even a simple dinner party helps mark the all-too-fast-moving years of childhood. And the best parties become an annual tradition.

At *FamilyFun* magazine, we know how important it is for every party to be a hit. Through the years, our readers, parents with kids ages three to 12, have come to depend on our party plans, whether they're for a slumber birthday bash, summer cool-off fest, neighborhood potluck, or block party. The plans we print are complete, from the invitations to the cake to the thank-you notes, and they are always tested out by families.

In this book, you'll find the best parties from *FamilyFun* magazine. Like Ella's first birthday, I hope the celebrations that this book inspires go down in your own family fun history.

— *Deanna F. Cook*

Party Planning

Party Worksheet

Once you have settled on a party in this book, copy the following list onto a large piece of paper and use it to track decisions about the party. Keep a shopping list running simultaneously.

✓ **Theme:**
✓ **Location:**
✓ **Date:**
✓ **Time:**
✓ **Guests:**
✓ **Prizes and favors:**
✓ **Helpers:**
✓ **Invitations:**
✓ **Decorations:**
✓ **Menu:**
✓ **Games:**
✓ **Crafts:**
✓ **Activities:**
✓ **Supplies:**

THROWING a successful party need not be expensive or exhausting — and the memories it will create can last a lifetime. Simple planning and family teamwork are the key. Invite your child to flip through the pages of this book to find a plan, then take a close look at the Party Stats (in the balloons) to make sure it fits your budget, works within your time frame, and is age appropriate. Here are some basic planning tips to get you in the party spirit.

Allow time for planning: A great birthday or block party can take as long as a month to plan at a non-stressful pace. So be sure to factor in ample time (use our estimated prep time as a guideline). To make it easier, divide the work into a series of after-school activities (make the invites one week, and the party crafts the next).

Enlist help: Ask your spouse, a neighbor, an older child, a relative, or a baby-sitter for support both for the planning and for the party. Of course, all during the planning stage, be sure to include your kids, who will have lots of ideas.

Pick a theme: Parties are fun when they revolve around a child's current passion or a family's personal interest, from ballerinas to beaches. A theme also helps spark your imagination when it comes to invitations, decorations, food, favors, and games. Suggest the theme and go over ideas with your family (to make sure no one has moved on to a new one). At the same time, not every party has to have a theme. You can mix and match games, invitations, and crafts from any of our plans for a successful party.

Choose an age-appropriate party: We have recommended an age range for each party, but don't let that number restrict you. For instance, if your eight-year-old would rather throw a doll's tea party than a mermaid bash, adapt a birthday party to suit her interests and abilities.

Settle on a budget that suits your family: In each party, we estimated the cost per guest, assuming three favors each would be plenty.

Use this figure as a starting point — if you feel like spending more, splurge on every favor on the list; if the estimate seems too steep, trim away. The easiest way to hold down costs is to make as much as you can, from the invitations to the decorations, favors, and food.

Choose a location: Home parties, either inside or in the backyard, are nice for any age and definitely work best for children ages four and under. Outdoor locales, whether a backyard or a skating rink, have the advantage of space and spare your house wear and tear. Still, it may be harder to control the boundaries, and events depend on Mother Nature. For more location ideas, see page 306.

Set a time limit: For birthday parties, a few hours of playing games, eating cake, and opening presents is plenty. Family parties, on the other hand, tend to have a looser schedule and can last an entire afternoon. When determining the length of a party, keep in mind your child's (or family's) energy level and plan accordingly.

Structure the party: Think of a party as consisting of segments: the welcoming activity, the games, the refreshments, and the closing activity. As guests arrive, plan an icebreaking activity, such as making party hats, for them to do until everyone shows up. When all guests are present, open with a game that lets the entire group interact. Thereafter, change the pace so that boisterous games are followed by calmer ones. Make the last game before refreshments a calm one and plan free play for the farewell activity.

Go with the flow: Once the party is in full swing, don't be afraid to repeat a game that was a huge hit — or scratch one you think won't go over well now that you know the mood of the party. The most important thing is to plan a structure before the party, then remain as flexible as possible once it is under way. Once you've settled on an order, write it down and use it only as a guideline. If something doesn't go as planned, roll with the punches and change activities, and your party will be a winner.

Memory Makers

Capture the spirit of your party on film with these photo tips:
- ☞ Before the party, make sure your camera battery and flash are working.
- ☞ Assign a roaming photographer, such as Dad, a sitter, or a teenage sibling, to take pictures.
- ☞ Turn party guests into photographers by passing out disposable cameras.
- ☞ Set up a photo backdrop for posing guests.
- ☞ Assemble all your party shots into a mini album as a keepsake.
- ☞ If you own or can borrow a video camera, film the party highlights.
- ☞ Be candid — too many posed shots may dampen the fun.

Planning a Party

Party Invitations

Creative Invitations

☞ **For a plane or train party, send "tickets" with boarding passes.**
☞ **Write the invitations on balloons, puzzles, paper chains, or the back of photos.**
☞ **Make one master invitation (a child's drawing, a collage, or a computer design) and photocopy it.**
☞ **Send a musical invitation — a cassette with theme music.**
☞ **Decorate the envelope with stickers to fit the theme.**
☞ **Deliver invitations dressed in a costume that relates to the party theme.**
☞ **Stuff the card with glitter or confetti.**

OME PARTIES, such as a special dinner for grandparents, might not call for invitations. A phone call or e-mail will do. Most parties, though, benefit from a written invitation. They set the tone for a party, establish the theme, and excite guests to come. Before sending out your invitations, review the designs we feature with each party plan, as well as the following hints.

Start with the guest list: When making the guest list, consider the size of your house (or yard) and how many guests you can comfortably manage. If you're throwing a children's party, you can use the old formula that the child's age determines the number of attendees (a five-year-old would invite five friends, for example), but if you think you can handle the entire class, by all means, do so.

Include party particulars: On your invitation, list who the party is for, what the theme is (if any), and where the party will be located (along with directions, if

necessary). You'll also want to include both the starting and ending times so parents know when to pick their kids up.

List special instructions: It's a good idea to mention if a meal will be served or if it's simply cake and ice cream. You should also list any items guests should bring along, such as a swimsuit for a pool party.

Request an RSVP: Include your phone number and a date you'd like a response by. When parents call to RSVP, ask if they plan on staying and if their child has any food allergies or conditions, such as asthma. For larger parties, write "regrets only."

Send invitations at least two weeks in advance: This allows guests plenty of time to respond while giving you the chance to finalize the amount of food or favors you need.

Party Decorations

APARTY CALLS for a festive atmosphere, so go ahead and dress up your space with balloons and streamers. For ideas, you may want to hit a party supply store (for resources, see page 306), but don't overdo it. When it comes to decorations, a little goes a long way, especially for younger kids.

Set up the space: A party is a good excuse to clean house, enlisting help, of course, as needed. In the room where games will be played, pack away any breakables and clear the furniture, too.

Hang balloons and streamers: Nothing says "it's a party" more than balloons and streamers. Choose colors that match your theme, such as orange and black for a Halloween bash or blue and green for a mermaid party. Hang them in the party room — and on the mailbox, too. Note: For preschoolers, purchase Mylar balloons (latex balloons are a choking hazard).

Turn toys into props: To keep costs down, dress up the party room with props you already own, strategically placed. Place a red wagon of stuffed animals on the porch for a farm party; hang a sombrero in the dining room for a Mexican fiesta.

Handcraft decorations: Paper chains, banners, and signs are simple decorations kids can make the week before the party.

Spiff up the table: Start with a colorful tablecloth, cups, and novelty plates (use paper for easy cleanup). Then get creative with napkin folding, centerpieces, and handcrafted place cards.

Think all-natural: For low-cost charm, spruce up your house with seasonal finds. Try a vase of spring tulips at an Easter party, pine boughs for a Christmas bash, or pumpkins and Indian corn at a fall festival.

Birthday Throne

FamilyFun contributor Pamela Glaven of South Deerfield, Massachusetts, found a novel way to make the birthday child or guest of honor feel like a king or queen. She decorates a special chair with streamers and balloons to look like a throne.

Party Food

The Best Party Cake Ever

If you have enough time to bake a cake from scratch, this classic yellow party cake is the one. It's rich and buttery without being too sweet, and sturdy enough to be cut into all of our cake shapes.

> 3/4 cup unsalted butter, softened
>   to room temperature
> 1 1/2 cups sugar
> 3 large eggs (for a white cake
>   substitute 6 egg whites)
> 3 cups all-purpose flour
> 2 teaspoons baking powder
> 1 teaspoon cream of tartar
> 1 1/3 cups buttermilk (or 1 cup
>   buttermilk and 1/3 cup plain
>   yogurt)
> 2 1/2 teaspoons vanilla extract

Preheat the oven to 350°. Butter and lightly flour your cake pans (see our list of pan sizes below). Cream the butter and sugar until light and fluffy. Add the eggs one at a time, beating well after each addition.

Sift together the dry ingredients. Mix the buttermilk, vanilla extract, and butter mixture into the dry ingredients, one third at a time, scraping the bowl frequently. Pour into the prepared pans and bake according to the times listed below, or until a toothpick inserted in the center comes out clean. Serves 10 to 12.

Our Best Party Cake Ever batter can be baked in all sorts of overproof pans and bowls. If you don't already own the pans we suggest for our cake designs, you can buy disposable versions (or borrow them from a neighbor). Pour the batter from one batch of this recipe into any of the following combinations of pans and bake as directed.

☛ Two 8- or 9-inch rounds or squares; bake for 20 to 35 minutes
☛ One 13- by 9- by 2-inch pan; bake for 35 to 40 minutes
☛ Two bundt or ring pans; bake for 20 to 30 minutes
☛ Two 12-cup cupcake tins; bake for 10 to 12 minutes

☛ Two 6-inch half spheres (available at cake supply stores) or two 1 1/2-quart ovenproof bowls (stainless steel or Pyrex); bake for 30 minutes
☛ Two rimmed 12- or 14-inch pizza pans; bake for 20 to 30 minutes
☛ Five mini loaf pans; bake for 20 to 30 minutes

The Icing on the Cake

This classic buttercream icing is quick and easy to prepare and can be flavored in any way the birthday child fancies.

> 1 cup unsalted butter, softened
>   to room temperature
> 3 cups sifted confectioners'
>   sugar
> 2 teaspoons vanilla extract
> 2 tablespoons light corn syrup
> 1 tablespoon milk

In the bowl of an electric mixer, cream the butter until fluffy. Add the remaining ingredients and beat until smooth. Makes 4 cups.

Chocolate Frosting: Substitute 1/2 to 3/4 cup of cocoa powder for an equal amount of confectioners' sugar.

Cream Cheese Frosting: Substitute 4 ounces of cream cheese for 1/2 cup of butter and use lemon juice instead of the milk. Beat in an additional 1 1/2 to 2 cups confectioners' sugar and omit the light corn syrup.

Strawberry or Raspberry Frosting: Add 1/4 cup seedless strawberry or raspberry jam to the basic frosting recipe. Add an additional 1/2 cup of confectioners' sugar and omit the light corn syrup.

A PARTY JUST isn't a party without good food. When planning your menu, keep things simple and stick with your theme. The following tips, and the recipes listed in each party, will help you prepare foods everyone loves.

Make it familiar: Parties are not the time to introduce new foods to children. Save yourself time (and peace of mind) by preparing the old standbys, such as sandwiches, pizza, tacos, and hot dogs. You can make these foods more impressive by jazzing up the presentation or the name to fit your theme. For instance, use cookie cutters to cut sandwiches into stars for a Fourth of July party; at a puppy party Pigs in a Blanket can be renamed Dachshunds in a Bed.

Serve finger foods: A rule of thumb for feeding crowds is to make everything small — crudités, finger sandwiches, mini fruit kabobs, and bite-size cheese and crackers. If you plan an assortment of, say, six hors d'oeuvres, plan two of each per guest. You may also want to have a big bowl of munchies, such as tortilla chips (and salsa), popcorn, pretzels, or party mix.

Choose dishes that can be made ahead: To spare yourself stress on the day of the party, prepare as much food as you can in advance. Bake and freeze the birthday cake or cut vegetables for crudités.

Balance sweets with nutritious snacks: Because kids tend to load up on too much cake and ice cream, be sure to serve nutritious snacks. Not only will this balance out your menu, but it will keep the games under control, too.

Serve drinks for thirsty guests: Offer guests a drink when they arrive — juice boxes or chocolate milk for a child or party punch for an adult — and keep guests hydrated during party games. To free space in your refrigerator, pack the drinks in coolers with ice.

Don't forget dessert: Behind every memorable party is a great cake. With creative cuts, our Best Party Cake Ever recipe at left can be adapted to fit any party theme.

Party Punch

FamilyFun reader Marianne Cashman of Binghampton, New York, served magic potion punch at her five-year-old daughter Shannon's princess party. In clear plastic cups, which she had decorated with glued-on jewels, Marianne served seltzer (ginger ale or any clear liquid would do, she says). With the drink, she distributed colored ice cubes and let each girl pick her own color. "As the ice cube melted," Marianne writes, "the drink magically turned into a colored potion." Note: We tried this successfully with grape juice and red raspberry cubes. And if we'd had ice cube trays with fancy shapes, we would have used those, too.

Party Games

15 Classic Party Games

- ◆ **Pin the tail on the donkey**
- ◆ **Musical chairs**
- ◆ **Costume relays**
- ◆ **Red light, green light**
- ◆ **Mother, may I?**
- ◆ **Blind man's bluff**
- ◆ **Hide-and-seek**
- ◆ **Hot potato**
- ◆ **Leapfrog**
- ◆ **Red rover**
- ◆ **Spud**
- ◆ **Duck, duck, goose**
- ◆ **Simon says**
- ◆ **Bingo**
- ◆ **Charades**

WHEN ALL is said and done, parties are remembered for the games that made everyone laugh and cheer. Here are some tips for choosing the best ones for your party.

Choose age-appropriate games: Provide the environment for a terrific time by choosing games that work well with the temperaments and ages of the guests. Preschoolers' short attention spans, for instance, mean they can be easily overwhelmed, so simplicity is key. This crowd enjoys duck, duck, goose, pin the tail on the donkey, Simon says, and musical chairs.

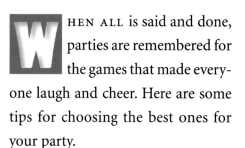

School-age kids, on the other hand, like to try new things and can follow more complex rules. Appeal to their sociability, too, with games that call for teamwork, such as Twister, blind man's bluff, and relay races. Preteens enjoy the privileges of getting older and like updated versions of grown-up games, such as name that tune, charades, and trivia games.

Rename classics to fit your theme: Most kids know the rules to the classics — a big advantage for the harried host. Brainstorm with your child to come up with variations, such as pin the patch on the pirate, musical beach towels, splash tag, or fish, fish, shark.

Plan extra games: Plan as many games as you can in case you have misjudged how long they take. Try not to let games go on so long that guests are waiting awkwardly for others to finish (10 minutes is ample time for a game); elimination games, in particular, create this problem. At the same time, allow winners a minute to bask in their glory before moving on to the next game.

Party Piñata

Piñatas are a smashing success at any children's party. Our hot air balloon design is easy to craft, and easy for kids to break. With a little creativity, the balloon can be modified into a dinosaur egg, basketball, or pumpkin.

1. In a bowl, mix up papier-mâché paste. Combine ½ cup flour and 2 cups cold water. Add that mixture to a saucepan of 2 cups boiling water and bring to a boil. Remove from heat and stir in 3 tablespoons sugar. Let cool.

For the base of the balloon, blow up a 14-inch balloon. For stability, place it in a 10-inch bowl. Fold a two-page spread of newspaper in half and then in half again. Tear (don't cut) 1½-inch-wide strips so they have a slightly rough edge. Drag a strip of newspaper through the paste, wipe off any excess, and place it at an angle on the balloon. Place the second strip so that it slightly overlaps the first. Continue until the balloon is covered with one layer, leaving a 2-inch-square hole at the top for adding the candy. Give it 24 hours to dry. Cover your leftover paste with plastic wrap so it doesn't dry out.

2. For the piñata's hanger, wrap the midpoint of a length of string around the bottom of the balloon, pulling the ends up to the top; tape it to the balloon in a few places. Knot together the ends of the string 6 inches above the top. Tape the top half of a 32-ounce yogurt container to the bottom of the balloon (for the hot air balloon neck).

3. Cover the balloon (including the string), the neck, and the bottom half of the yogurt container (which will become the balloon basket) with a

layer of strips of comics dipped in papier-mâché. Place the strips at a different angle from the first layer. Allow the second layer to dry.

4. Cover the balloon, neck, and basket with strips of plain newsprint going in a third direction. Smooth over rough edges as you work. Dry thoroughly.

5. Punch four holes into the neck of the hot air balloon and four into the basket. Attach string to the neck to later suspend the basket about 3½ inches from the base of the balloon.

6. Dot the corners of a tissue paper square with a glue stick and place it just to the side of the 2-inch square on the top of the balloon. Follow with other squares in the same color, working your way diagonally down around the balloon. When you get to the bottom, start at the top again in another color to create a houndstooth pattern.

7. Cover the basket with squares of tissue paper. Attach the basket to the balloon. Puncture the uncovered balloon at the top of the piñata and remove all of the balloon fragments. Make sure the inside of the piñata is dry before you fill it, so the candy won't stick to the sides. Fill it about halfway with the candy. Cover the opening with some tissue squares, and it's ready to hang.

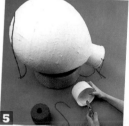

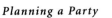

Party Crafts

Photo Frames

FamilyFun reader Bee Jones of Poway, California, came up with imaginative favors for her granddaughter's birthday party. As the guests arrived, she took a photo of each one with the birthday girl. Once everyone was there, she also took a group picture. While her daughter ran the party, Bee took the film to a one-hour developer. In the meantime, the children made and decorated Popsicle stick picture frames. When she returned, each guest glued her photo into her frame, and the birthday girl put the group shot into hers. Everyone went home with a special party memory.

WHETHER YOU'RE decorating a baseball hat at a sports party or painting clay pots at a flower party, crafts are often a showstopping activity. They also serve a dual purpose — as a party activity and a take-home favor. Most of the parties in this book feature at least one craft. If you plan on using any of our ideas, review these tips first.

Plan a craft as a welcome activity: Guests typically arrive at different times — and they may not know one another — so ease them into the party with an art project. Invite them to sign in on a newsprint mural, decorated thematically (an empty ocean for a mermaid party or haunted house for a Halloween party). Or, let them craft something to wear at the party, such as hats, headbands, or masks.

Test craft projects before guests arrive: To avoid disappointment, give all art projects a test run. That way, you'll get a sense of how easy the craft is to execute, how long it takes, if it's age appropriate, and most importantly, if it's fun.

Set up a work space: Lay out all the materials for the craft on a low table with comfortable chairs. If it's a messy activity, cover the area with newspaper, or better yet, set up outdoors. Have a few old shirts on hand for kids to wear as cover-ups over their party clothes.

Turn crafts into favors: The best party crafts are keepsakes that remind the guest of the special occasion. Kids ages seven and up enjoy using puffy paint or fabric markers to decorate T-shirts at an art party, pillowcases at a slumber party, or stockings at a Christmas party. Other crafting hits include making jewelry, toys, or photo frames.

Homemade Party Hats

At children's parties, kids love to costume themselves in festive hats, from birthday crowns to princess tiaras to witches' hats. Set out hatmaking supplies, such as construction paper, markers or crayons, glue sticks, sequins, pasta noodles, glitter, buttons, and feathers. Enlist the help of a creative teenager or friend to craft the basic hat shapes to fit, then let guests decorate the wearable art. The hats will instantly put guests into the party spirit.

Party Activities

G AMES, CRAFTS, and even cake and ice cream are all highly supervised elements of children's parties. The following activities, on the other hand, relieve the host from directing the party and invite guests to simply enjoy each other's company.

Allow time for free play: At parties, allot time for kids to do what they like best: play. At a construction party, set up toy dump trucks in a sandbox; a backyard cookout calls for Frisbees or a croquet set. Unstructured play time gives kids the freedom for make-believe and impromptu games.

Sing and dance: Background music adds atmosphere to any party, and it may even motivate guests to get up and cut a rug. For a birthday party, play or sing children's songs; at an Italian dinner, crank up Italian opera; and at a Christmas party, gather around the piano for carols.

Watch a show: If you feel like splurging, hire an entertainer, such as a clown, magician, storyteller, or musician (see page 307 for resources). Or, enlist the help of an entertaining friend, such as a teenager who happens to have a few tricks up his sleeve or a dad who plays the accordion.

The Ultimate Treasure Hunt

A treasure hunt is often the favorite event at parties for two reasons: it includes everyone and everyone loves loot. But the real appeal of the hunt (though no hunter would admit this) lies in its delayed gratification. Each new clue brings the search party closer to a prize that the seekers are half hoping they never find. Here are some tips on executing the perfect treasure hunt.

☞ Hunts adapt beautifully to any theme. Instead of being generic, have the clues, the chest, and the treasure relate to the party. For instance, at a bug party, hide plastic ants, gummy worms, and bug stickers in a picnic basket.

☞ Preparation is key. Walk around and note clever places where you could hide clues (the mailbox, a flowerpot, the tire swing).

☞ Start in reverse. Hide the treasure first, picking a spot in your yard or house where you want everyone to end up. Write the clue that will bring kids to this location (it's easier to do this on the spot rather than from another vantage point). Next walk around your yard to find a hiding place for this clue. Right then and there, compose the clue that describes this new place. Repeat this process until you have hidden all your clues.

☞ Write clues that test the seekers' sleuthing abilities ("I once swung people, but now I'm re-tired" is a tire swing). Make a list of each clue and where each is hidden, in case you yourself forget where they're hidden or if one has disappeared and must be read aloud in order to send the seekers on.

☞ Make sure boundaries are well defined, especially outdoors, to keep kids from wandering into restricted areas or all over the house.

☞ Clues can take on many forms — riddles, coded messages, or drawings.

☞ Everyone wins. Whatever is found, whether sought by one group or teams, should be divided evenly and handed out.

Party Etiquette

Giving Thanks

FamilyFun reader Jan Foley of Albany, New York, discovered a creative way to coax her son to write thank-you notes after his birthday parties. She orders double prints of photographs taken during the event, and her son incorporates them into homemade cards. He chooses which photo to include in each note and then pastes it inside colorful paper. Next he writes a brief message. Guests — and their parents — enjoy the photograph sent in a timely fashion.

Another way to show appreciation with pictures is to take a photo of your child wearing or playing with the gift and include it inside the thank-you note sent to the giver. Distant relatives will especially cherish the up-to-date keepsakes.

S ANY PARENT knows, children's parties are more than just fun and games. They are one of a child's first introductions to social situations and, as such, raise delicate issues for kids and parents alike. Before your party, give your child a quick briefing on all things mannerly.

Make guests feel welcome: Encourage your child to greet each guest as he arrives, and to see to it, as best as he can, that the guest has a good time during the party. It's also important that the host thank each guest for coming at the end of the party.

Be tactful with invitations: On your child's party guest list, he should include his best friends as well as anyone who might feel left out. Siblings close in age should be invited but discouraged from upstaging the birthday child. If the guest is under five, you can expect him to bring a date, namely his mother.

Let every guest win at least once: If your child

wants to play competitive games, try to orchestrate them so that every child wins convincingly at least once. Better yet, plan a few cooperative games, in which the whole gang faces a challenge, such as following a treasure map, then splits the loot evenly.

Accept gifts with a smile: It can take an entire childhood to learn the art of receiving gifts. The receiver should say something nice about each gift as it is opened and act grateful, even if it is a toy or book he dislikes or already owns.

Send thank-you notes: Although thank-you notes have fallen by the wayside with some time-pressed families, it's important to teach your child that thank-you notes are always the rule after birthdays and holidays.

Favors & Prizes

AT MOST BIRTHDAY and holiday parties, favors are a must. These sweet surprises are a gift from the hosting family to friends, and they should be fun to receive and to give. In many of our parties, we list favor ideas for you to pick and choose from. Use the list — and the following pointers — and your prizes will shine.

Give all guests the same favors: It's easiest if everyone gets the same party favors, including the host child. Buy favors in bulk at party stores or from catalogs, such as the Oriental Trading Company (see page 306). Or, purchase sets that can be divided up among the guests, such as a child's tea set for a tea party.

Opt for cleverness over priciness: In choosing favors, it's better to use your wits than your money. Offer some wonderful surprise that has to do with the theme, such as a gold medal for a sports party or a whistle at a police party.

Stick to reliable standbys: You can't go wrong with the classic party favors, such as penny candy, yo-yos, coloring books, magnets, markers, bubbles, plastic animals, and jump ropes.

Craft favors: Favors don't need to be store-bought. Have your child make baked goods, a computer-generated coloring book, or play clay. Send party crafts home as favors, too.

Leave room for prizes: Party favors don't all have to come packaged in a bag. They can be received as prizes, collected from a treasure chest, or scooped up under a piñata.

Party Bags

Sure, store-bought party bags are quick and easy, but they're expensive, too. Here are some clever homemade versions.

◆ **Balloon Bags:** For older kids, tuck an assortment of favors into a balloon, then blow it up.

◆ **Colorful Bags:** Purchase colored paper bags at a craft store, then personalize them with stickers or stamps.

◆ **For other creative favor bags, see the Take-Home Tackle Box on page 209 and the Bunny Bag on page 279.**

Mermaid Party, page 42

Chapter Two

Birthday Bashes

Pony ★ Wizard ★ Jungle ★ Race Car ★ Dinosaur
Mermaid ★ Puppy ★ Spy ★ Ladybug ★ Clown School
Fishing ★ Cinderella ★ Construction ★ Painting
Pirate ★ Tea ★ Sports ★ Slumber

FOR MANY parents, planning a birthday party is an annual tug-of-war between our idealism and our pragmatism. We want our child's birthday to be a blast — a person turns six only once, after all — but we don't want to have to break the bank or take a week off from work to do it.

In hopes of finding a happy middle ground, we at *FamilyFun* magazine have put together this birthday party chapter with 50 pages of ideas for throwing parties that won't throw you.

First, with the help of experienced party parents (and their willing kids), we cooked up themes with kid appeal, from a puppy party for frisky preschoolers to a spy party for that ever mysterious group, preteens. In choosing invitations, favors, games, and food, we focused on ideas that are high in fun but low in work and cost.

Also in this chapter, we feature fabulous birthday cakes that will garner *ooh*s and *aah*s but that won't take all day to bake and decorate. And should you want your partyers to burn off energy bashing a piñata, check out our hot-air balloon (page 171).

So, go ahead and tear the wrapping off this birthday package, beginning with the tips below. We think it's a gift that should delight both party planners and partygoers alike.

Start planning early: About six weeks before your child's birthday, start planning his or her party. Together, flip through this chapter and pick a theme

Birthday Bashes

Birthday Party Checklist

Before guests arrive, make sure you're ready to party with this handy checklist:

- ✓ Supplies for crafts, games, and activities
- ✓ Prizes
- ✓ Favor bags
- ✓ Cake and ice cream
- ✓ Birthday candles
- ✓ Camera (and extra film)
- ✓ First aid kit
- ✓ Party clothes

that suits his or her current passion, whether it's princesses or pirates.

Don't break the bank: Once you've settled on a theme, adapt the party so it works within your budget. To cut costs, use just one or two of our favor or craft ideas; if this is the year you want to go all out (remember, you'll have to top it next year), take our ideas and run with them.

Customize the party plan: If your four-year-old would rather be a purring cat than a puppy, you'll find these themes (and any others in this book, for that matter) easy to modify. Get creative and mix and match any of our games, foods, or favors.

Involve the birthday child: Preparing for a party can be as entertaining as the event itself. In the week prior to the party, give the birthday child a task to complete each day, such as crafting a decoration or assembling favor bags. Not only will they make fun after-school activities, but they'll also harness a child's excitement for the big day.

Be flexible hosts: No matter how much planning you do, birthday parties take on a life of their own. Picky eaters, sore losers, and kids revved up from too much cake are par for the birthday course. Have tricks up your sleeve — noncompetitive games, familiar foods, and extra prizes — as well as a sense of humor and a positive attitude, and the party will be the hit of your child's year. For more party planning tips, see page 164.

Puppy Party, page 196

Magical Pony Party

L ITTLE GIRLS won't be able to resist the charm of this birthday celebration. The props and decorations are sparkly, the games are sweet and inviting, and the cake and lemonade are deliciously pink.

Invitations

Y OU'RE IN LUCK! That's what it means when the tips of a horseshoe are pointing up — and your child's friends will feel lucky indeed when they receive one of these invitations. To make each card, simply fold in half a 5½- by 8½-inch piece of white card stock. Then cut out a horseshoe from pink craft foam or construction paper and glue it to the front of the card. Apply gold glitter dots for horseshoe nails. Use colored markers to add the message and any decorative details you wish, then print the party details inside.

Pony Invitation

Pony Party Decor

T URN YOUR HOME into a beautiful pony palace! Decorate with pink and lavender balloons and streamers and strings of white twinkling lights.

Create a giant pink birthday box to hold all the birthday gifts. Remove the top of a big box and cover the sides with pink wrapping paper and bows. Set it in a central location so guests can put their party gifts into it when they arrive.

During the party, play some spirited classical music for your pony guests to prance to.

Pony Props

P ARTY GUESTS WILL get a real kick out of donning these pony headbands and tails when they arrive. Fashioned from felt and yarn, they make perfect props for prancing through the pony games.

Headbands: For each ear, fold a 9- by 2½-inch piece of white felt in half

A

Pony Headbands

Magical Pony Party

Pony Party

Barn Dance

FamilyFun reader Vicki Haugen of Hawley, Minnesota, took a cue from her son's favorite book, *Barn Dance!* by John Archambault and Bill Martin, Jr., and threw a barn party. They converted their garage into a barn with straw bales, feed sacks, horse tack, and cornstalks. Two old-time musicians brought the "barn" to life, luring guests dressed in western attire to kick up their heels.

B

so that the shorter edges match up. Trim the sides and top (but not the fold) of the doubled felt to resemble a pointed ear. Sandwich the cutout around a child's headband, using double-sided tape to stick the inside surfaces together (A). Then cut out pink felt ear linings and tape them to the fronts of the ears. For a forelock, arrange eight 12-inch strands of yarn in a bunch and tie it (as if it were a single strand) around a 10-inch length of yarn. Tie 5 more bunches to the 10-inch length. Drape the ensemble around the base of an ear, tying the ends snugly behind it (B). Make a matching ensemble for the other ear.

Tails: To fashion a pony tail, arrange 6 dozen or so 2-foot strands of yarn into a bunch. Tie a 3-foot string or doubled length of yarn around the center of the bunch (C) and tie the ends around your child's waist.

Magic Pony Wands: These glittery wands add a touch of enchantment to the festivities. Before the party, paint foot-long wooden dowels with pink or lavender acrylic paint. You'll also need an assortment of inexpensive silk flowers (sold at most craft stores) with the stems trimmed to about 1½ inches long, curly ribbon, and glitter glue. At the party, let each girl choose a flower she likes. Tape the stem to the upper dowel, then wrap ribbon over the tape. Once the flowers are attached, the girls can use glitter glue and more ribbon to finish decorating their wands. After all, Magic Pony Wands are unique — just like their owners!

Pony Playtime

Horse, Horse, Pony: Have everybody sit on the floor in a circle with their wands for this equine spin-off of duck, duck, goose. One girl plays the part of the Pony, trotting around the outside of the circle and using her wand to lightly tap her friends on the back, saying "horse, horse, horse . . ." as she goes. When she taps someone and says "pony," that girl jumps up and trots behind her around the circle and back to the empty space. Then the first girl sits in the empty spot and the second girl becomes the Pony.

Prancing Ponies: Divide the

180

e girls into pairs and explain that each team will be a pony: one girl will be the front (she should wear her headband) and the other girl will be the back (she should wear her tail and place her hands on the waist of the girl in front). Line up the ponies along a pink-ribbon starting line. When the music starts, the ponies must prance to the finish line. Once the race is over, the girls in each pair can swap roles and prance back to the starting line.

Magical Merry-go-round: You don't have to grab the ring to win a prize in this pony game — everyone who participates gets one. Before the party, package a party favor for each guest in a small decorative box or gift bag. When the party winds down, have the girls form a circle and turn on some music. Hand each person a package and ask the girls to pass them around and around the circle until the music stops. Then everyone gets to open the one they're holding and take home the trinkets inside.

Magical Menu

J UST LIKE PONIES, party guests will love nibbling on peeled baby carrots and apple slices. Serve them with a light lunch of sandwiches cut into star shapes and glasses of pink lemonade. For dessert, serve this fanciful pony cake, sprinkled with a little magic — a dusting of edible glitter.

Pink Pony Cake

2   baked dome cakes (baked in a 1½-quart bowl)
2   cups pink frosting
    Edible pink glitter or coloring dusts, available at party stores or www.sugarcraft.com

Pink Pony Cake

Pink sour tape (mane and eyelid)
3   Milk Duds (eye and nostrils)
    Good & Plenty (ear lining)
    Black and red shoestring licorice (eyelashes and mouth)
    Silk flowers

Place one dome cake rounded side up. Cut and arrange the second cake as shown to create the pony's snout and ears. Ice the entire cake with pink frosting, then dust it with pink edible glitter. Curl strips of pink sour tape by wrapping them around a wooden spoon handle. Arrange them in place to create a flowing mane. Complete the pony with a Milk Duds eye and nostrils, Good & Plenty ear lining, shoestring licorice eyelashes and mouth, and a sour tape eyelid. Adorn the mane with silk flowers (and don't forget to remove them before serving!).

Favors

Party guests will love taking home ponytail holders, pony stickers, and miniature toy ponies (sold at many craft stores or dollar stores).

Wizard Party

PARTY STATS
Ages: 7 to 10
Size: 8 to 14 kids
Length: 2 hours
Prep time: 2 to 3 hours
Cost: $4 to $6 per guest

BECAUSE KIDS have an inherent love of mystery and magic — witness the ever-growing fascination with a certain young wizard from the Hogwarts School, for example — it's safe to predict that this birthday theme will prove positively bewitching. The agenda includes a mix of exciting activities and quieter craft projects, perfect for setting a manageable pace for wizards in training, who can get a bit high-spirited in group gatherings.

Wizard Hats and Magic Beans

Crystal Ball Invites

Crystal Ball Invite

SPREAD THE WORD about this party in true sorcerer's style — with a crystal ball that reveals all there is to know about the upcoming event. For each one, start with a CD that you no longer use. On the unprinted side, attach a sticker star to the center, then use a permanent marker to print on the words "Prediction: A Magical Time" and the date of the party. Next, tape or glue the lower edge of the CD onto a colored-paper crystal ball base, as shown. Cut out a paper circle, write on the rest of the party information, and glue or tape it to the back of the CD.

Wizard Decor

WITH A FEW decorating props — fake spiderwebs, strings of twinkling lights, and plastic bugs and frogs — you can turn any room into a wizards' lair.

Fun & Games

Magic Wands: What's a wizard without his wand? Before the party, use a craft knife to cut ½-inch clear unflexible plastic aquarium tubing (sold in pet stores) into 1-foot lengths (one for each person). Seal one end of each tube with a bit of modeling clay. Then each child can fill his own tube with wiggle worms (metallic pipe cleaners) and dragon scales (sequins or glitter) before sealing the other end with clay.

Wizard Hats: For each hat, lay a sheet of newspaper on a flat surface. Sandwich the sheet between two pieces of glossy gift wrap. Treating the stack as if it were a single sheet of paper, shape it into a large cone and tape the overlapping edges. Roll up the lower edge of the cone to create a brow band. Then each kid can adorn his hat with stars cut from bright-colored Con-Tact paper.

Search for Magic Beans: A job is always easier when great wizard minds join forces. In this case, that means solving a series of cleverly cryptic clues to find a stash of magic beans (a fanciful container filled with multiflavored jelly beans). To set up the hunt, first choose four to six successive hiding spots around your house or yard (the last one being where you hide the treasure). Then write a clue that leads to each one. For example, the first clue, which might direct the kids to look under a pot of marigolds, could be printed backward so that they will have to hold it up to a mirror to read it. The second clue, hidden under the flowerpot, might lead them to the mailbox. This time you could write the clue with a white crayon on white paper and leave it with a colored marker and instructions to scribble all over the paper to reveal the message. For the remaining clues, consider posing a riddle, coming up with a numeric code and a key to translate each number into a letter, or even creating a word search puzzle.

Wizard Eats

SET UP A BUFFET of disappearing tortilla chips with midnight (black bean) dip, celestial sandwiches (cut into star and crescent moon shapes), lizard tongues (baby carrots), eyeballs of newt (chilled red grapes), and Wizard Cupcakes.

Wizard Cupcakes

> Cupcake baked in an ice-cream cone
> Skin-tone icing
> Edible decorations (sugar eyes, decorator's icing, shoestring licorice, colored sugar, mini pretzel sticks, ice cream cones)

Place a scoop of icing on top of the cupcake to make the head. Add sugar eyes, icing hair, and a licorice smile. To make the wizard's hat, use scissors to cut a sugar cone down to 2 inches. Coat with icing and decorate with candy stars, edible glitter, or colored sugar. For the magic wand, coat a mini pretzel stick with icing, sprinkle with edible glitter or colored sugar, and attach the sugar star with a dab of icing. To finish, place the hat on the head and arrange the wand nearby.

Party Favors

These crystal ball party favors are sure to cause a stir among attending wizards. In the center of each one is a sparkly sorcerer's stone. Here's how to make one. Use your hands to mold some polymer clay (such as Sculpey III) into a small mushroom shape, then press plenty of glitter onto the clay surface. Next, press the bottom of the clay "stem" onto the inner lid of a small clean jar, as shown, so that it is firmly attached. Fill the jar almost to the top with water and stir in a few drops of glycerin (sold at most pharmacies) and ½ teaspoon of glitter. The glycerin will increase the density of the water and cause the glitter to fall more slowly. Finally, tightly screw the lid onto the jar and invert the globe.

Wizard cupcakes

Jungle Party

A SK ANY PRESCHOOLER what he or she would like to be, and the answer is bound to be something four-legged, hairy, and hopelessly noisy — which is precisely why jungle parties are such a roaring success. In this party, kids get to pretend they're wild animals by dressing in animal headbands, hunting for peanuts, and parading around the house. Tarzan, watch out.

PARTY STATS

Ages: 3 to 5
Size: 4 to 8 kids
Length: 2 hours
Prep time: 2 to 3 hours
Cost: $5 to $8 per child

Elephant Invitations

S END OUT the call to your child's favorite party animals with an unfolding pachyderm. From an 8½-by 11-inch sheet of gray paper, cut out the shape of an elephant's head and trunk and draw in the eyes and tusks. Fill in the party information, including a request that each child bring a

Elephant Invitation

favorite stuffed animal. Fold up the trunk accordion style, then fold in each ear and place in an envelope.

Jungle Decorations

T URN YOUR house into a deep, not-so-dark jungle with balloons, streamers, or strings of lights in tropical colors. Cordon off an area of the party room with string and hang a sign labeled "Jungle Petting Zoo." When guests arrive with stuffed animals in tow, they can set them in a comfortingly nearby spot.

Party Animal Costumes

A S ANY four-year-old will tell you, it's the stripes that make the zebra. With quick-to-make headbands, kids can decorate and don their animal alter egos as soon as they

Party Animal Costume

Catch the Lion by the Tail

Stuffed Animal Safari

If your kids have a whole zoo's worth of stuffed animals, let them host a safari, like *FamilyFun* reader Linda Schrupp of Auburn Hills, Michigan, did for her kids, Kimberly and Matthew.

First Mom hid the animals. Then the kids made paper safari hats and cardboard tube binoculars. They wore safari belts with walkie-talkies and canteens of jungle juice and set up camp — a small tent and two laundry basket cages. The "hunters" used flashlights to spot the animals, then they brought them back to "camp" and put them in the "cage." When all the animals were caught, the kids sat around camp. The animals were then free to go back to their natural habitat.

hit the party. Before the event, cut out one poster board strip (roughly 3 by 20 inches) for each guest, adding the ears for a particular animal (rounded ears for a tiger, say, or ears and horns for a giraffe). At party time, set out the strips on a newspaper-covered table or bench and scatter around a pile of crayons or water-soluble markers. Children can pick whichever blank headband they like, then color it. Measure the band around the child's head, then staple the ends so that it fits snugly. A touch of face paint — for whiskers, stripes, spots, or a black nose — completes each child's costume.

Wild Games

Jungle Charades: A great mixer for new arrivals, this game gets even the bashful hissing and howling. Before the party, cut out pictures of animals from magazines and paste them on index cards. At the party, each child gets a turn to pick a card. She must then act out her creature (no words are allowed, but animal noises are encouraged) until the others shout out her identity. When the animal is guessed, the rest of the party-goers get to jump up and act out the same animal together.

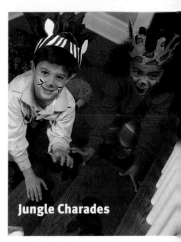
Jungle Charades

Jungle Party

Jungle Favors

Any favor that is striped or spotted is golden with this preschool crowd (two or three prizes still feel like a big haul to them). Shop for small animal figures, jungle noses, animal stickers, animal coloring books, tropical-flavored candy, or boxes of animal crackers. The plastic sand pails used in The Great Peanut Hunt make durable favor bags.

Catch the Lion by the Tail: Like most winning games, this twist on duck, duck, goose combines suspense, action, and make-believe. Kids sit in a circle on the floor. One partygoer, the lion, tucks a tail (a yellow piece of fabric with a knot in one end) into his waistband and begins circling, touching each child on the head and saying "Lion." Then he touches one player on the head and shouts "Hyena!" The lion then must dash around the circle and take the hyena's spot before the hyena can grab the lion's tail. If his tail is not snatched, he remains the lion; if it is, the crafty hyena becomes the new king of the jungle.

The Great Peanut Hunt: Before the guests arrive, hide unshelled peanuts around the yard or house. At the party, explain to the kids that they, as elephants, must go out in search of a tasty meal. Give each child a plastic sand pail, then send them out to forage. Offer a prize for the partygoer who harvests the biggest crop.

Jungle Parade: A fine finale, this activity lets little ones cap off the party with a wild forest chorus. Before the party, the host parent sets up a "pawprint" trail throughout the house (poster board cutouts taped to the floor). Come parade time, partygoers gather their stuffed animals and line up behind the birthday child at the beginning of the pawprint trail. When the host parent puts on music (*The Jungle Book* sound track, for example), the kids and their pets begin their march through the jungle, continuing until the music ends.

Tiger Cake

Safari Lunch

A T ANY PARTY for preschoolers, it's smart to stick to a simple and familiar menu. Serve up peanut butter and banana sandwiches, animal crackers, jungle juice (fruit punch), and end with a roar — the tiger cake.

Tiger Cake

    1 9-inch baked round cake
    2 baked cupcakes
      Orange frosting
      Tube of chocolate decorator's icing
      Decorations: green hard candies, peppermint patties, chocolate dots, black jelly beans, and black shoestring licorice

Arrange the cooled round cake "face" on a platter with two cupcake "ears." Frost with orange icing. Zigzag chocolate piping on the face for stripes. Add green candy eyes, assorted chocolates and jelly beans for the nose and ears, and black licorice strings for the whiskers.

Jungle Charades

Race Car Party

OR KIDS WHO like to be on the go, this party plan puts you on the fast track to fun. Readers of *FamilyFun* magazine liked the simple design and pit-stop-fast assembly of the invitation, race car games, and the speedy raceway cake.

Race on Over Invitation

HIS STAND-UP tire invitation will get kids revved up for a good time. First, draw a 5-inch circle on thin cardboard to use as a template. Cut straight across the top and bottom to create a tire shape that's 4¼ inches tall. Next, fold an 8½- by 11-inch sheet of black construction paper so that the longer edges match up.

Place the template atop the paper so that the top lines up with the fold.

Trace around the sides and bottom, then cut along the lines (you should get 2 invitations from each sheet of paper). Cut out an oval hubcap (2 inches wide by 3½ inches tall) from yellow paper and glue it onto the tire slightly left of center. In marker, print "Race on Over!" on the hubcap. Use a white crayon or marker to add zigzag tire treads and to print the party specifics inside.

Race On Over Invitation

Raceway Decor

OR DECORATIONS, shape fluorescent orange poster board into road cones and hot-glue each to a square cardboard base. You also can use them to mark a course for the Hot Rod Relay. Use crayons or markers to transform a plain paper tablecloth into a racetrack for Matchbox cars.

Race Car Fun

Hot rod relay:. So what if you're five years old and you don't have a license? All it takes is a 450-horsepower imagination and fast feet to win this cardboard car relay. Beforehand, you'll need to make a car for each team. Trim off the top and bottom

Race Car Fun

flaps of a cardboard box (the box shown here is about 14 inches square) and cut a handle hole in each door panel. Paint the cars, adding your child's favorite racing numbers. Then tape on yellow paper headlights and front grills fashioned from ¾-inch-wide strips of aluminum foil. At race time, the first kid from each team dons a helmet and goggles and steps into his team's car. On cue, the drivers race around a designated landmark, such as a picnic table, tree, or large rock, and back to the start, where they quickly turn their gear over to the next person. The race continues in this manner until all the members of one team finish the course and win the game.

Pit passes: At the track, pit passes are reserved for drivers, crews, press, and superimportant guests — like all of the race car fans attending your child's birthday. Take an instant photo of each kid as he or she arrives. Punch a hole in the top of the picture and string a length of ball chain through it. With a permanent marker, print the words "Pit Crew" at the bottom ("Crew Chief" for the birthday child).

Fast Food

FOR LUNCH, cut pumpernickel and white bread sandwiches into squares, then arrange them on a platter to resemble a checkered flag. Serve with frosty glasses of your child's favorite soft drink and, for the grand finale, a Racetrack cake.

2 baked 9-inch round cakes
3 cups white icing
1 to 2 cups finely crushed chocolate cookie crumbs

Racetrack Cake

1 to 2 cups green sprinkles
   White Good & Plenty candies
   Checkered paper or ribbon
2 toothpicks and tape
   New toy cars, washed with soap and water

Cut a small semicircular notch from one cake, then position the cakes as shown and cover them with the white icing. Place a small bowl in the center of each cake and sprinkle cookie crumbs around them to create the track. Remove the bowls and sprinkle ¼ cup of sprinkles onto each icing circle, then press the remaining sprinkles onto the sides of the cake for grass. Lay a white Good & Plenty dotted line along the track and use a pastry bag to pipe a white icing border around the edge of the cake. Create racing flags by taping small squares of the paper or ribbon to the toothpicks and place them on the track along with the race cars.

Speedway Favors

Race car fans will be jazzed to take home Matchbox cars, whistles, key chains, and racing stickers or patches.

Pit Passes

PIT CREW
PIT CREW
PIT CREW

Dinosaur Party

F YOU HAVE A PRESCHOOLER who loves stomping the house like a dinosaur, throw him a party where he and his friends can turn into over-sized reptiles for the afternoon. Our dinosaur party makes prehistory come alive with towering brachiosaurus hats, helium balloons, and an edible volcano.

Dinosaur Balloons

Dino Invitations

ET THIS PARTY off on the right foot by sending out giant dinosaur print invitations cut from a roll of wrapping paper or newsprint. (You can enlarge this one to use as a pattern.) On each one, write the party specifics, then fold it up so that it fits in a letter-size envelope.

Dino Decor

HEN IT COMES to dinosaur decorations, think big: giant chalk dinosaur prints that lead up the driveway to the front door. You can also greet guests with a balloon bouquet of smiling dinosaur faces tied to a mailbox or fence post. Later, you can let each guest take one home. Just inflate a bunch of quality large round latex balloons or, even better, purchase helium-filled balloons at a party store (generally, they cost about $1 apiece). Turn each balloon knotted side up, then pull the string down along the back and tape it to the bottom of the inverted balloon. With acrylic paint, decorate the front of each balloon with two large eyes, circular nostrils, and a U-shaped row of zigzag teeth.

Dino Invites

Get this party off on the right foot by sending out giant dinosaur print invitations cut from a roll of wrapping paper or newsprint. (You can enlarge this one to use as a pattern.) On each one, write the party specifics, then fold it up so that it fits in a letter-size envelope.

Prehistoric Fun

Jurassic Hats: Head up this party itinerary by fitting visiting dinosaur-lovers with one of these brachiosaurus hats. If you precut the necessary pieces, the kids can even assemble their own caps with just a little help from you. For each one, you'll need a 5- by 28-inch brow band, two googly eyes, and the following colored paper cutouts: four 4-inch-long rec-

Jurassic Hats

tangular legs with pointed feet, an 11-inch-long tail that measures 4 inches across the top and tapers to a point, and a 9-inch-long head and attached neck that resembles a giant finger.

Wrap the brow band around the child's head to fit, then staple together the overlapping edges. Now the child can tape or glue the legs and tail to the brow band. Use the edge of a ruler to curl the top of the dinosaur's neck so that the face points downward, then glue on the googly eyes and draw on nostrils and a mouth. Finally, tape or glue the base of the neck to the inner brow band.

Dino Egg Relay: You never really know a dinosaur until you've walked in its shoes — and this wacky contest lets kids do just that. Each team member must wear a pair of cardboard-and-foam dinosaur "feet" while he completes his leg of the race.

Making the feet: For each foot, simply tape closed the open end of an empty cereal box (or cracker box for small feet), then cut a 4½-inch-wide circular foot opening in the front panel. Next, cut out a dinosaur footprint from craft foam (it should be bigger than the box) and make two 5-inch criss-crossed snips in the center of the print. With a low-temperature hot glue gun, attach the print to the box surface so that the cuts in the foam are directly over the circular opening in the cardboard. For a finishing touch, hot-glue foam "claws" onto the dinosaur toes.

Starting the race: Divide the kids into two teams and set a chair across from each group at the far end of the racing area. Have the first person from both teams put on dinosaur feet,

Dino Egg Relay

then hand each of them a wooden spoon with a plastic egg (a rubber ball will do in a pinch) balanced on it. On cue, they must quickly stomp around their respective team chairs and back to hand off the spoon and then the shoes to the next runners. If a child drops the egg en route, she must retrieve it before going on. The first team whose players have all successfully completed the course win the relay.

Dino Diner

F OR LUNCH, serve dinosaur eggs (cherry tomatoes or grapes) in a nest (shredded lettuce), dino-dogs (hot dogs with all the fixings), monster mash (gummy bugs, peanuts, and raisins), and the following dinosaur cupcakes.

Dinosaur Cupcakes

1 baked cupcake per person
   White frosting
   Shredded coconut
   Green food coloring
   Small plastic dinosaur

Frost the cupcake. To make the "grass," place a handful of shredded coconut in a ziplock bag, add a few drops of food coloring, seal the bag, and shake it. Cover the frosting with grass and top with a dinosaur.

Pail-eolithic Dig

Digging up favors for this party is a cinch. Just pick up a package of toy dinosaurs and bury them in a giant bucket of sand. Before they go home, guests can take turns using a plastic beach trowel or fork to see what creatures they unearth — Tyrannosaurus rex, allosaurus, or diplodocus, perhaps? Have a dinosaur book on hand, too, so you can help the kids identify their favors.

Mermaid Party

THROW YOUR birthday child this underwater fantasy party, and she'll dive right in. Add six to 12 mermaid-crazed friends, hidden treasure, and a slew of games and races, and she may never want to come up for air. When we ran this party in *FamilyFun* magazine, the real showstopper was the Mermaid Cake (see page 194).

Deep-Sea Invites

LURE PARTY GUESTS with an underwater message. Write the details on a 5- by 6-inch piece of green construction paper with a wavy top edge. Slip it into a ziplock sandwich bag. Sprinkle sand, glitter, and confetti (available at party stores) inside. Fold in half and mail in a blue envelope.

Deep-Sea Invite

Crown Crafting

Crown Crafting

Decorations

THIS PARTY has plenty of decorations — you essentially turn one room into an ocean — but they're basic and inexpensive. First, drape a sheet over a chair to make a mermaid rock. Then hang a long green streamer, clothesline style, across part of the ceiling, attaching the ends securely with tape and thumbtacks. Cut a half-dozen fish and starfish shapes out of poster board and tape each to ends of 4-foot lengths of blue crepe paper. Hang these, plus some plain streamers, from the suspended green streamer. Litter the floor underneath with blue balloons.

Crown Crafting

THIS QUIET icebreaker gives arriving guests a chance to settle in. Ahead of time, cut out 5-inch-high poster board crowns. On a table, set out saucers of glitter, confetti, or stickers, along with glue sticks and water-based markers or crayons. Ask partygoers to decorate their crowns. Size each by wrapping it around the child's head and stapling the ends together. Then, set the creations aside to dry for the Mer-race (see page 195).

Mermaid Games

Trail of Treasure: Nothing piques grade-schoolers' curiosity like a treasure hunt. This one relies on pictures instead of words, so the game moves quickly. To make the treasure chest, cover the outside and inside of a small Styrofoam cooler with aluminum foil. Glue two strips of black construction paper, as shown, to simulate straps. Fill with a mixture of uncooked pasta shells (large or jumbo stuffing-size works best), cooked spinach linguine "seaweed" (the gross-out factor is priceless), costume jewelry,

Trail of Treasure

Mermaid Party

Mermaid Cake

The Kimmel family of Montebello, New York, sent the blueprint for this outstanding Mermaid Cake to *FamilyFun* magazine. The cake is large enough to feed a big group of kids and still have leftovers.

1 baked 8-inch round cake
1 baked 13- by 9- by 2-inch cake
12 baked cupcakes
8 cups frosting (white, blue, and yellow)
Necco wafers (pink, green, and purple)
2 green Necco wafers and 2 blue M&M's for eyes
Shoestring licorice eyelashes
Fruit by the Foot mouth
Colored sugar

Cut and arrange the cakes as shown above. Frost the mermaid's tail blue and cover it with Necco wafers. Frost the head and body white (or whatever skin color you choose) and the bikini top blue. Add the candy eyes and mouth. Frost the cupcakes yellow, then sprinkle on colored sugar for a marine sheen.

Sea Food

Anything ocean related, and preferably punny, makes a great catch of the day for this party — peanut butter and jellyfish, potato boats, or shell pasta sprinkled with "sand" (grated Parmesan). Serve with blue Gatorade and Goldfish crackers. For dessert? A bowl of blue Jell-O and gummy fish or the Mermaid Cake above.

plastic ocean creatures, or chocolate coins.

To set up the hunt, collect eight beach items — a swim mask, a shell, a flip-flop, and so on. On small pieces of paper, draw a picture showing the location of each item and of the treasure chest. (Hide the chest in a spot where all the kids will be able to gather easily.) Place the picture of the chest inside, say, the shell and hide that. Tape the picture of the shell inside the flip-flop, and so on, until you've hidden all but one clue. Give the remaining picture to the kids and instruct them to follow the clues in order. When the

chest is found, each child gets a turn reaching into it and fishing for one or two treasures.

Skin the Eel: Kids have to work together to complete this flexibility challenge. First line up everyone single file. Each child bends forward and places his right hand back through his legs and with his left hand grasps the right hand of the player in front of him. The player at the back of the line lies down on his back while everyone else walks backward over him. The next player lies down, then the next, until everyone is on their back. The last player to lie down gets up and walks forward, pulling the rest of the line with her, until all are standing and still holding hands.

Mer-race: This game made a big splash with our kid-testers, who stayed all wrapped up for the rest of the party. First outfit each child with a mermaid tail by having him or her step into a heavy-duty drawstring trash bag. Tie the bag loosely around the child's waist, then secure it in place with a belt of duct tape. Wrap a second strip of duct tape around the knees to create a fin effect, then lay the children down on their bellies across the room from your mermaid rock. Scatter the crowns around on the rock. At the "Ready, set, dive" signal, kids squirm and flap their way to the rock, don their crowns, and race back. Afterward, photograph each child, then serve lunch. (Cut a few small airholes in the bags, so the kids don't end up with slimy fish feet.)

Thank-You Notes

K IDS ALWAYS love seeing pictures of themselves in costume. To make a thank-you card, fold a piece of construction paper in half, cut four angled slits on front, and slip in a photo of each child as a mermaid. Add a silly message like "Nice to sea you" or "Come back off fin!"

Favors & Goody Bags

After a day at the beach, send kids home with a plastic or tin pail full of treasure — squirty fish, ocean stickers, fish pencils, real shells, and chocolate coins. Top it off with a sprinkling of sand or glitter.

Skin the Eel

Puppy Party

FOR KIDS WHO ARE dogmatically canine, this party gives them license to bark, roll over, and gnaw on bones. From start to finish, it's got a message that will thrill them: hey, little lads and lassies, today you aren't just pretending to be a pack of Rovers — you *are* the dogs.

Puppy Party Invitations

PARTY STATS
Ages: 3 to 5
Size: 4 to 8 kids
Length: 2 hours
Prep time: 2 to 3 hours
Cost: $5 to $7 per child

Call In the Dogs

INVITE THE party animals to join in the fun with this invitation. Cut two matching paper squares and tape them together along the top edge. From the top one, cut away the center part and round the ears. Decorate the bottom one with a face and collar, then clip on a detachable dog tag cut from the bottom of an aluminum pie plate (bend back the tag's sharp edges). Write the child's name backwards on the tag's reverse side (so the type is embossed). Put the party info under the earflaps and ask guests to come with license in paw.

Doggy Decor

TO SET UP this party, you don't need to work like a dog. Decorate the front door with a discreet "Kennel Club" sign. Inside, set up a table as the groomer's salon, with a sign to that effect and a mirror. Fill the playroom with doghouses made from large cardboard boxes — one for each kid with his name over a simple cutout door (wait until the kids arrive if you think they'll choose special puppy names). Even simpler to make are doghouse facades, cut from the sides of a box and leaned against a wall. With the addition of clean dog bowls — gauche, but they'll love it — the scene is set for playtime, games, and snacks.

Welcome Wag

196

Welcome Wag

AS KIDS COME in the door, have grown-up "groomers" turn them into puppies. Use face paint and dog ears (fabric or fake fur fastened to the child's hair with hair clips). Lay out dog-collar-making baubles including beads, buttons, string, and extra dog tags. Let the pups string their own (help them center the tag). It'll be your job to make sure no body's necklace gets turned into a choke collar. Have an instant camera handy for portraits.

Dog Games

YOU WON'T NEED any formal games for this pack of dogs. Two hours of dressing up and remaining in character is enough to keep them howling for days about the party. Still, here are two activities in case you've got a roving pack on your hands.

The Snoop: Hide about 40 cardboard bones at "dog height" and have the puppies hunt on hands and knees. Found bones get buried in a bag at the end of the game in exchange for treats.

Dog Trainer Says: Based on Simon says, this game has the kids doing dog tricks but only when the leader prefaces the command with "Trainer says…" The trainer will need a cheat sheet to remember appropriate dog commands: Sit. Lie down. Roll over. Speak. Jump. Shake. Stay. Three-year-olds may have trouble keeping the rules straight. For them, forget the "Trainer says" part and just pretend to teach them tricks like Sit or Run around the yard, backwards. Five-year-olds might like the game better if you add silly commands like Growl, Wag your tail, and Bark your head off. All good puppies get treats for learning their tricks.

Dog Trainer Says

Doggie Bags

Send each pup home with — what else? — a doggie bag, either plain or decorated with spots. Stuff it with the child's photograph (puppy name and breed underneath with some remark like "Loves bones" or "Beautifully groomed"). Throw in a dog figurine, stickers, a ball, and a bone cookie. And of course, leave room for the collar.

Puppy Party

A Party for the Dogs

If your dog is your family's best friend, throwing a birthday party for him is not all that far-fetched. Invite a few human friends and stuffed animals over (canine pals might cause chaos). Spruce up the guest of honor with a bath. And if he's tolerant, crown him with a birthday hat. And don't forget about the cake. Mold his favorite dog food into a one-serving torte, garnished with a dog biscuit "candle."

Canine Cake

Puppy Chow

BEGIN LUNCH with fruit leather "chews," then serve hot dogs or cheese or bologna sandwiches made with soft white bread and cut with a bone-shaped cookie cutter. For a side dish, make kibbles from those cheese- or peanut-butter-filled pretzels that look like dog treats (such as Combos). Garnish with sticks (pretzel rods). For extra fun, serve the entire lunch in a clean dog bowl (or just a regular bowl).

Canine Cake

2 baked 9-inch round cakes
2 baked cupcakes

4 cups white frosting
Red Fruit by the Foot
1 green Necco wafer
Junior Mints
Small mint patties
Black shoestring licorice
2 gray Necco wafers

Frost the cake rounds and the two cupcakes. Wrap the Fruit by the Foot around the top edge of the cake to make the dog's collar. For the doggie tag, add a green Necco wafer. Place three Junior Mints on the edge of each cupcake paw, one on the top of the cake for the nose, and the rest in a random pattern all around the cake.

Fill out the spots with a few mint patties, outline the ears and jowls with the shoestring licorice, and add a fruit leather tongue. Finally, frost the M&M's to the gray Necco wafers for a pair of sweet puppy dog eyes.

Thank-You Note

SEND A MESSAGE from the birthday pup in dog language. For example, on the front, you might put a picture of your child with a cartoon dialogue balloon: "Woof-woof, arf, Batcar, grrrrr, woof-WOOF! Rrrr, Ralph." Translation inside: "That means, 'Thank you for the great Batcar for my birthday! Love, Ralph.'"

Spy Party

A THEME PARTY for preteens? The concept may seem suspect, but it holds a hidden lure: kids can hide behind personas and act sneaky. Some clues for parents: keep things loose (don't try to map out everything). And most importantly, hone your own stalking skills; while keeping an eye on things, let the kids think you've made like ink and disappeared.

Sleuthing Games

Invitations

Anything marked "Top Secret" will grab a partygoer's attention. For each special agent, cut down a manila folder to about 4 by 5 inches. On the inside, write the party details backwards (so invitees will need to use a mirror to read it). Pen the agent's name on the file tab, stamp the folder "Confidential," then slip the missive into an envelope for mailing.

Top Secret Invitation

Spy Party

Mystery Gifts

FamilyFun reader Judy Miller's ten-year-old son, Tim, loves reading mysteries. So during his detective theme party in Urbana, Illinois, the gifts were hidden for him to find. As he found each one, he would play 20 questions with the gift-giver. All the guests had a chance to ask questions, and, says Judy, the boys had a ball guessing what each gift was.

Detective Decorations

LEAD GUESTS up to your front door with footprints drawn in chalk and by hanging a few fake "Police Line: Do Not Cross" banners.

Sleuthing Games

Who Am I?: Before the party, cut out pictures of celebrities. Each guest gets an identity pinned to his back, so that everyone but him can see it. Then, by asking yes or no questions, each child must figure out who he is.

Shadowing the Suspects: One at a time, usher guests into a private room, where they don a spy suit — a hat, trench coat, and a pipe. Stand each child in profile in front of a large piece of paper mounted on the wall. Shine a light on her, trace her outline, then write her name on the back. When all suspects have been traced, gather the kids in one room to guess who's who.

Clueless: For this takeoff on Mad Libs, compile a few short mystery stories. Copy or type out each tale, leaving blank several key words — such as a noun, a verb, or an exclamation. (Note above each space the type of word to be filled in.) Kids can take turns soliciting verbal entries to fill in the blanks — then reading aloud the hilarious results.

Lie Detector: While this bluffing card game won't prepare kids to be a spy, it gives them practice at keeping a poker face. The object is to get rid of all your cards — and catch a comrade in a lie along the way. Each player gets seven cards, and the rest are turned facedown in a drawing pile (you can use more than one deck, if necessary). The dealer lays a card or cards from his hand facedown on the table, declaring the value (for example, "Three sevens"). The next player has to add a card or cards of the next highest value (in this case, eights). If he or she has no such card, the choice is either to pick from the drawing pile — or to fake it. Any player can challenge by saying "Lie detector," and when the truth is told, whoever is wrong inherits the discard pile.

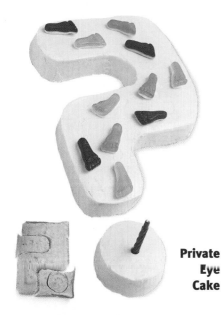

Private
Eye
Cake

Mystery Meal

WITH FOOD, anything too cute is a crime to preteens. They may prefer munchies like nachos or hot-on-the-trail mix (pretzels, raisins, and Cheez-its). For more serious eats, try pizza with the pepperoni rearranged like a question mark. As a finale, serve the Private Eye Cake.

Private Eye Cake

1 baked 13- by 9- by 2-inch cake
4 cups yellow frosting
Gummy feet

Cut the cake as shown above. Frost with yellow icing, then walk gummy feet across the cake for footprints. For a sleuthing surprise, hide a charm in the cake before frosting it and see which spy is the sharpest (warn kids of the charm so that they eat carefully).

Thank-You Notes

BEFORE DEPARTING, each guest must ink his or her fingertips on an inkpad and leave a set of prints on an index card. Your child can use these for thank-yous later.

Shadowing the Suspects

Goody Bag

For a mysterious take-home favor, stamp "Top Secret" on the front of a manila envelope for each party guest. Inside, your gumshoes will find a pack of gum (natch), as well as top secret notepads to record evidence gathering, a pair of cheapo sunglasses, and a disguise, such as a fake nose. And don't forget the candy — even Kojak needed a lollipop to keep his observational skills sharp.

Ladybug Party

PERFECT FOR A PRESCHOOLER'S first foray into the birthday zone, this party idea will have you seeing spots — and a lot of smiles. For *FamilyFun* reader Dawne Carlson of Eagan, Minnesota, who created the party for her preschooler, Abigail, the biggest attraction was its simplicity. "At that age," she says, "a little fun goes a long way."

Adorable Antennae

Fly-Away Invitations

THIS SIMPLE ladybug invitation will guarantee that your child's birthday is a lucky day. To make one, trace a 32-ounce yogurt lid onto white card stock for the ladybug's belly, and draw an outline of her head above the circle. Cut along the lines, then color the ladybug's face with markers and write the party details on her belly. Next, make the ladybug's wings by

Fly-Away Invitations

tracing the lid onto red construction paper and cutting out the circle. Decorate the circle with black spots (trace pennies for a guideline). Trim the top of the circle, cut it in half to create wings, and attach them with paper fasteners.

Red and Black Decorations

ANYTHING RED and black — streamers, balloons, a tablecloth — will set the stage for this party. Dawne's guests *ooh*ed and *aah*ed over the homemade Ladybug Plates on her party table. To make one, simply decorate a red plastic plate with shoestring licorice legs and antennae (or pipe cleaners, for a non-candy version). Four chocolate cookies make up the edible spots.

Adorable Antennae

AT THE DOOR, greet each child with a set of his own antennae, or the materials to craft one. To make a set, twist red pom-poms onto the ends of black pipe cleaners. Next, loop the opposite ends, and tape under the brim of a black hat. Alternatively, twist the ends onto a headband.

Ladybug Games

WITH ANY LUCK, flying around the yard in ladybug antennae will keep the partyers entertained. But here are a few structured games to heighten the fun.

Stick the Spot on the Ladybug: For young kids, you'll probably want to do away with the blindfold. Just challenge them to pin a black construction paper spot onto a poster board ladybug.

Dance the Jitterbug: It doesn't matter if the guests don't know the steps; simply put on some tunes and let them make it up as they go.

Ladybug Cake

READER CAROL ZEMANEK of Shoreline, Washington, gave her four-year-old a dose of good luck with this adorable Ladybug Cake (she baked the cake in a stainless bowl).

    1 baked dome cake (made in a 1½-quart bowl or 6-inch sphere)
    1 baked cupcake
    3 cups red frosting
    12 Junior Mints

Ladybug Cake

    2 green gumdrops
    Black shoestring licorice

Turn the cake and cupcake upside down and frost them with red icing. Place the mints on the body for spots. Add the green gumdrop eyes and the licorice antennae. Serves 8 to 10.

Party Favors

GETTING TO WEAR the antennae home may be enough of a treat for this set, but you could also give each ladybug a bag with some black and red jelly beans, ladybug stickers, or Eric Carle's *The Grouchy Ladybug* (HarperCollins Juvenile Books).

Bug Party

FamilyFun reader Dana W. Fiore of Hopatcong, New Jersey, chose a Goin' Buggy theme for her son's fourth birthday party. She filled the house with yarn spiderwebs and giant balloon bugs. The kids crafted bugs with foam ball bodies, pipe cleaner legs, and googly eyes, and played Pin the Antenna on the Bug. They even made a bug piñata! The biggest hit was the treasure hunt for a picnic basket full of goodies.

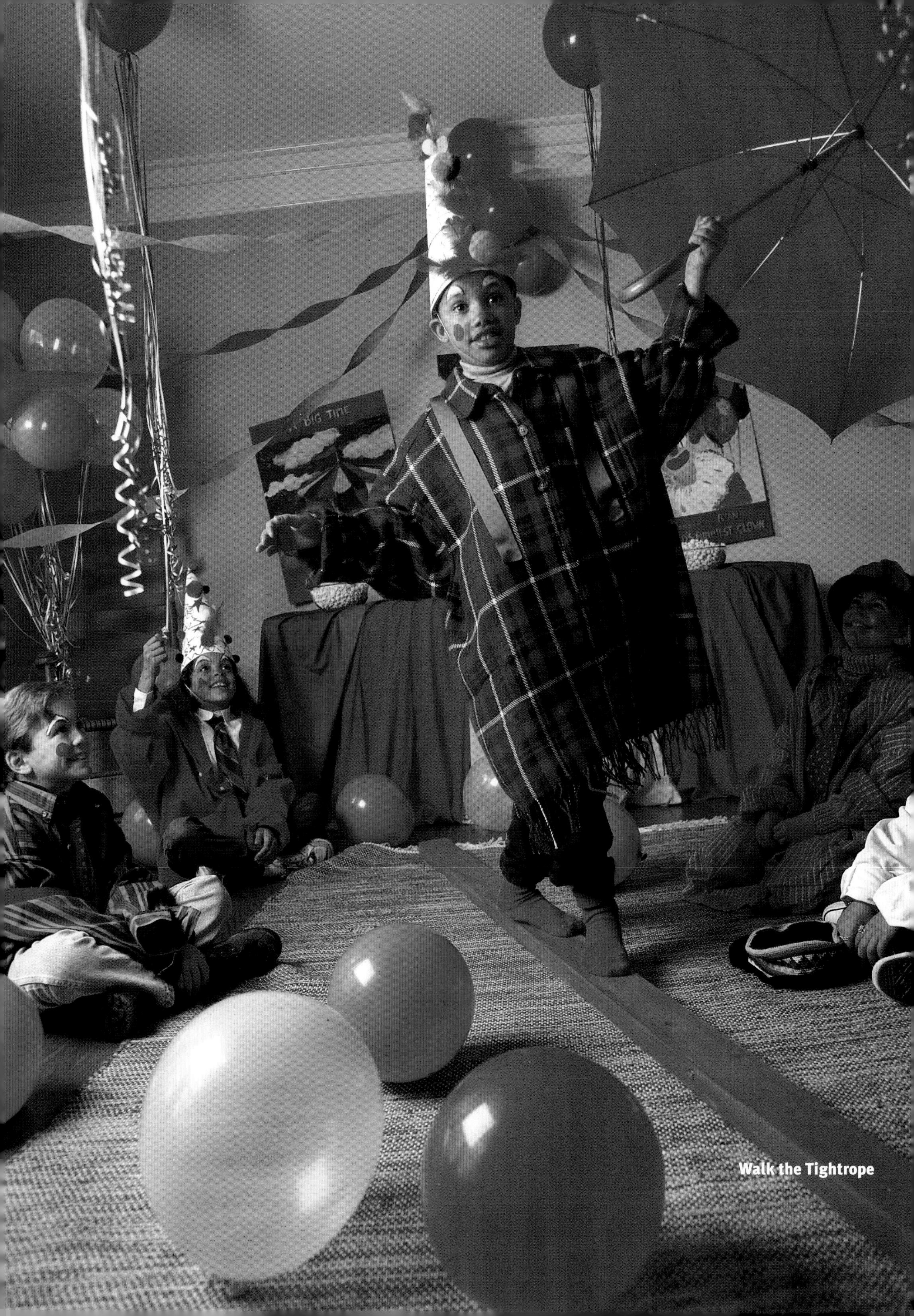

Walk the Tightrope

Clown School

To COMICALLY inclined kids, life is a three-ring circus. No trick is too silly, no joke too dumb. Our clown school party is a mix of the finest circus games, events, and snacks — just the right atmosphere for a hilarious, if over the (big) top, birthday afternoon.

Balloon Invitations

WHAT BETTER herald of an arriving circus than bright balloons? To make the invitations pictured on page 161, blow up a pair of balloons for each guest and write the relevant information on the outside with permanent markers (don't knot the balloon). Deflate and place them in a bright envelope with a handful of confetti.

Circus Decorations

SPLASHED with red, blue, and yellow balloons, streamers, and tablecloths, an ordinary room or porch takes on the gaiety of a circus tent. If you have time, make posters portraying guests as three-ring circus performers. "Ladies and Gentlemen … we bring you Paul the Fire-Eating Kid!"

Clown Costumes

Clown School

Clown Costumes

AT HER DAUGHTER Jennifer's clown party, *FamilyFun* reader Lucy Hutchison of Hayes, Kansas, gave guests the option to come dressed as clowns, and they did. If your guests don't show up in clown gear, have lots of clownlike clothes and accessories — oversize shorts, shirts, jackets, gloves, suspenders, and bow ties — on hand. A parent or teen can run a face-painting table, where each child receives the necessary red nose, arched brows, pink cheeks, and exaggerated smile or frown.

Heads Up

Clowning Around

Heads Up: To play this catching game, each child will need a special hat you make ahead of time plus a small, soft ball, such as a beanbag or Koosh ball. To make one hat, glue two plastic bowls bottom to bottom and fashion a chin strap by either stapling on an elastic band or looping one through tiny holes. To play, put kids in pairs about 4 feet apart. At the whistle, the first player to toss the soft object into his partner's hat wins. For another variation, kids are on their own. The first child to toss the object into her own hat wins (a photo opportunity if there ever was one).

Walk the Tightrope: Even acts of daring are funny business when you are a clown. To set up this high-wire routine, place a 2 by 4 on the floor or ground and gather your materials: an umbrella and a large-format (but not too thick) hardcover book. In this elimination game, each contestant first crosses the high wire with an umbrella in hand. All who survive make it to round two: crossing with a book on their heads. All who live through that ordeal go to round three: crossing with the book on their heads and the umbrella in their hands. All masters of the high wire win a prize.

Balloon Sandwich: This race, a feat of cooperation, is best held outside or in a spacious room. Begin by choos-

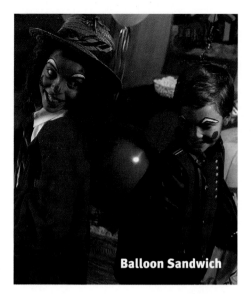

Balloon Sandwich

Circus Food

ALL CLOWNS get hungry for a little circus food, so serve up hot dogs, along with a circus snack — popcorn, peanuts, or Cracker Jacks — and Ice-Cream Clown Cones.

Ice-Cream Clown Cones

This dessert proves that birthday cakes need not always take center stage. For easier handling, make the cones in batches of four. Place four scoops of ice cream on a cookie sheet lined with waxed paper, then wedge on chocolate-dipped ice-cream cone hats. Decorate each face with candy and coconut.

Freeze for at least 2 hours, then peel off and place on dessert plates. Alternatively, you can let partyers dress up their own ice-cream clowns for dessert.

How do you paint a rabbit? With Hairspray

Clown School Favor

Favors & Prizes

IN HONOR of the legendary hobo clown, favors and prizes can go in a bandanna on a stick. Load it up with gag gifts, small joke books or jokes handwritten on slips of paper (a good project for the birthday child or an older brother or sister), clown and circus animal stickers, noisemakers, candy, and funny dress-up items, such as bulbous clown noses or fake eyelashes.

Ice-Cream Clown Cone

ing partners and lining them up back to back at a starting line. Place a balloon between the partners so that they must squish it to keep it off the ground (no hands!). At the sound of a whistle, the pairs must take off in this position, shuffling their way toward a finish line. If the balloon pops or drops, they must return to the starting line for a replacement. The first sandwich to cross the line wins.

Clown Class Relay:

Here's another game for a spacious area. Ask all the kids to strip back down to their original (well-fitting) clothes and stocking feet, then divide the crew into two relay teams positioned at a starting line. At the finish line, place two similar clown outfits that include giant shorts, suspenders, a jacket, a hat, and the biggest pairs of men's shoes you can find (clomp, clomp). When the starter whistle blows, the first person from each team runs and puts on the outfit (over his clothes), runs back, strips, and tags the next player, who puts on the outfit and runs and touches the finish line, runs back, strips, and so on. The team to complete the relay first is victorious.

POPCORN "1 TICKET

Backyard Big Top

Every year, *Family Fun* reader Mindy Malone of Naperville, Illinois, organizes a backyard circus. The stars are ten neighborhood kids. Each child chooses an act and meets at Mindy's house for rehearsals.

Their circus personalities have included a ringmaster, popcorn man, lion and lion tamer, bareback rider (on a bouncing hobbyhorse), tightrope walker (on a balance beam), strongman, tattoo man, snake charmer, acrobat (performing on a swing set and rings), and, of course, clowns. The shows are lots of fun, and everyone looks forward to the next time the circus comes to town.

Fishing Party

WE FELL HOOK, line, and sinker for this party, which *FamilyFun* reader Amy Diaz of Kingwood, Texas, threw for her five-year-old son, Christopher. The fledgling anglers in your own family are sure to be lured to this backyard fishing fest.

Go Fish Invitations

Paper Plate Fish

WRITE THE PARTY information on a cutout paper fish with a small bag of gummy worms pinned to its mouth.

Fishing Fun

GO FISH, PIN THE HOOK on the fish, and other classics work for this theme, but for Amy's crew, the most popular game was Go Goldfishing — a chance to land a real fish.

Sail High Seas: Create a fishing boat play area by spreading out a blue tablecloth and setting an overturned table on top. Drape sheets over the legs to form the hull and rig with ropes. Give kids paper towel tubes for spyglasses, a compass and map for direction, and let them sail away on a pretend boat ride. For added fun, tell tales about Sinbad the Sailor or cast for fish with magnets.

Magnet Fishing: Haul in the catch of the day by angling for paper fish with paper clip mouths. Use heavy card stock to create fish (make some temptingly bigger than others). Scatter them in an empty blue kiddie pool or painted box and hand kids poles (sturdy sticks with yarn "lines" and magnet "hooks").

Go Goldfishing: Put live goldfish in a kiddie pool of water and let the kids watch them swim around. Toward the

Magnet Fishing

Fish Cake

end of the party, each child can fish one out with a net and take it home in a ziplock bag along with fish food. (Note: Parents may not be thrilled by an unexpected pet. You can keep it a surprise for the kids, but make sure parents are comfortable with the idea when they call to R.S.V.P.)

Salty Eats

COVER YOUR TABLE with a fishing net and turn paper plates into fish by adding paper fins, tails, and heads. Serve fish and chips followed by this Fish Cake.

Fish Cake

   1 baked 13- by 9- by 2-inch cake
   2 cups orange-yellow frosting
   6 cups blue frosting
   1 peppermint patty
   1 gummy fish
      Necco wafers

Cut and arrange the cake as shown. Frost the cake blue and add yellow-orange fins and tail. Place the Necco wafers on as scales. Add the mint as an eye and the gummy fish for the mouth.

Take-Home Tackle Box

YOUNG ANGLERS will deem this grown-up-looking tackle box "reel" cool. Before the party, spray-paint Styrofoam egg cartons, then glue a cardboard handle on top. At the party, set out bowls of rubber fish, gummy worms, and tiny toys and let each child select a handful to go in his box. Send this tackle box home with the partygoer along with the bag of fish food for the goldfish.

Take-Home Tackle Box

Cinderella Party

O N Samantha Miller's sixth birthday, a fairy tale came true. Her parents, *FamilyFun* readers Jim and Sara Miller of Aurora, Ohio, helped reenact the Cinderella tale, with each partygoer playing the belle of the ball. Samantha is older now, long past Cinderella parties, but she still keeps on her bedside table the little corked jar of fairy godmother dust from her party.

Fairy-Tale Invitations

K EEP THE invitations simple for this grand affair. Photocopy a picture of Cinderella. Ask guests to come dressed in "rags"and be prepared to get transformed into princesses.

The Party Plot

Cinderella Housecleaning

When the guests arrive, announce that each girl is now Cinderella and give each one a rag or feather duster to clean up a room in your house. (Sara reports that the guests loved this part.)

Castle Cake

Cinderella Snapshots

FamilyFun readers Mike and Sherry Branch of Fort Worth, Texas, held a ball in honor of daughter Rebecca's sixth birthday. They solved the tale's transportation problem by creating a magical "carriage" to take guests to the castle. The coach was made by mounting a cardboard facade to a wagon (you can also use Fome-Cor). The girls really enjoyed being pulled by the Duke from one room into the "ballroom" and having their pictures taken. Be sure to have doubles of the photos developed. Slipped into the thank-you notes for each girl, the pictures are wonderful reminders of being a "Princess for a Day."

The Duke Arrives

While the Cinderellas are busily dusting, the Duke (Dad dressed in a tuxedo) should knock at the door and drop off the royal invitations (in gold ink with a crown drawn on top) to the Prince's Ball.

Dressing for the Ball

The girls' excitement over the mysterious Duke will end when they realize they have nothing but rags to wear to the ball. So let them make their own gowns — simple, sandwich-board-style dresses that can be cut beforehand from extra-wide sheets of crepe paper bought from an art supply store. They can glue faux jewels, sequins, and beads on their dresses and tie a long piece of lace around their waists. Give each girl a party store tiara to keep.

Ballroom Dancing

When all the Cinderellas are dressed for the ball, play the "Nutcracker Suite" and let them dance around a living room-turned-ballroom. From time to time, turn off the music and present a prize to "the best twirler" or "the most elegant couple." (For her daughter's party, Sara had written out these awards ahead of time; everyone received a prize: a Cinderella paper doll with little rags and little gowns to wear.)

The Strike of Midnight

During the last dance, the clock strikes 12 (an alarm clock that chimes). Instruct the girls to run, leaving one shoe (slipper) behind. Back in poor Cinderella's room, they strip down to their "rags."

Find the Lost Slipper

Meanwhile, the Duke should gather up the lost slippers and fill them with party favors, such as candy and penny jewelry. Then set out a trail of aluminum foil footprints leading to the slippers. The girls should follow the footprints to their surprises.

Party Food

WHEN EACH girl has her slipper back (they fit perfectly), it's time to celebrate. At the table each girl receives a small jar of fairy godmother dust (sparkles) and a slice of Castle Cake (with ice-cream-cone towers, a graham cracker drawbridge, and candy decorations).

Wizard of Oz Party

If your kids are into playacting at parties, reenact *The Wizard of Oz* as *FamilyFun* reader Kathy Lecate of Richmond Heights, Ohio, did for her daughter's sixth birthday. The kids followed a crepe paper rainbow downstairs into Oz, where they picked a lollipop from a tree in a cardboard Munchkin Land and played Pin the Badge on the Lion. The kids were truly amazed. Imagine an entire kindergarten class skipping around a painted yellow brick road in the basement singing, "We're off to see the Wizard!"

Construction Party

G IVEN THEIR NATURAL INCLINATION to build, it's a wonder all children don't grow up to be city planners. This outdoor party invites kids to create a pretend city booming with buildings, roads, and bridges. At noon, they break from work to enjoy a builder's lunch — complete with a dump truck full of birthday cake.

PARTY STATS

Ages: 3 to 5
Size: 4 to 6 kids
Length: 2 hours
Prep time: 2 hours
Cost: $4 to $6 per guest

Road Sign Invitations

D IRECT CONSTRUCTION workers to your site by sending out road sign invitations. To make one, cut two identical squares of yellow paper, place a Popsicle stick in between (as a signpost), and glue together. In black capital letters, write the party details on both the front and back, including a request for workers to bring

Road Sign Invitation

their favorite construction toy (forklifts, dump trucks, and front-end loaders encouraged) and to dress in work clothes.

Building Site

T RANSFORM YOUR backyard into a construction zone with yellow caution tape, orange cones, and any construction toys your child owns. If you're feeling ambitious, you might also hang homemade poster board street and traffic signs (the humor of "Children at Play" and "Go Slow: Children" signs may be lost on kids, but not on their parents). In the event of rain, clear space in your biggest room and set up the construction party there.

Fun & Games

Build a City: Near a sandbox in your backyard, set up boundaries, approximately 8 by 10 feet, for a bustling city-to-be. Before the guests arrive, set out materials and build just enough of the city to inspire the kids to take over. You might begin constructing

Build a City

Dump Truck Cake

brick, race a specified distance, and lay their bricks down to begin the wall. Each child in line continues until one team completes their contract.

Bag Lunch

D ELIVER sandwiches and chips to the construction site (in brown lunch bags, of course). Then let the workers dig into a plastic dump truck loaded with cake and cookie crumb "dirt."

Dump Truck Cake

2 baked 8- or 9-inch cakes
2 3-ounce packages prepared
   chocolate pudding
3 to 4 cups chocolate cookie crumbs
Clean dump truck and shovel

Cut the cake into 3-inch chunks. Layer the cake, pudding, and crumbs in the clean dump truck and serve with the shovel. Serves 8 to 10.

Favors

F OIL-COVERED chocolate cars, tiny plastic trucks, and car stickers are all favors that can be handed out in a plastic hard hat (with a black marker, you can write the party guest's name above the brim).

a cardboard box building, a wood chip road, or Popsicle stick railroad tracks. For a pond, bury a bowl of water in the sandbox. Invite each arriving guest to contribute to the new city. Once the whole crew is assembled, allow enough free time for kids to complete the city.
Foreman Says: Follow the same rules as Simon says, but the child in charge should call out construction commands. He might say, "Dig with a shovel," "Use a hammer," "Mix the cement," or "Drive a truck."
Brick by Brick Relay: Partygoers race to be the first team to construct a pretend brick wall. In the weeks before the party, save empty cereal boxes, shoe boxes, and other cardboard packaging to use as "bricks." Divide the bricks into two piles and have the kids break into two teams. The first players grab a

Plane Party

For her son Drew's fourth birthday, *FamilyFun* reader Carol Schmidt of Mukwonago, Wisconsin, took off on a plane theme. For invitations, she made tickets, complete with boarding passes. To greet guests, a door sign read "Gate 4." Inside, decorations included empty suitcases and paper clouds. She turned the dining room table into a runway by unrolling a strip of paper down the center and drawing lines and arrows on it. A strand of white Christmas lights on each side of the runway illuminated the landing strip. Favors were plastic wings, chocolate planes on a stick, and packets of roasted peanuts.

Lego Mania

At age nine, *FamilyFun* reader and Lego maniac Katie Lemberg of Bernardsville, New Jersey, threw a Lego birthday bash. For decorations, she hung streamers in bright colors and put heaps of Legos on the floor. The kids played pin the Lego on the Lego, guessed how many Legos were in a jar, and built the tallest tower they could in 2 minutes. The hit of the party was the cake: a sheet cake topped with eight cupcakes and frosted bright blue.

Painting Party

PARTY STATS
Ages: 9 to 12
Size: 3 to 10 kids
Length: 2 hours
Prep time:
2 to 3 hours
Cost: $4 to $6
per child

ART IS A NATURAL building block for a children's party — and it's no surprise. After all, what child wouldn't love the basic concept of messing around? Painting murals, T-shirts, and even a birthday cake will make a big impression on the visiting artists.

Invitations

SET THE STAGE by sending out painter's palette invitations. Cut poster board palettes, color with "paint" dabs, and write all the party details — plus a reminder for guests to dress in old clothes or smocks.

Artsy Fun & Games

Mural Painting: At a party for *FamilyFun* reader Jill Driscoll's son, Christopher, the guests got a kick out of creating a giant mural. Instead of using butcher paper, Jill went to her local newspaper for "end roll paper" (long rolls of paper that many newspapers give away or sell for just a few dollars) and stapled it to a large fence in her yard.

Splatter T-Shirts: For a craft that doubles as a party favor, hang white T-shirts out on a clothesline, away from unintended targets, and hand out fabric paint and brushes. Then let kids flick, splatter, and sling to their hearts' content. For a funky alternative, fill plastic water guns or spray bottles with paint that's been watered-down just enough to prevent nozzles from clogging, then aim and squirt. While they have the fabric paints out, guests may also enjoy decorating inexpensive painter's caps from a hardware store.

Pictionary: For a mess-free artistic game, play a homemade version of Pictionary. Before the party, make up slips of paper that name a person, place, or thing and put them in a bowl or hat. Also gather colored markers, butcher paper, and a timer. To play, tape the butcher paper to a wall and

Mural Painting

Paintbrush Puppets

break guests into two teams. Each round, a designated drawer selects a slip and attempts to illustrate the word (no speaking!) for his team to guess before time runs out.

Paintbrush Puppets: All it takes is a few brush strokes to get one of these bristle-headed puppets ready for a birthday party show. To make one, begin by applying a base coat of acrylic paint all the way around the upper handle and metal band of a paintbrush. Add facial features, creating a different expression on each side of the brush. Once the paint dries, it's showtime!

Artistic Lunch

E VEN LUNCH can have artistic flair at your painting party. Let party guests paint bread for sandwiches and dig into slices of the Artist's Palette Cake for dessert.

Sandwich Art

Using slices of white bread as a canvas, party guests can create masterpieces that are good enough to eat. Fill several paper cups with a few tablespoons of milk, then stir in drops of food coloring to create edible paint. Using the colored milk and new paintbrushes, have the kids paint pictures and designs on the bread. Toast lightly. Now the party guests can use the slices to build their own sandwiches from a platter of fixings.

Artist's Palette Cake

> 1 baked 9-inch round cake
> 2 cups white icing
>   Gel frosting, assorted colors
>   Fruit leather
> 1 licorice twist

Cut cake as shown and frost with white icing. Using a 1½-inch round cookie cutter, cut a thumb hole in the center of the cake. Use the cutter to lightly mark the circles on the cake, then fill with various gel frosting "paints." To make the brush, wrap the fruit leather around the base of the licorice twist and fringe the ends.

Party Favors

F ILL A PAINT BUCKET with a selection of art supplies, such as a paintbrush, watercolor set, play clay, crayons, or a coloring book.

Artist's Palette Cake

Pirate Party

SINCE YOUNG KIDS have a natural inclination to pillage and plunder, pirate parties are always in fashion. *FamilyFun* readers Connie and Tony Bonaccio of Shelburne, Vermont, were hooked by the flexibility and swashbuckling fun of this theme. It made their son Ben's birthday a blast.

PARTY STATS
Ages: 6 to 8
Size: 4 to 12 kids
Length: 2 hours
Prep time: 2 to 3 hours
Cost: $4 to $6 per child

Shipwreck Invitations

ROUND UP THE pirates for the party with a message in a bottle. Along with the invitation, add a few seashells and a pinch of sand to an empty soda bottle, then hand-deliver.

Hook Hands

Swashbuckling Fun & Games

ORGANIZE YOUR party around two principles — that pirates are an energetic lot, and that they like to take home lots of booty.

Treasure Hunt: Hand the Captain (the birthday child) a map covered with decades of dust (a pinch of flour). Write a message inside about a stash of treasure hidden somewhere in your yard or house. For example: "As any pirate ought to know, this is where tomatoes grow." Each guest gets to guess the answer to a riddle, and as a pack, the guests can run to wherever the clue leads and find another one. At hunt's end, be sure to hide a suitable prize, such as a stash of candy coins or the Treasure Chest Cake.

Walk the Plank: The Bonaccios secured a board across a kiddie pool with duct tape. They set toy alligators in the pool for ambience, then each child got to walk across. Upon reaching the other side, the pirate was awarded a plastic hook hand. To make one, cut a slit in the bottom of a plastic cup. Cut a hook shape out of cardboard, wrap with aluminum foil, and slip it through the slit in the cup.

Make Spyglasses: Have kids cover the end of a toilet paper tube with

FAMILYFUN'S PARTIES

a square of colored cellophane and fix it in place with a rubber band.

Ticktock, Find the Croc: With a little imagination, an egg timer makes a suitable crocodile. Have pirates try to locate the hidden croc by its tick, before the bell rings.

Musical Islands: Set as many hula hoops on the floor as you have guests and play music. Pirates must walk around the hoops until you turn off the tunes, at which point they must be standing inside one of the "islands" or they're out. Every few minutes, take away a hoop, until only one seafarer remains.

Pirate Grub

KEEP THE LUNCH simple, with hot dog boats (spear a paper sail with a wooden skewer and set it in a hot dog), Goldfish crackers, and the Treasure Chest Cake.

Treasure Chest Cake

    1 baked 13- by 9- by 2-inch cake
    6 cups chocolate frosting
      Edible treasures, such as chocolate coins, Rolo candies, chocolate almond kisses, or Necco wafers
      Red Fruit by the Foot
      Mini jawbreakers
      Candy jewels, such as candy necklaces and rock candy

Cut two triangular wedges through the center of the cake; the two remaining pieces will form the bottom and top of the chest. Place the wedges on the bottom half of the chest, as shown, to keep the chest wedged open, then frost.

To add further support for the top of the chest, stand a few large gold coins under the lid. With the "hinged" end (right side of photo) at the back, place the top of the chest on the bottom and frost. Wrap the fruit leather straps around the chest and press mini jawbreaker "nails" into the frosting along the straps. Fill the chest and the surrounding area with edible treasures and jewels.

Take-Home Loot

YOUR PIRATES can leave with quite a haul, such as gummy fish, temporary tattoos, chocolate coins, or candy jewelry. They can dig these treasures out of the treasure chest at the end of the hunt (just be sure everyone gets an even number of prizes).

More Treasure

For directions on how to set up the ultimate treasure hunt, see page 173.

A Child's Tea Party

ONCE KIDS, especially little girls, discover the magical sound of china tinkling against china, setting up tiny cups and saucers often becomes a favorite pastime. That's why we pored over *FamilyFun* contributor Cynthia Caldwell's idea for her four-year-old daughter, Isabelle: an afternoon tea at which guests dress up in proper party fashion and get their fill of friendly chatter — and fancy finger foods.

Invitations to Tea

A TEA PARTY calls for invitations that look like fine china. For each one, cut out a colorful paper teacup and then use a gold or silver marker to outline the rim and handle. Print all the party particulars, along with a note that reminds guests that "Dolls and stuffed animals are welcome."

A Table Set for Tea

REMEMBER, the fussier the table, the more the guests will like it. So, break out the ornate tablecloth, crocheted doilies, matching cups and saucers, and dessert dishes. Of course, you'll also need a teapot, a creamer, and a bowl of sugar cubes with tongs for serving one lump, or two. And don't forget to set places for teddy bears, too.

Teatime Activities

Sign In: Set out a feathered pen and a guest book (a small spiral-bound notebook with one of your child's drawings glued to the cover will suffice). Encourage each child to sign her name *and* her doll's.

Dress Up: Raid your closet for costume jewelry, old party dresses, gloves, and high heels. If you come up short, you can probably pick up a few inexpensive outfits at a thrift shop. Then let partygoers dress to the nines.

Make Dolls: Give each child an old-fashioned clothespin and lay out fabric scraps, lace, yarn, sequins, ribbons, and markers to make tiny fancy ladies to sit at the tea party table.

Silver Tea

It wouldn't be a tea party without a spot of tea. About five minutes before the guests are ready to be seated, steep a pot of decaffeinated tea. Then, to be sure the tea isn't too steaming hot, ask each child to fill her teacup halfway with milk before pouring. Add a spoonful of sugar and enjoy.

A Child's Tea Party

Tiny Tea Foods

Peanut Butter Pinwheels

Peanut Butter Pinwheels

Spread creamy or chunky peanut butter and a little bit of honey, fruit preserves, or apple butter on a fresh flour tortilla. Sprinkle with granola, roll up the tortilla, then slice it into bite-size pinwheels.

Shrunken Sandwiches

Shrunken Sandwiches

These cracker sandwiches are just the right size to share with stuffed animals. To make them, cut ham and cheese into small rounds. (You can use a clean bottle cap as a cutter to make it easy.)

Place ham rounds on the crackers, then the cheese. Cover each with another cracker.

Animal Cookies

Animal Cookies

For dessert, serve a plateful of sweet animals on parade. To make each one, you'll need three cookies of the same animal. Spread jam or peanut butter between them to make a three-layer filled cookie that will stand up on the serving dish.

Party Favors

BUY A CHILD's tea set and present one cup and saucer with a tea bag and a sugar cube to each guest. Or, give out candy jewelry, play makeup, and nail polish.

Sports Jamboree

WITH QUICK BOUTS of football, basketball, and Wiffle ball to test your mettle, winning sports favors, and fare that's strictly ballpark, this bash is just the ticket for enthusiastic sports fans. It's also perfect for an end-of-the-season celebration for your child's athletic team. Your backyard or a nearby playground serves as the playing field, and the guests are the ballplayers.

Tag Football

Sports Invites

BEFORE YOU send out invitations, try to assess the athletic abilities of the guests in order to select two evenly matched teams that can compete throughout the party. "Draft picks" then can be announced on the invitations. To make the invitations, cut T-shirt shapes out of white paper. With crayons or markers (a different color for each team), accent the necklines and draw stripes above the hems. Then print the party details and a reminder for guests to dress for playing sports.

Decorations

BOLD BANNERS (in the teams' colors), pom-poms, and pennants make great pep rally props. You also can post a team roster on which sports fans can sign their names when they arrive — both their real ones *and* their sports nicknames of choice.

Play Ball

Tag Football: You'll need at least two kids on each team for this friendly, tamer version of big league football. The game begins as in tackle football, with a midfield lineup and kickoff. The receiving team attempts to run the ball back across the opponent's goal line to score a touchdown. Instead of tackling the player who's carrying the ball, members of the opposing team need only to tag him or her. If anyone is successful, play stops and the teams line up again where the runner was tagged. The team with the ball gets four chances (or downs) to score a touchdown before the ball passes to the other team.

Indoor Baseball

When her son, Michael, insisted that his sixth birthday party (which happened to be in November) reflect his passion for baseball, *FamilyFun* reader Rhonda Cloos of Austin, Texas, planned an indoor party that would keep her lamps intact. The boys pinned paper numbers to their jerseys, played Pin the Baseball in the Glove, and tossed a beanbag through a piece of poster board into which she had cut four bases.

Sports Jamboree

Sports Fan Favors

There's no striking out with these party favors: fill inexpensive baseball caps with whistles, sports cards, rubber balls, or chewing gum.

O-U-T! A day on the basketball court is not complete without a game of O-U-T (or any other word your kids want to spell). One player starts by shooting the ball from anywhere on the court. If it goes in, the other players must shoot from the same place (determine a shooting order in advance). Successful players are safe; those who miss get an O (the first letter of O-U-T). If the first player misses his first shot, the second player takes over the lead spot. Players must drop out when they get all letters of the chosen word; the last one in the game wins.

Chase the Dog: To join in this group game, each child will need a basketball and a bandanna tucked into a pocket (to resemble a tail). While staying within a designated area and continually dribbling their balls, players try to grab each other's bandannas. As soon as a player loses his tail, he is out. The game continues until only one child, the top dog, is left with his tail.

Three-Inning Baseball: For this mini match, follow the rules of traditional baseball with these exceptions: use a Wiffle ball and a plastic bat (no mitts needed) — and a lawn chair set up behind home plate in place of an umpire. The backrest defines the strike zone handily — if the ball hits it, it's a strike. Each team is at bat for just three innings.

Chase the Dog

Ballpark Menu

WHAT COULD BE better, or easier, to serve at a sports party than a classic ballpark lunch? For an extra treat, follow up with a dessert that's sure to score with kids: a cake that's shaped like a baseball cap.

Spicy Sports Popcorn

⅓ cup vegetable oil

1 cup popcorn kernels

1 1-ounce package taco seasoning mix

1 12-ounce jar unsalted dry-roasted peanuts

In a large pot, warm the vegetable oil over medium-high heat for a minute or two. Add the popcorn kernels. Cover and cook, shaking the pot, until the kernels stop popping.

Remove from the heat and pour half of the popcorn into a large paper bag. Add the taco seasoning and the peanuts. Add the remaining popcorn, fold over the top of the bag, shake, and serve. Makes about 20 cups.

Stadium Lunch

Serve grilled or steamed hot dogs and buns with mustard, catsup, or relish and cans of ice-cold soda.

Baseball Cap Cake

1 baked 8-inch round cake

1 dome cake (baked in a 1½-quart bowl or 6-inch sphere)

2 cups blue frosting

1 cup red frosting

Red shoestring licorice

1 red gumdrop

Red M&M's

Cut the 8-inch cake so that it is shaped like a brim and arrange it next to the bowl cake. Frost the hat blue and the brim red. Add shoestring licorice to the crown with a gumdrop button. Outline your child's initial in M&M's.

Baseball Cap Cake

Hot Seats

These sporty benchwarmer favors let party guests reserve cushy seats at the next big game. To make them, use a craft knife to cut handholds (adults only) in gardener's kneeling pads (sold at department stores for about $3). Let the kids print their names and slogans and draw sports symbols with permanent colored markers.

Slumber Party

ASK ANY GROUP OF GIRLFRIENDS: you just can't beat a chance to hang out in your pj's and chat all night long. The good news for parents is that with a few activities like the ones that follow and *lots* of munchies, a sleep-over generally throws itself. So, if you do lose sleep, it won't be over keeping the kids entertained.

PARTY STATS

Ages: 9 to 12
Size: 2 to 8 kids
Length: Overnight
Prep time: 2 hours
Cost: $4
per child

Invitations

MINI PAPER pillows make cute invitations for a sleep-over party. For each one, cut a pair of 4¼- by 3-inch rectangles from white stationery. On one, print the party specifics and a reminder to bring a sleeping bag and pillow (you might add whether dinner is part of the party). Glue a couple of cotton balls to the center of the matching rectangle. Then glue the two rectangles together.

Nail Painting

ONCE THE GIRLS have arrived, they can catch up on all the news while they brush up on the latest in fingernail fashion. Here's a handful of designs for inspiration. One tip: A tiny watercolor brush (size 00) is great for detailing.

Plaid: Apply a base coat of polish. Once dry, add lines of a different color.

Starry Night: Top a dark undercoat with a glittery gold star.

Checkerboard: Start with a coat of red. Add staggered rows of black squares.

Pot of Gold: Paint a miniature rainbow at the tip of the nail.

Tiger Stripes: Apply an orange or gold undercoat. Add irregular black stripes.

Flower Garden: Top a base coat of green with daisies or tulips.

Polka Dots: Apply a base coat of polish. Dab on drops of another color.

Cow: Paint the nail white, then top with big black patches.

Lightning Bolt: Top a blue base coat with a bright yellow zigzag.

Red Delicious: Paint on a tiny apple complete with a stem and leaves.

Nail Painting

Rag Rolling

Rag Rolling

AFTER THE GIRLS dress in their pajamas, they can try this old-time hairstyling technique that will take them from rags to ringlets.

1. Tear fabric scraps into thin strips (8 to 10 inches long).

2. Using a spray bottle filled with water, dampen a guest's hair and comb out any knots.

3. Starting at the top of her head, lift a section of wet hair and place a fabric strip across its end. Roll the hair and the rag toward the scalp, then tie together the ends of the rag roller in a bow.

4. Repeat step 3, working down the back and sides, until the entire head of hair is rolled in rags. Leave the rollers in overnight.

5. In the morning, untie and unwind the rag rollers to unveil a headful of curls.

Bedtime Boxes

When her great-aunt turned 90 years old, *FamilyFun* reader Donna Conti and her family, from Quogue, New York, spent the whole weekend with the birthday girl, essentially turning the celebration into a family slumber party. To give all of the kids their own special spot for storing sleeping bags, pillows, teddy bears, and the like, they created bedtime boxes. First they cut the top and front panels off large cardboard boxes and glued paper to the inside back panels. Then the kids used colored markers and crayons to decorate the papered panels with their names.

Slumber Party

Activities for Night Owls

◆ Pop in a dance lesson video and learn how to line dance or do the Macarena together.

◆ Braid embroidery floss into friendship bracelets or mix and match beads from old jewelry to make new necklaces.

Scrapbook

Scrapbook

THIS PASS-AROUND scrapbook lets sleep-over guests do what they love best: discuss what's cool. Each page is dedicated to a topic on which kids can share their opinions. Make one for each child, and they double as mementos of the big night.

For each book, you'll need a spiral sketchbook or a few sheets of unlined paper with holes punched along the side and bound together with ribbon.

Ask your child to print a different heading on each page, such as Our Favorite Animals, Best Movie, or Most Popular Saying. She can even pose a question, for instance, "What do you want to be when you grow up?" Next, divide each page into equal sections, one for each child to write in.

When the guests arrive, hand out the books and set out a bunch of colored markers everyone can use to jot down or draw their answers in each other's books.

Sleep-Over Cake

Since slumber parties aren't really about sleeping, let your wide-awake partygoers decorate cookies to look like their own faces, then tuck them into this sweet bed.

      1 baked 13- by 9- by 2-inch cake
      6 cups frosting (pink and light pink)
      Twinkies, marshmallows, and vanilla or chocolate wafers (1 for each guest)
      Gel icing (pink and green) and mini jawbreakers
      Pink and green Fruit by the Foot

Turn the cake upside down and lightly frost it. Cut the Twinkies in half lengthwise and center the tops, cut-side down, on the cake. Frost a pink sheet on the upper third of the cake. Flatten the marshmallows for pillows and place them above each Twinkie. Decorate the wafers (curly hair and big smiles can be made with gel icing; mini jawbreakers are perfect for eyes) and place the faces on the pillows. Frost a light-pink blanket over the Twinkies and the rest of the cake. Add gel icing flowers and a ruffled Fruit by the Foot bed skirt.

Slipper Socks

Slipper Favors

THESE ZANY Slipper Socks make a great slumber party craft. Each child gets to paint her own pair with bold, colorful designs. Then, left to dry overnight, they're ready to slip on the next morning.

To make each pair, you'll need cotton socks (pre-wash and dry them ahead of time, but do not use fabric soft-ener), cardboard, a pencil, scissors, and nontoxic three-dimensional fabric paint. The paint, which is sold at most craft or fabric stores, comes in a variety of colors and costs about $3 for a 1-ounce bottle.

Have each child set her shoes on top of a piece of cardboard and trace around them with a pencil. Cut out the two shoe shapes with the scissors. Then fit the cardboard feet into a pair of the cotton socks so that they are pressed flat against the soles of the socks.

Now the kids can paint stars, fish, letters, or any other designs they like on the sock bottoms. Most three-dimensional paints can be applied straight from the bottle — just press the nozzle gently against the fabric to make sure the paint sticks.

Let the paint set overnight before removing the cardboard and wearing the slippers. You'll also want to wait about three days before you machine-wash and dry them (refer to the bottle for the proper heat settings).

Breakfast Sundaes

The morning after, tempt sleepyheads to rise and shine with fresh fruit sundaes. In parfait glasses, layer sliced peaches, bananas, melon, berries, and plain or flavored yogurt. Top with granola or finely chopped nuts and a cherry.

Family Olympics,
page 250

Chapter Three

Crowd Pleasers

Cool-off Party ★ Block Party ★ All-Star Carnival ★
Beach Party ★ Family Olympics ★ Fall Festival ★
Skating Party

E VERY YEAR, *FamilyFun* contributor Charlotte Meryman and her family welcome spring with a big, boisterous bash. And every year, the party gets a little bigger — and better. Last year, nearly 100 guests (half kids and half adults) gathered the week-end after Memorial Day on her Massachusetts farm for an old-fashioned day of fun, games, and food that lasted long after dark.

Large gatherings, like Charlotte's annual bash, do take a lot of planning. To throw a successful big party, she says, you need to start with a basic game plan that has something for everyone — games, activities, and food for all ages. Once the guests arrive, Charlotte lets the party take on a life of its own. The best moments, she says, are often unexpected.

In this chapter, we've featured eight parties that please a mixed-age crowd of 20 to 100 guests. If you're up for host-ing a big bash, start by choosing one of our party plans that appeals to your fam-ily's tastes, from the wintry Skating Party on page 260 to the All-Star Carnival on page 240. Once you have set-tled on a theme, mix and match ideas from other parties and toss in your own unique twists (asking key guests for input).

Admittedly, large events take more effort, but they also have a greater payoff. Charlotte loves it when people start asking about her party months ahead of time. She says, "I know we're creating the kind of memories I treasure from my own childhood."

Start early: Allow several weeks to several months for at-home parties. If you need to book a space elsewhere or if guests will be traveling from out of town, start

Beach Ball Invitation, page 246

Crowd Pleasers

Family Reunions

No matter how connected we are in today's information age, there's nothing like seeing your family face to face. Any of the parties in this chapter can be adapted to suit a large family gathering. Use an entire theme, such as the Family Olympics on page 250, or a mix of games and activities from this chapter.

planning six months ahead.

Set a date: Notify guests right away for a good turnout. For annual events, establish a permanent date, such as the first Saturday in May. Resist the temptation to reschedule, no matter how many regrets you receive. (If there are guests you consider essential, check with them early.) For weather-dependent events, set an alternate date, too.

Spread the work around: A good host knows how to delegate. Make a list of the tasks that need to be done (including deadlines), from the invitations to the menu to the cleanup. Then divvy up the respon-

sibilities with members of your family or a party committee. Check in regularly and reassign jobs that aren't getting done.

Plan activities for all ages: Soliciting ideas from people of varying ages will help ensure that there are activities to satisfy everyone. Plan an icebreaker, such as a group game, early in the party to help draw guests together and get the party rolling.

Arrange for child care: Hiring a few neighborhood teens to entertain toddlers can make the party more fun for them and give their parents a chance to participate in the activities.

Make the food potluck: Not only are potlucks the easiest meal to prepare, but they have the added advantage of giving guests a chance to contribute. If someone makes a dish you've enjoyed in the past, consider requesting it again; you'll probably find they're more than happy to oblige.

Don't forget to document: Stock up on film before the party and assign a few "photographers," or hand out disposable cameras. A group shot is a terrific way to remember the day.

Write it all down: Take advantage of the inevitable post-party review to jot down notes for next year's bash, such as how many people attended, what they consumed, and where and when the supplies were rented, plus note any great ideas from guests.

Skating Party,
page 260

Cool-Off Party

PARTY STATS

Ages: All
Size: 10 to 20 guests
Length: 2 to 4 hours
Prep time: 2 hours
Cost: $3 per guest

WHEN IT'S 90 DEGREES in the shade, don't sweat it out alone. Lure friends and family away from their air conditioners and over to your house for a rollicking cool-off party. What follows are water games, cold foods, and favorite tricks that will leave everyone smiling, splashing, and feeling as cool as cukes.

A Hot Spot

THE MOST IMPORTANT thing you'll need for this party is sizzling hot weather, so plan on hosting it in the heat of the summer. Choose a date (and a rain date) and invite a bunch of kids and their parents via telephone. If you aren't lucky enough to have a pool in your backyard, plan the party at a public swimming area, pool, or lake. Alternatively, ask guests to bring their own wading pools and create a big pool party in your backyard. No matter where you host the event, you'll want to haul out the pool toys, water balloons, and squirt guns, then get ready to dive right into the coolest celebration around.

Splash Tag

Crowd Pleasers

Cool-Off Party

Cool Pool Competitions

- ☞ Dive for a penny at the pool bottom
- ☞ Throw an underwater tea party
- ☞ Hold a chat at the bottom of the pool
- ☞ Do a cartwheel underwater
- ☞ Grab a greased watermelon
- ☞ Style a wet and wacky hairdo

Musical Sprinkler

IN THIS AQUATIC adaptation of statue, a sprinkler takes the place of music. One great thing about the game is that everyone is a winner, because everyone gets cool. Begin play with the sprinkler turned off. Players must move around the sprinkler area, jumping, dancing, or striking funny poses. When the sprinkler is turned on, they must freeze in position — and get drenched — until the sprinkler is turned off again.

Musical Sprinkler

The Great Foot Freeze

The Great Foot Freeze

HERE'S A SILLY group icebreaker that will cool your guests off in a hurry. Fill a child's plastic wading pool with water, then add lots of ice cubes. Now supply each contestant with a plastic bowl. (All bowls should be roughly equal in size.) Players sit around the edge of the wading pool with their feet poised over the water. At the word "Go," they race to move ice cubes out of the water and into their bowls within a designated time period. The catch is, they can only use their feet. The winner — by a foot, of course — is the person who has the most ice cubes in his bowl when the time is up.

Foot Freeze is one game where kids have a distinct advantage over grown-ups: not only do their feet seem to be much more dexterous, kids also aren't nearly such wimps about plunging their toes into the (eek!) icy water.

Parent Polo

THEY SAY NOBODY knows you like your mother, but is that really the case? Just go to the grocery store and see how many women turn around when just one child cries "Mom!" In this variation of the classic pool game Marco Polo, first mothers and then fathers have to find their own children in the pool on the basis of voice alone. Parent Polo can be played in a swimming pool or lake; otherwise your only requirement is to have a lifeguard on duty to watch the kids.

When you're ready to play, have all the kids and their moms get into the pool. (In the second heat, it's the dads' turn to dive in.) Each parent closes his or her eyes, then the adults count to ten in unison while the kids spread out in the water (shallow end only, unless the kids are all strong swimmers), with siblings grouped together. The moms now begin to search for their own children by listening to their voices. Kids call out "Mommy!" and the moms must respond "Polo!" The first mom to touch her slippery kids wins. Follow with a round of Daddy Polo.

Parent Polo

Cool-Off Party

Relative Relay

Relative Relay

FAMILIES GO for the gold in this Olympic-style swimming relay, which focuses more on the sillies than the strokes.

Line up all the families in the starting area (the race can be conducted in a pool, a lake, or a pond). If some families have more members than others, even out the teams. If possible, try to match dads against dads, moms against moms, kids against kids. Once you get your teams straightened out, you're ready to begin.

At a signal, the first member of each family dives in to swim a single lap. As soon as that person finishes, the next family member jumps in and swims hers, and so on, until the whole team has finished. The first family to complete all its laps wins.

The contest proceeds just like any other relay, really, except with one big catch: racers must perform a feat while swimming. For example, in lap one, all the moms must push beach balls across the pool using only their noses. In lap two, cousins must paddle on water noodles. For lap three, the grandmothers must frog-kick behind kickboards. In lap four, kids must dog-paddle while singing "Yankee Doodle." For the anchor lap, the dads must do the breaststroke with rubber ducks balanced on their heads. Make up your own rules. The zanier the better.

On the face of it, you might think that competitive swimmers would hold a decided advantage over their less aquatic friends in the Relative Relay. After all, this is a swimming contest, right? Not so fast. Ever try to do an expert backstroke when you're giggling hard enough to make waves in the pool? It ain't easy.

Cool Cuisine

Every host likes her guests to think her menu is cool, especially during a party such as this one. If it's really hot outside, your guests may not feel like eating at all, but make sure they stay hydrated with plenty of water and party drinks. If they do work up a hunger, offer them cold cuts to build their own sandwiches along with an Arctic Orange and a slice of Sunshine Cake.

Arctic Oranges

Arctic Oranges

4 oranges

4 cups orange juice

4 cherries, pitted

8 raisins

4 apple slices

Cut the tops off the oranges in a zigzag pattern. Hollow out the insides, remove the seeds, and combine in a blender with the juice. Set the rinds in a muffin tin and fill with the mixture. Drop a cherry inside each orange. Freeze for 2 to 3 hours. Use toothpicks to apply raisin eyes and apple slice mouths. Let the kids eat their way down to the surprise cherry. Makes 4.

Sunshine Cake

Sunshine Cake

2 8- or 9-inch round baked cakes

Yellow frosting

7 to 9 sugar cones

Yellow crystal sugar

Frost the top of one cake, then add the second layer and continue frosting. Ice the outside of one cone and roll it in the sugar. Push the open end into the side of the cake, using more frosting to hold it in place, if needed. Repeat with the other cones, positioning them around the cake like sun rays. Serves 8 to 10.

Frozen Favors

Frozen Favors

Cap your cool-off party with this frosty favor. For each child, insert a small toy or piece of plastic jewelry into a balloon. Fill the balloon with water, knot it, and freeze solid. Before giving out the goodies, cut away the balloon. Now young guests can push the ice ball around a kiddie pool and watch it melt into a surprise.

Block Party

PARTY
STATS

Ages: All
Size: 25 to 100
guests
Length: 3 to 5 hours
Prep time: 5 to
10 hours
Cost: $3 per
guest

A BLOCK PARTY is your chance to move beyond the nodding acquaintance you may have with the people next door. When you serve up food and fun, you'll be swapping recipes and baby-sitters' phone numbers in no time. The following block party plan, sent in by the folks who live on Tucker Street in suburban Natick, Massachusetts, is one neighborhood's recipe for success.

Festive Mailboxes

Decorate for your block party on a neighborhood scale. Ask all the families on your street to cover their mailboxes with helium balloons, ribbons, and signs. At the party, vote on who owns the fairest mailbox in the land.

Party Preparations

THE FIRST THING you need to do is solicit volunteers for a planning committee — this is not a project you want to tackle solo. The party chairman (a job that should be rotated every couple of years) must request, in advance, town permission to block off the street. Subcommittees can plot out food, games, and the much-anticipated variety show.

Mail Flyers

ONCE YOU HAVE settled on a date and time, invitations can be sent out (3 to 8 P.M. will ensure that dinner can be served around 5 o'clock followed by the talent show). Have a subcommittee member write out all the party info by hand or on a computer, then reproduce the invites at a copy shop. Now all you have to do is stuff them in the mailboxes.

Mail Flyer

The Kick-Off Parade

THIS EARLY afternoon event sets the mood for the later festivities. The kids proudly present their bikes, strollers, and wagons decorated with anything they can think of. Have plenty of decorations on hand, such as streamers, helium balloons, bows, and ribbons. Notch playing cards or slit straws down their sides and slip over wheel spokes. Tape pinwheels to the handlebars and watch the parade begin.

Rock Around The Block

ADD AN INSTRUMENTAL ambience to the day's activities by trying this idea provided by Robin Conti of Natick, Massachusetts. Tune radios up and down the block to a common station (chosen by committee, of course) and bring speakers outdoors or aim them out opened windows.

The Kick-Off Parade

Crowd Pleasers

Block Party

Fun & Games

Cool-de-Sac Classics

Please the neighborhood gang with one of these tried-and-true classics:
- Horseshoes
- Croquet
- Badminton
- Wiffle ball
- Dodgeball (try kids versus parents)
- Lawn golf
- Red rover
- Kick the can

Rowdy Races: At the Tucker Street block party, Robin said it was amusing to see how many of the men participated in the relay races. They actually had to have a separate men's division. Along with relays, try three-legged races (an adult class featuring married couples hobbling together is hysterical), wheelbarrow runs (one person holds up the legs of another person walking on his hands), and trash bag sack hops.

Lawn Mower Race: Dads will need little incentive or instruction to participate in this game. Simply line up riding or push mowers, stand back as engines roar, and point the contestants toward the grass.

Know Thy Neighbor: In this game, families find out how well they know the neighborhood. Hand out copies of a map of all the houses in the surrounding area and challenge players to fill in the names of who lives at each. At the end of the game, answers should be read aloud, so people can fill in any blanks. Add phone numbers, and the completed map now serves as an impromptu neighborhood directory.

Treasure Hunt: At the party planning stage, a subcommittee can be charged with thinking up the clever clues to lure family teams to a hidden pile of loot in the neighborhood. (For complete directions on staging treasure hunts, see page 19.)

Rowdy Races

Blockbuster Menu

TEN DOLLARS per family buys barbecue meats and drinks (and contributes to the rental of "military-size grills," as Robin puts it). One side of the street is charged with making salads, the other, desserts.

Variety Show

ONE OF LIFE'S great thrills is a stage curtain lifting — even if the curtain is a bedspread and the stage a bit grassy. To form an easy performance space at your block party, run a clothesline between two large trees and drape sheets over the line. Add a portable mike and a spotlight, and the show is ready to go on.

Before the party, have parents help kids find a particular talent they want to show off: Is it training the family dog? Doing impressions of her parents? Playing the kazoo? Bear in mind that the key to a successful show is raw enthusiasm and an appreciative audience, not polished performances.

Consider anchoring the show with one big number that involves the whole cast. This way, the kids will have an excuse to get together regularly for rehearsals before the party.

If you're long on neighborhood talent but short on plot ideas, take your script from stories the kids know. They can stick to the original or — for a fun twist — modernize or adapt it. What if Cinderella lived in the nineties or Clifford was a big, red cat?

Once the dinner dishes are cleared, let the talent show begin. For an extra touch and a souvenir of the event, have the kids pass out programs that have been made on a computer.

Neighborhood Fun

There are more ways than one to throw a block party. Any of these ideas can be worked into your gathering.
Show Off Your Pets: Have kids present their loyal pals for prizes at the party — Most Bashful Guppy, Happiest Dog, Sleepiest Cat, and so on.
Watch a Movie: Rent a movie projector and play it on an outdoor screen — a white sheet hung on the side of the house. Alternatively, have neighbors bring a handful of slides from a favorite family vacation to share.

Catch Community Spirit: Add a can or clothing drive element to the block party — or make group plans for future volunteer projects.

All-Star Carnival

PARTY STATS
Ages: All
Size: 15 to 75 guests
Length: 2 to 4 hours
Prep time: 5 to 10 hours
Cost: $2 per guest

GAMES, CONTESTS, PRIZES, music, sweets, and sunshine. Put them all together, and you get the most memorable event of the summer — a carnival. Whether you make it a neighborhood street fair or use a few ideas for a birthday party, the principle is the same: you dream up the festivities, then invite carnivalgoers to wander from booth to booth, playing games, trying their luck, and, well, clowning around.

Set Right Up

FOLLOW *FamilyFun*'s tried-and-true formula for throwing a carnival: keep things simple, sweet, and silly. You will need a group of willing friends and an open area (a field, backyard, or park) with access to a hose and faucet. Decide which booths and contests you want to set up, then choose a date and a rain date. Divvy up the planning and enlist kids to help with the booth-making and decorating — carnival construction is half the fun. Then put up a few carnival posters and wait for the eager crowds to pour in.

Ticket Booth

The Booths

THE BACKBONE of any carnival is an array of enticing booths. To make one, start with a bench, table, or cardboard box, then drape it with a bright tablecloth or sheet. Attach balloons, streamers, pinwheels, or flags, and, most importantly, a hand-painted sign listing the booth's name and the ticket fee. Staff each booth with an adult or teen attendant with a basket of prizes.

Ticket Booth: As an entrance fee to the big event, ask carnivalgoers to bring a donation of $1. (This pays for the prizes — penny candy, stickers, rubber balls, and other inexpensive toys.) When the donation is made, the booth manager hands out a paper bag with 20 tickets. Throughout the fair, kids can pay a ticket to enter an event. When they receive a prize, they can stow it in the bag.

Wet Sponge Toss: Armed with a garbage can lid, a valiant parent at this booth must defend himself or herself from kids who get three chances to make a direct hit with a large, wet sponge. Depending on the weather, parent volunteers can don rain gear or swimsuits. Provide a bucket of water and at least three thick, soft sponges and mark off a line behind which the

Wet Sponge Toss

assailants must stand. The target can duck, twist, or wield the shield to avoid the wet missiles — but must remain with feet planted as kids pitch. A hit wins the contestant a prize.

Guess Your Weight: Nothing pleases young carnivalgoers more than outsmarting a grown-up. Decked out in full academic regalia, a dad or mom masquerading as Professor Guesser must try to guess the weight of children who step up to his or her scale. If the professor's guess is within five pounds, the child wins nothing. If the guess is more than five pounds over or under, the child wins a prize. A full-size, stand-up scale lends drama to the game — but if Professor Guesser is enough of a natural-born ham, any size scale will do for this fun and suspenseful contest.

Guess Your Weight

Face-Painting

Ask an artistic teen to be in charge of face-painting the not-too-squirmy carnival attendees. Before-hand, buy a high-quality face paint kit, such as Professional Snaz-aroo Face Painting Kit, which is available at depart-ment and party stores for about $15. Then paint faces with stars, flowers, rainbows, hearts, clown noses, or animal stripes.

All-Star Carnival

Ready, Aim, Fire!

steps up to the line, and gets three tennis balls — and three chances to try her luck on any of the targets.

Speedy Delivery: For a ticket, kids can send a surprise (a balloon? jelly beans? a lollipop?) to a parent or pal. After picking a prize and writing an accompanying note, the gift-giver can sneak to the sidelines to watch as a courier, decked in a sandwich board, delivers the surprise with a flourish.

Penny Splash: This event requires an aquarium filled with water, two or three tall glasses, and a bowl filled with pennies. Set the aquarium on a sturdy table and sink the glasses so they sit upright on the bottom of the tank. Contestants then try to drop pennies into the glasses. Award a prize for every lucky penny that makes its mark.

The Contests

WHAT'S A GOOD carnival without a few sporting events? Next to the ticket booth, set up a poster listing all the contests, their locations, and their starting times (you may want to run a number of heats throughout the carnival so that everyone can participate). When kids arrive, they can sign up for one or all of the contests, then meet at the appointed spot at game time. An adult or teen can monitor each event, explaining the rules and making sure the competition stays fair and friendly.

Outrageous Obstacle Course: For this game, two relay teams race through identical obstacle courses — the first team that completes its run wins. The obstacle course at your

Guess the Joke

At fourth grader Katie Clark's carnival in Jackson, Michigan, kids paid a ticket for a chance to get lucky ... with laughter. Booth attendants got out their joke books, wrote down their favorites, then put all the questions in a hat. For a ticket, carnival revelers got to pull one out and try to guess the punch line. If they guessed right, they received a prize. Stumped? They got a consolation prize — and a good laugh when they heard the answer.

Ready, Aim, Fire! Players in this throwing contest will need a strong arm and a sense of aim that is right on the money. To set the stage, use pieces of string or twine to hang a series of targets from a long tree branch or a clothesline. Make your targets a variety of shapes and sizes, using paper plates, aluminum pie pans, hula hoops, beach balls, wind chimes, cowbells, spinning targets, or anything else you can think of. Label each target, indicating how many prizes a successful hit is worth (anywhere from one to four, depending on the difficulty), then mark off a line 10 to 15 feet away. Each contestant pays a ticket,

Speedy Delivery

Outrageous Obstacle Course

carnival can be as wild as your imagination and resources permit, but here are a few ideas to start with. Racers can crawl through hula hoops, bounce balls, step in and out of tires, jump over a sleeping alligator (a hay bale), step into a sack and jump a few yards, shoot a water gun, or pitch a Frisbee disc through a hoop. When each runner has completed the obstacles, she must run backward (not through the course) and tag the next runner on her team. The winning team gets a prize apiece.

Balloon Stomp: This event requires a few packages of medium-size round balloons, string, lots of eager participants, and a small field marked off with cones. Competitors should blow up two balloons and tie one to each ankle. The object is to stomp other people's balloons while keeping yours intact. The judge yells "Go!" and all players start stomping, remaining on the field at all times. The last person to remain unpopped wins a prize — and the right to pop her own balloon.

Spin & Run: Absurdity rules the day in this game, which requires nothing but a bunch of baseball bats and a finish line. To play, each contestant must grip a bat and hold it upright so the top rests on the ground. Then players must bend over, place their foreheads on the ends of the bats, and spin around ten times. After this, they drop the bats and attempt to race for the finish line (a more difficult task than you might expect). Don't play with too many kids or you'll have to rename it Spin & Collide.

Spin & Run

All-Star Carnival

Water Balloon Toss: Here, kids try to toss water-filled balloons to each other over increasing distances without breaking them. Have pairs of kids face each other in a line and give one child in each pair a filled balloon. On the starting whistle, the child must toss the balloon to her partner. If her partner can catch the balloon without breaking it, both children take a step backward. On the next whistle, the sequence is repeated. If a balloon bursts, that pair of kids is eliminated. The pair that can toss its balloon from the greatest distance wins a prize.

Cracker Whistling: The familiar schoolyard expression "Say it, don't

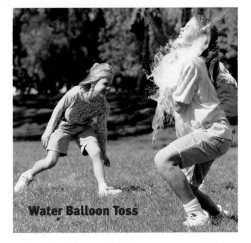

Water Balloon Toss

spray it" definitely does not apply to this silly contest. In fact, players must whistle a simple tune even though they have a mouthful of crackers. To set up the contest, you will need a table, chairs, small paper plates, and a couple of boxes of crackers. Seat each contestant in front of a plate with two crackers. At the starting whistle, players must chew as quickly as they can, then try to be the first one to whistle a few bars of a specified tune for a prize. Have a few glasses of water handy and — a word to the wise — stand clear.

Bucket Brigade: This race requires two evenly numbered teams, one bucket for each player, a filled wading pool with a running hose inside it, and two washtubs (or trash cans) with a tennis ball tossed into each. Team members must coordinate the fastest method for filling their washtubs with buckets of water. The first group to make the tennis ball spill out of the tub wins.

Cracker Whistling

The Food Booth

With the scent of barbecue in the air, contestants will converge on this booth quickly. Cover a table with a cloth and set out plates, utensils, condiments, and a cooler of drinks. Place a grill nearby and let the chef du jour preside over hot dogs and hamburgers (charge 10 tickets for dogs, 20 tickets for burgers, and 5 tickets for juice boxes or soda). For dessert, set up a decorate-your-own-cupcake table, where kids can indulge a sweet tooth with frostings and sprinkles for 5 tickets.

The Toddler Corner

Doll Show

TREAT THE YOUNGEST carnival-goers to a play area with games and contests that are just their speed (older siblings and parents are admitted by toddler invitation only). Station a few parents or teens to collect tickets, run the fun and games, and hand out a prize to each child who completes an event.

Music-Makers Tent

Music-Makers Tent: Here, a magical tent sets the stage for dressing up and making music. Dolled up in play clothes, hats, and paper leis, kids can pound on drums, tootle on harmonicas, rattle maracas, and dance the day away. Pitch a camping tent, set out the supplies, and let the kids make some noise.

Tricycle Races: Soup up a few three-wheeled hot rods with streamers and bows, and the racers will be lining up for a chance to pedal to victory. Make a finish line by hanging crepe paper between two poles and use traffic cones or milk jugs weighted with sand to delineate the racecourse.

Doll Show: For this event, little children get to dress up one of their favorite dolls or stuffed animals. They bring along their dolls, and you provide a box of doll clothes, ribbons, bows, and hairbrushes. After thoroughly primping

and adorning their charges, the kids can parade before a panel of friendly judges. Every contestant's entry receives a prize — for fanciest dress, funniest hat, cutest smile, longest hair, fuzziest fur, or best button nose.

Bubble Factory: When little kids see bubbles flying through the air, they'll flock to this event. Fill pie plates with store-bought bubble soap and hand out a selection of wands, from giant bubble makers to mini wands.

Edible Jewelry: This activity combines two all-time favorites: stringing beads and eating sweets. Offer kids Fruit Loops and shoestring licorice and let them string themselves an edible necklace.

Art Show: For a kids' carnival mural, hang a roll of newsprint from a clothesline or tape it to a garage door and offer paint and brushes (keep a hose nearby for cleanup!).

Tricycle Races

Carnival Booths for Little Kids

Magnet Fishing: Stock a dry kiddie pool with paper fishes with paper clips attached to their mouths. Let kids fish with a magnet tied to a fishing pole.

Lucky Lollipop: Stick lollipops in a Styrofoam cone. For a ticket, kids get to pull one out. If it has a red mark on the end, they win a prize; if not, the lollipop itself is a happy consolation.

Dig for Buried Treasure: Bury hidden treasures (inexpensive prizes) in a sandbox. One ticket lets kids dig until they discover a prize.

Tire Target: Hang an old tire from a tree and let kids try to toss a football through it.

Beach Party

PARTY
STATS
Ages: All
Size: 10 to 20
guests
Length: 2 to 4
hours
Prep time: 2 hours
Cost: $4 to $6
per guest

THE SEASHORE — with the waves rolling in, the cloudless sky, the gulls winging overhead — offers a picturesque setting for a family party. Young shell-seekers will find plenty to do, from decorating sand castles to playing tic-tac-toe, while their parents drink in the view from beach chairs. All the activities can take place right on a pub-

Beach Ball Invitations

THE IDEA of a day at the beach should be inviting enough, so get guests in the party mood with a beach ball invitation. Inflate inexpensive plastic beach balls and use a permanent marker to write down the party info. Ask guests to pack their beach bags with towels, bathing suits, beach chairs, and sunscreen. Deflate the balls and send in manila envelopes.

Beach Ball Invitation

Shell T-Shirts

AS GUESTS ARRIVE, invite them to print summery designs with seashells on white T-shirts or tank tops. Place newspaper inside the T-shirts to keep the paint from leaking through. Next pour fabric paint onto a sponge. Press the outside of a shell into the paint and then onto the shirt. Repeat, experimenting with different colors. At home, guests should heat-set the paint according to package directions.

Shell T-shirts

Sand Sculpture Contest

THE KIDS at your beach party will probably take one quick plunge in the water, bounce around in the surf for about 30 seconds, then want to spend the rest of the afternoon digging sand sculptures on the beach. So why not stage a Sand Sculpture Contest as the focal point of the party?

Keep the contest rules straightforward: a sculpture can be made with any available tools or materials — driftwood, shells, beach pails, plastic shovels, even boogie boards — and it should represent the collaborative efforts of a family or parent-child team. Sand sculptures might include a dune buggy (like the one pictured at right), a sea lion with a seaweed mane, or a motorboat with a (real) waterskiing dad getting towed behind.

Award prizes for the goofiest, most artistic, sandiest, and most creative use of beach finds. For prizes, present disposable underwater cameras or plastic sunglasses.

246

Sand Sculpture Contest

Beach Party

Beach Bowling

Beach Hunt

Send teams of beach-combers on a scavenger hunt. Depending on where you live, the list might include:

- ☞ **Blue sea glass**
- ☞ **Driftwood**
- ☞ **10 types of shells**
- ☞ **A sand dollar**
- ☞ **3 types of seaweed**
- ☞ **8 smooth sea stones**
- ☞ **A crab or starfish**
- ☞ **10 pieces of trash**
- ☞ **A found penny**
- ☞ **A snail**

Note: Remind kids to return living things to their natural habitat.

Beach Games

Musical Towels: Lay out beach towels — one fewer than players — on the sand and turn up the music on a portable stereo (we recommend the Beach Boys or any surfer sounds). When the music starts, players dance around the towels. When it stops, players must stretch out on a towel like a sunbather. The player left without a towel is out. Remove one towel each round until there's only one remaining beach bum.

Beach Bowling: First, build ten pins by filling a cup with moist sand. Carefully turn the cup over and lift it off. Set up the pins in a triangle with one pin in front, two pins in the next row, three in the next, and four in the back row.

Next draw a starting line in the sand about 6 or 8 feet from the pins. Now take turns standing behind the line and rolling a softball or other small ball toward the pins to knock them over. Each player gets to roll the ball twice. Count how many pins you knock over, set them up again, and keep score in the sand.

Tic-tac-toe: Make a nine-square grid in the sand and draw the X's and O's with driftwood. If you have enough partygoers who want to play, make teams and ask human markers to sit in the squares.

Hopscotch: To give this playground classic a seaside flavor, each player can scavenge a beach-related marker to toss: a clamshell, a plastic shovel, or a colorful flip-flop.

Darts: Draw a dartboard with six concentric circles and give each ring a point value. Each player should choose three markers that look the same (three clamshells, three pieces of green sea glass, and so on). Take turns tossing the markers at the dartboard and keep score in the sand.

Beach Bowling

Sandy Food

PACK A COOLER with juice boxes and bottled water — and a variety of picnic salads and sandwiches. For a sweet surprise, bring along the Pail of Sand Cake (below).

Seashore Snacks

For a party snack mix, fill a large paper bag with 1 cup each of dry chow mein noodles (seaweed), pretzel sticks (driftwood), Cheddar Goldfish crackers, roasted peanuts (beach pebbles), and Cheerios (life preservers). For sweetness, add 1 cup of raisins and ½ cup of dried pineapple slices cut into bite-size wedges. Fold over the top of the bag and shake to mix.

Pail of Sand Cake

This novel cake, topped with crushed cookie "sand," will be the hit of your beach party. After your kids eat it up, scrub the pail and let them fill it with real sand (no eating allowed).

    1 baked 8-inch round cake
    1 8- to 9-cup capacity new plastic
        sand pail
    24 ounces unsweetened applesauce
        (or 1 3-ounce package pudding,
        prepared)
    ¾ cup crushed graham crackers or
        vanilla cookies
    Shell candies
    1 plastic shovel

Cut the cake into 1-inch pieces. Fill the pail, alternating layers of cake pieces and applesauce, ending with applesauce. Sprinkle on the crushed cookie sand and top with shell candies. Now dig in with the plastic shovel.

Indoor Beach Party

Being snowed in is just another day at the beach for *FamilyFun* reader Cathy Rickarby of Stratham, New Hampshire. When her kids had a snow day from school, they hosted an indoor beach party. While Cathy packed lunch in a cooler, Carly, age five, and Kirstin, age three, dug out beach hats, towels, pails, and shovels. They set up their beach tent and towels on the floor and put on their bathing suits. They had a great time eating lunch and playing games at their pretend beach. Even ten-month-old Charles joined in the fun.

Party Favors

FILL A PLASTIC bucket with some of the day's necessities, including a shovel, sun visor, bottle of water, and snacks (shell candy, gummy fish, Goldfish crackers, and saltwater taffy), cheap sunglasses, and sunscreen.

Pail of Sand Cake

Family Olympics

THIS SUMMER COMPETITION, developed by *FamilyFun* contributor Jenifer Harms, pits family against family in a series of low-cost games the world-class event will never see. The event deserves a motto all its own. Forget "Faster, higher, stronger." These games are "Wackier, funnier, friendlier."

Opening Ceremony

SPARK THE OLYMPIC spirit with an official opening ceremony, where family teams carry a poster board pennant affixed to a broom and parade down the street to a taped rendition of the Olympic theme. After some inspirational words from the host, kids can race a foil and tissue paper torch across the playing field (a neighborhood or public lawn), and let the wacky games begin.

Olympic Torch

Olympic Torch: To make an official (albeit fake) torch, poke a hole in the center of the bottom of a plastic cup. Working from the center, make outward cuts like you would slice a pie. Next poke a hole in the center of a large yogurt lid and cut three "pie" slices. Now assemble the torch by slipping the lid up onto a paper towel tube, then slipping the cup down to meet the lid. Wrap foil around the entire torch and light it with tissue paper flames.

Winning Party Plans

When it comes to organizing games, the International Olympics Committee has nothing on Jenifer Harms. A mom and *FamilyFun* writer, she's been spearheading her neighborhood's Family Olympics for years. Here are her tips for making everything run like clockwork.

◆ **Choose your location early.** Jen held last year's games in a church gym. This year she'll move it outdoors and use traffic cones and ribbons as boundaries.

◆ **Use referees.** Jen recruits two grandparents and two college students to run the show.

◆ **Manage your time.** Jen hands each team an activity schedule on arrival and gives referees copies of the rules. She starts the games at 3 P.M. and ends them two hours later.

◆ **Pay attention to details.** The more authentic touches you can introduce into the events, the more memorable they will be. Give the referees whistles; hand out prizes; ask families to come in uniform.

◆ **Use a megaphone or a microphone.** It's the only way you'll be heard over the din.

◆ **Learn to love chaos.** Even good planning can't eliminate the craziness generated by a horde of kids.

Olympic T-Shirts

Awards Ceremony

Piggyback Parent

Tunnel Gopher

FAMILY
OLYMPICS
1996

Family Olympics

Honorable Mentions

An Olympics without medals is like a birthday without cake. To make your own, write *first*, *second*, and *third* on plastic lids. Attach colored ribbons — blue for first, red for second, and white for third. Or, order real ribbons from a trophy store, such as Ribbon Ranch, Inc. (303-936-0231).

Mom-Calling Contest

I N THIS CONTEST, blindfolded mothers (or fathers) race to find their children, who are standing in a row and calling to them from a designated distance. Just imagine the roar of 50 kids bellowing all at once, "Mom, Mom, hey Mom!" (Crafty competitors have been known to cut through the clatter with a whistle, a move of debatable legality. Your Olympic committee will have to set its own guidelines.)

To get started, just line up all the parents and blindfold them. Next sta-

Mom-Calling Contest

tion the kids across an open expanse, making sure no obstacles come between them and their seeking parents. At a signal, the kids start screaming. The first parent-child team to make contact wins.

Piggyback Parent

I N THIS VARIATION on the 50-yard dash, parents have to carry their kids across the finish line. For single-child families, this will be a cinch. The dad who has to swing a seven-year-old on his back while wearing five-year-old twins on either hip faces a stiffer challenge.

As far as materials go, this event requires virtually nothing — just a start and a finish line. Competitors do need plenty of heart, however, since they can move forward only when their wee ones are completely off the ground. Here's one back-saving multichild strategy: shuttle the kids one at a time.

Piggyback Parent

Tunnel Gopher

THIS RACE IS the opposite of leapfrog. Instead of jumping over the backs of teammates, players must tunnel through their legs toward the finish line.

Once again, all you need to get going is a start and a finish line. Begin by lining up families so they're facing the finish. At the start of the race, the last family member in line drops to the ground and crawls through the legs of everyone in front of him. Not until he stands up and spreads his feet can the next person at the end of the line begin. The team continues tunneling in this way until it reaches the finish line.

Tunnel Gopher

Free-Style Relay

Free-Style Relay

THIS RACE HAS as many legs as your largest family has members. Got a Brady Bunch among your friends? If so, each team must run eight legs. One more catch: Each leg consists of a different movement. For example, Leg 1: Cartwheels; Leg 2: Crab-walking; Leg 3: Skipping. Team members choose which lap or laps they want to run (it helps to keep track of the order on a sign board). The first family to finish a full round — one leg at a time — wins.

Olympic T-shirts

To make your competition more realistic, have participating families create and wear their own uniforms. T-shirts can be printed, hand-painted, or simply color-coded.

Family Olympics

Wacky Olympics

FamilyFun reader Robin Williams of La Verne, California, gives family games a zany twist. Her event — the Wacky Olympics — opens with a neighbor's scorching electric-guitar solo of the Olympic theme and includes a shoe-kicking contest. "Flip-flops won't even move," Robin advises. "But tennis shoes really fly."

Shoe Pile Scramble

IN THIS GAME, children have to find their shoes and put them on. So what's the big deal? Don't we try to get them to do this at least once a day? Well, here the shoes of all the participating kids are scrambled in one big, sloppy heap.

To begin, players remove their shoes and pile them together. Mix everything up so no one pair is intact, then have the children stand side by side at the starting line. When the whistle blows, the kids race to find their shoes and fasten them before running back across the line. Children with siblings have to finish as a family.

Shoe Pile Scramble

Tug-of-War

A FAMILY-VERSUS-FAMILY tug-of-war is the crowning event of this contest, the marathon of the local Olympics.

A length of rope with a piece of tape marking the middle will get you started. Hint: The thicker the rope, the easier it is to hang on to and the less likely it is to cause rope burns. To avoid injury, do not let contestants wrap rope around waists or wrists.

To begin, set two families at opposite ends of the rope and center the rope over a tape mark on the ground. Have the families step back 6 feet to another line marked with tape. At a signal, each family strains to pull the other across to its mark.

Run the contest like a tournament, picking family names out of a hat to determine who goes head-to-head in the first round. Winners keep advancing until only two families are left to square off for the championship.

Tug-of-War

Cake-Decorating Contest

Cake-Decorating Contest

T HIS EVENT MAKES the grade because it calls on creativity rather than athleticism. Plus it's always nice to have cake around.

Each family is allotted an identical premade, unfrosted, 9-inch, single-layer cake and a lump of white frosting. Participants also have access to a community supply of decorative frostings, berries, and candies, which they can use in whatever way they please.

Blow a whistle to start, then watch the frosting fly. Teams have 10 minutes to complete their works of art. The winner is decided by an open vote.

Jell-O Eating Contest

Crowd Pleasers

Jell-O Eating Contest

I N THE FINAL EVENT of the day, invite one member of each team to enter this silly, no-hands Jell-O Eating Contest. Prior to the party, prepare several packages of Jell-O as directed and bring them to the Olympic grounds in a cooler. Pack a measuring cup and several paper plates as well. Before the contest begins, the judge should put one cup of Jell-O per contestant on a plate and instruct each player to sit on his hands. When the judge calls "Go," players race to eat all the Jell-O. The first one to clean his plate wins a ribbon — and a full belly.

Awards Ceremony

A FTER EACH EVENT, winners stand atop cloth-draped milk crates to receive their medals (see Honorable Mentions on page 124). For an extra layer of authenticity, you can even play a tape recording of the familiar Olympic theme song. When the last medal has been awarded, tuckered out athletes traditionally tuck into a potluck supper — with prizewinning decorated cakes for dessert.

A Family Triathlon

For his tenth birthday, *FamilyFun* reader Kyle Campbell of Providence, Utah, planned a family triathlon. To prepare, he made a race number for each person, a finish line, and prizes. Contestants swam 25 laps in their backyard pool, raced mountain bikes up a rocky trail, and ran two laps around the block. Before crossing the finish line, they guzzled a can of soda. They celebrated with a backyard cookout.

Awards Ceremony

Fall Festival

APPLES, PUMPKINS, a lawn covered with leaves — when autumn is at its peak, there's no better time to round up the troops for a flurry of fun. Ask neighbors to bring their best apple pies to a cook-off, invite the kids to stuff a scarecrow, and for the grand finale, pile up all the leaves, and jump in and send them flying

Fall Scavenger Hunt

Like squirrels, kids go nuts foraging for fall objects. Send the gatherers out with a list of things to find and a time limit. Depending on where you live, the list might include acorns, bark rubbings, berries, bird feathers, cattails, cocoons, cornstalks, birch or maple leaves, insects, milkweed pods, mushrooms, pinecones, river stones, seeds, and sticks. Remind young children not to eat anything they find — and to return living things to their natural habitats.

Autumn Atmosphere

YOUR BACKYARD will look a lot like an autumn party when you set out Indian corn, hay bales, and pumpkins on picnic tables or benches (have a display table for guests' own garden wonders, too). Welcome friends to your fall festival with signs that read "Fall Festival: Food, Games, and Fun." Tape the signs to sticks, push the sticks into a hay bale, and surround with a pile of leaves.

Hayrides

KICK THE PARTY off with a hayride through the backyard. Simply fill a wagon or riding mower trailer with hay. Then pull the kids around the yard and through the leaves. If a real hayride at a local orchard or farm is an option, reserve space for your group ahead of time. Ask guests to meet there before the party.

Leaf Pile Games

DON'T BAG UP those fallen leaves — instead, treat your guests to a round of leaf games. If you end up scattering the foliage even more during the festivities, don't despair. The final game, a leaf bagging contest, will leave your yard spotless.

Leaf Pile Hurdle: Arrange a row of leaf hurdles by raking up a series of small piles. Heap up a much bigger pile at the end of the row. One at a time, let the kids run and jump over the small piles and into the big one.

Leaf Labyrinth: When leaves cover the lawn, rake a classic maze path with rows and dead ends throughout. Then challenge the kids to find their way through the twisting paths.

Musical Piles: Make a circle of small leaf piles, one less than the num-

Leaf Pile Hurdle

ber of players. Follow the same rules used in musical chairs, playing a portable radio and raking away one pile each round.

Leaf-Blowing Contest: Ask each player to collect one large leaf, then assemble everyone side by side. Tell participants to tilt back their heads, hold their leaves just above their mouths, and puff heartily. The person whose leaf flies highest overhead wins.

Bag Them Up: Pair up players and place a supply of plastic lawn bags in a central spot. See which team can fill the most bags in a set amount of time.

Bob for Prize Apples

WHAT FUN WOULD a fall party be without bobbing for apples? Here's a variation on the basic rules of the game: Wash about ten apples and mark one with a special carving, or slice it deeply with a knife (a parent's job) and insert a foil-covered chocolate coin deep into the slit. Then set the apples in a big tub of water. To play, bobbers take turns trying to latch onto an apple with their teeth. The player who grabs onto the prize apple wins.

Pumpkin Painting

FOR A FALL art project that doubles as a party favor, let kids paint goofy, surprised, or creepy faces on pumpkins. Cover a picnic table with newspaper (tape it down so it doesn't blow away). Set out liquid tempera paints, paintbrushes, and plastic yogurt containers filled with water for rinsing the brushes, then paint away.

Scarecrow-Making Party

One way *FamilyFun* reader Patricia Vara of Gaithersburg, Maryland, celebrates the fall season is by getting friends together for a scarecrow-making party. She plans her party for early October when people are starting to think Halloween. Invitations instruct guests to B.Y.O.C. — Bring Your Old Clothes — for their scarecrow to wear. (The Varas supply the straw and head supplies.) Attire possibilities are endless: a tattered farm jacket, painter's overalls, a flashy suit and tie, flannel pajamas, an old Halloween costume, a secondhand prom dress, or an outgrown baseball uniform. Accessories, like a corsage, tiara, sunglasses, or a hat, add to the fun. Once all contestants have tucked the last bit of straw into their scarecrows, a warm potluck supper awaits them. The next day, scarecrows are proudly perched on front stoops — or standing on their heads — ready for Halloween.

Fall Food

KEEP THE FOOD simple — and familiar — at your party. You can provide hot dogs, fixings, and hot cider while guests bring side dishes or apple pies. Build a bonfire, pull up lawn chairs, and wait for the stars to come out.

Hot Dog Roast

When it's getting close to dinnertime, stoke the bonfire or prepare the coals for grilling. Set out hot dogs, buns, and all the fixings on a picnic table. Then guests can roast their own on the bonfire, or the designated parent can cook them on the grill.

Cinnamon Hot Cider

For the freshest taste, pick up gallons of pasteurized cider at a local orchard before the party. Serve it cold or hot in thermoses. To make spiced hot cider, pour 1 gallon of cider into a large saucepan. Tie 16 whole cloves, 10 allspice berries, and 2 sticks of cinnamon in a coffee filter and add to the cider. Cut 2 oranges into quarters and toss into the saucepan with the cider. Warm for 8 to 10 minutes over low heat. Serves 16.

Classic Apple Pie

No harvest celebration is complete without apple pies — and everyone claims his or her family's recipe is the

Caramel Apple Pie

Crowd Pleasers

best. So why not put it to the test? Cap the meal off with a pie tasting, then line the kids up for a no-hands pie-eating contest. Here's a recipe to get you started.

> 7 apples, peeled, cored, and sliced very thin (about 9 cups)
> 2 teaspoons cinnamon
> 3 tablespoons brown sugar
> 2 teaspoons all-purpose flour
> 1 unbaked piecrust (top and bottom)

In a large bowl, combine the apple slices, cinnamon, brown sugar, and flour. Line a 9-inch pie pan with piecrust, leaving a 1-inch overhang. Spoon in the filling. Roll out the remaining dough and set the whole crust (or lattice strips) on top of the fruit. Trim the edges, then fold the overhang under and crimp to seal the dough. Cut slits in the crust and add apple ornaments (made by cutting apples out of piecrust with cookie cutters). Preheat the oven to 400° and bake for 45 minutes, or until bubbly and golden brown.

Caramel Apple Pie: Follow the directions for the Classic Apple Pie, but make a lattice-top crust. While the baked pie cools, whip up a caramel sauce. In a small nonstick saucepan, melt 20 caramel candies with ¼ cup milk over low heat, stirring occasionally until smooth. Drizzle over the lattice-top pie, or cut individual slices of pie and pass the sauce.

The Apple Corps

To celebrate one of their favorite times of year, *FamilyFun* reader Karla Paterson and her daughters invited friends for an autumn sleepover in their hometown of Grayling, Michigan.

In the evening, they decorated white T-shirts by cutting apples in half, brushing fabric paint on the surface, and pressing the fruit on the shirts. (Some of the kids personalized their T-shirts by taking a bite out of their apples before brushing on paint!) They accented the apple prints by painting on black seeds, green leaves, and brown stems. The next day, they wore their new shirts to go apple-picking.

Skating Party

GROWING UP IN New Hampshire, *FamilyFun* contributor Sam Mead would spend hours playing hockey on frozen Squam Lake with his brothers and sisters. Over the years, the gang perfected the outdoor skating party — a daylong event that includes plenty of friends, food, games, and, of course, a rinkside bonfire for warming numb toes.

Nice and Icy

YOU DON'T NEED to prepare for this party. Just wait for a day that's cold and crisp — and ice that's smooth and thick. Then make phone calls to invite friends, fill your thermoses with chicken soup and hot cocoa, and head to a local pond or lake. Clear a large area, lace up your skates, and let the games begin.

The Ice Train

THE PARTY officially begins when the Ice Train pulls out of the station. To form this conga line of skaters, just line up and grab the hips of the person in front of you, making sure to hold on tight. Of course, the lead person is the locomotive, so it's a good idea to position one of your stronger-skating adults at the head of the slithery line.

The Ice Train

Ice Skating Fun

SOMETIMES, the best games to play on the ice are the ones we're used to playing on dry land. Variations on tag are especially well suited to ice play.

Frozen Maze Tag: A layer of snow on the pond and a couple of shovels are all you need for this a-maze-ing game. To start, shovel lots of crisscrossing paths through the snow. When you've finished making your labyrinth, play the game like normal freeze tag. The only catch is that skaters have to remain within the cleared areas.

Skaters' Obstacle Course: Players get to show off all their moves in this game. To play, just set up an obstacle course by creating paths through boots, hockey sticks, sweaters, and any other items on hand. Try balancing sticks on top of boots for skaters to step or jump over. Or, two people can hold a stick at hip level that skaters pass under. To finish, all skaters must glide through a human tunnel, made by spectators.

Fox and Geese: Prepare for this game by shoveling a wagon-wheel shape in the snow, complete with hub and spokes. When you're ready to start, one player is designated the fox. His job is to chase the other players, the geese, in and around the wheel using the spokes (cleared paths) to cut across the circle. When the fox tags a goose, that person becomes a fox and joins in the hunt. The game is played until all the geese are caught. The last one to be tagged becomes the lead fox in the next game.

Skaters' Obstacle Course

Frosty Fashions

Partyers can step onto the ice in style by jazzing up their skates with pom-poms and beads. Offer them giant yarn pom-poms rinkside to tie onto their skate laces at the toes, or colorful pony beads (available at most craft stores) to string between the lace holes. The giant pom-poms make terrific party favors, too.

Skating Party

Quick Pick

To make teams, players toss their hats into a big heap. The hats are then randomly split into two equal piles — one for each side.

Hockey Play

A HOCKEY GAME often is the main event of a skating party. Before facing off, try warming up with these drills.

Monkey in the Middle: This icebreaker gives skaters a chance to practice their passing and puck control. Up to eight skaters form a big circle with one person standing in the center. The object is for the people around the circle to pass the puck without letting the monkey (in the middle) intercept it.

Broomball

Two safety rules: All sticks must be kept below the knees, and absolutely no flicking the puck in the air.

Sharpshooter: To test puck marksmanship, have all the players stand in the mouth of one hockey goal (formed by snow boots). One at a time, contestants take three long-distance shots on the goal at the opposite end of the rink. Having extra pucks helps keep the game moving.

Broomball

ONE OF THE BEST ways to introduce young skaters to the thrill of hockey is through broomball — in which young players use brooms and a rubber ball instead of sticks and a puck. A ball that's about the size of a bowling ball, or slightly smaller, and very light and bouncy makes the contest particularly fun. With a good wallop, players can send it ricocheting off knees and arms without worrying about anyone getting hurt. Set this game up like a hockey game, complete with snow boot goals (about 6 feet apart) and an equal number of players on each team (six is ideal). Start the game with a face-off at center ice.

Monkey in the Middle

Sled Race

Skating Races

ICE IS IDEAL for all kinds of sliding and towing races. These games are a great way to build skating muscles.

Sled Race: For this two-person team event, you'll need your blade sleds. One person sits on the sled while his partner pulls it over the ice. The object is to be the first team around the rink.

Backwards Hockey Pull: Another race (also good practice for skating backwards) is the hockey stick pull. Two team members face each other, holding the ends of two sticks between them. The puller skates backward, towing his partner along like a water-skier.

Ice Bowling

ON THE NIGHT before the party, fill ten (or more) clear plastic quart or liter bottles and several gallon jugs with water. Add a bit of food coloring to each, then put them out to freeze. To play, set out the quart containers as bowling pins, back up 10 feet or so, and use the frozen gallon jugs to topple the quarts.

Ice Bowling

Cold Feet?

Don't let numb toes slow you down. Warm your skates next to a woodstove or a heating vent before heading outside. Try a pair of silk socks instead of wool ones — the more room your toes have to breathe, the longer they stay warm.

Skating Party

Rinkside Dining

Triple-Axel Hot Chocolate

PROVIDING HEARTY nourishment off the ice is the secret to hosting a long, enjoyable party. And while a delicious cup of Triple-Axel Hot Chocolate (made with chocolate milk, chocolate chips, and cocoa powder) may warm a cold skater, it's more substantial foods like Chicken Soup with Rice that provide the energy to keep everyone's legs moving.

Because the bonfire will be used largely for warming hands and giving everyone a place to chat, set up a food table nearby and create the spread there.

Triple-Axel Hot Chocolate

A thermos of this hot cocoa, made with three kinds of chocolate, will give skaters an extra spin around the rink. For a double axel variation, you can omit the cocoa and sugar. Bring out Styrofoam cups and lots of mini marshmallows or whipped cream for serving the hot chocolate.

> ½ gallon milk
> ⅔ cup milk chocolate chips
> 6 tablespoons cocoa powder
> ⅓ cup sugar
> 1 quart chocolate milk
> Miniature marshmallows or
> whipped cream (optional)

In a large saucepan over low heat, combine 1 cup of the milk with the chocolate chips, cocoa, and sugar. Whisk constantly until the mixture is smooth and the sugar is dissolved. Add the remaining milk and the chocolate milk and heat until steaming, but do not boil. Pour the drink into a preheated thermos, which will ensure that the drink stays hot. (To preheat a thermos,

Triple-Axel Hot Chocolate

fill with boiling water and let it sit for 5 minutes. Pour the water out, then fill with hot chocolate.) Before serving, shake the thermos to mix, pour into individual mugs, and top with marshmallows or whipped cream, if desired. Serves 12.

Chicken Soup with Rice

Before serving up this soup, challenge guests to recite Maurice Sendak's *Chicken Soup with Rice.* To refresh their memories, recite these lines: "In January / it's so nice / while slipping / on the sliding ice/to sip hot chicken soup / with rice. / Sipping once / sipping twice / sipping chicken soup / with rice."

>   3 large carrots
>   1 large onion, diced
>   2 ribs celery, sliced ½ inch thick
>   1 tablespoon vegetable oil
>   10 cups low-sodium chicken broth
>   1 cup converted long-grain rice
>   3½ cups cooked chicken meat
>   (1 pound uncooked), shredded or
>   cut in 1-inch chunks
>   2 tablespoons chopped parsley
>   Salt and pepper to taste

Chicken Soup with Rice

Peel the carrots, slice into thin rounds, then cut into mini flowers using an aspic cookie cutter (or simply dice the carrots). In a large soup pot, sauté the carrots, onion, and celery in the oil over medium-high heat for 10 minutes, stirring occasionally. Add the chicken broth and rice, bring to a boil, then reduce the heat to low and simmer for 15 minutes. Add the chicken and continue cooking until the vegetables are tender, about 15 to 20 minutes. Add the chopped parsley, salt, and pepper and pour into a preheated wide-mouthed thermos (see directions under Triple-Axel Hot Chocolate). Serves 12.

Sled Race

Toasty the Snowman

This cute snowman on a stick can be roasted over the fire or eaten raw.

>   3 marshmallows
>   2 thin pretzel sticks
>   Currants
>   Apricots cut into small pieces
>   Miniature M&M's
>   Miniature chocolate chips

Roast all three marshmallows on one skewer until golden (a 2-foot-long green stick is the safest length for kids to use when cooking over a campfire). Carefully press the pretzel sticks, fruit, and chocolates into the toasted marshmallows for arms, eyes, a nose, and buttons.

Note: If you don't have a bonfire, just eat the decorated snowmen raw. If you have trouble getting the eyes and buttons to stay, snip small slits in the marshmallows, then insert the decorations. Serves 1.

Toasty the Snowman

Christmas Carnival,
page 206

Chapter Four

Holiday Cheer

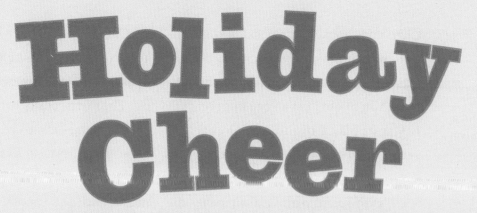

New Year's Eve ★ Valentine Workshop ★ Easter Party
Fourth of July ★ Halloween Party ★ Thanksgiving Feast
Christmas Carnival ★ Hanukkah Party

WITH ALL the excitement in the air, the holidays are a natural time to entertain. Our homes are dressed in their holiday best — jack-o'-lanterns line our porches on Halloween, tiny white lights brighten our windows on Christmas, and American flags sway over our front lawns on the Fourth of July. We get to indulge in our favorite holiday foods, from pumpkin pies on Thanksgiving to potato latkes on Hanukkah. And our homes are filled with friends and out-of-town relatives who are all in the party spirit.

So let the celebrations begin. In this chapter, we showcase eight party plans for all the major holidays of the year, from New Year's Eve to Hanukkah. You can host your party the weekend before the holiday with friends and neighbors — or work the party games, crafts, and foods into your family's private celebration.

Don't say we didn't warn you: if you try a few of our ideas this year, your kids may insist that you repeat them again next year. Thus a *FamilyFun* holiday tradition will begin.

Get into the holiday spirit: Kick off the holiday season by gathering with your friends to prepare for the big day. You might decorate your house for Christmas at a tree-trimming party or help kids make cards at a valentine workshop. These get-togethers will give your family the chance to slow down, visit with friends, and heighten holiday cheer.

Turn a family gathering into a party: When your extended family arrives for Thanksgiving, Easter, or

Holiday Cheer

The Best of the Holidays

FamilyFun contributor Maggie Megaw found a festive way to organize her daughter's birthday party: she borrowed an activity from all the holidays of the year. The kids wore Halloween costumes, trimmed a Christmas tree, dyed Easter eggs, and sat down to a Thanksgiving feast.

Christmas, make the day extra special by planning games, crafts, or activities to precede or follow the meal. You might host an egg hunt on Easter or play a round of Colonial games on Thanksgiving. These activities can help make the time your kids get to spend with faraway relatives all the more memorable.

Make holiday parties hands-on: While parents are busy socializing, keep little hands occupied with a simple holiday craft, such as decorat-

ing Christmas cookies or making New Year's hats. Get older kids into the act by asking them to supervise the activity. The party crafts or foods make excellent take-home favors, too.

Create a festive atmosphere: To promote the holiday spirit, play music, such as a spooky sound track for a Halloween party or carols at a Christmas carnival. You might also greet guests at the door in costume, donning a Pilgrim hat for Thanksgiving or a red, white, and blue crown on the Fourth of July.

Deck your halls: A few jack-o'-lanterns, a Christmas tree, or an American flag may be all it takes to spruce up your home for a holiday party. Ask your kids to help you hang balloons and streamers in the holiday theme colors, too. Note: If you plan on hosting the same party next year, store your decorations in clearly labeled boxes. You might also stock up on decorations, which are often discounted the day after the holiday.

Don't overdo it: A party during the holidays can be a hit just by offering good food and good fellowship. So keep things simple. Use the holiday decorations you already have in place, serve dessert instead of a sit-down dinner, or phone friends to invite them to your party rather than sending out handcrafted invitations.

Halloween Party, page 288

New Year's Eve

PARTY STATS

Ages: All
Size: 8 to 20 guests
Length: 4 hours
Prep time: 2 hours
Cost: $2 per guest

O
N NEW YEAR'S EVE, have a ball with your kids and your friends — without ever leaving your home. With this party plan, you can time the festivities to begin well before midnight, allowing even the youngest revelers to join in. So invite a group of friends to put on silly hats, blow party horns, raise glasses, and toast to a happy New Year

Timely Decor

T
O DECORATE your house for a party on the last day of the year, don't hold back. Start with streamers, balloons, and Happy New Year banners, then litter the floor with confetti. Homemade hats and noisemakers are a must, too. To play up the countdown to midnight, pull out all your ticking clocks (shift midnight to an earlier hour if you'd like little ones to hit the sack early) and draw clock faces on all your balloons.

New Year's Eve

Party Drinks

WHEN ALL YOUR guests have arrived, toast to the New Year with a colorful cocktail.

New Year's Sunrise

- 4 ounces seltzer
- 6 ounces orange juice
- ½ ounce grenadine syrup
- 1 orange slice
- 1 lemon slice
- 1 Maraschino cherry
  Plastic toothpick

In a tall glass, mix the seltzer and orange juice. Slowly pour the grenadine into the center of the glass, allowing the syrup to settle on the bottom (which it does thanks to its greater density). Garnish with the orange, lemon, and cherry, stacked and skewered with the toothpick. Serves 1.

Triple-Red Shirley Temple

- 1 ounce grenadine syrup
- 6 ounces cranberry juice
- 4 ounces cranberry ginger ale
- 1 paper umbrella
- 3 Maraschino cherries
- ½ orange slice
  Ice (optional)

Mix the syrup, cranberry juice, and ginger ale in a tall glass. Open the umbrella and slide the cherries on the handle. Balance the umbrella on the glass rim in front of the orange slice. Serves 1.

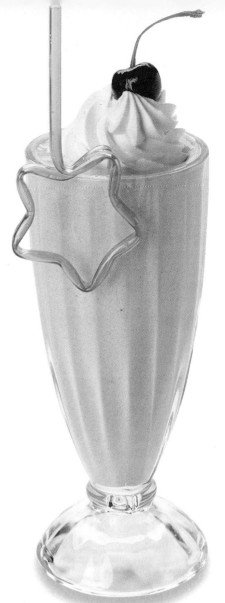

Strawberr Smoothi

Strawberry Smoothies

- ½ pint fresh strawberries
- 1 banana
- 2 8-ounce containers nonfat strawberry yogurt
- 1 cup lowfat milk

Wash the strawberries, hull them, and pat them dry. Peel the banana and slice it in quarters, then place all the fruit in an electric blender. Spoon the yogurt into the blender, the pour in the milk. Blend until smooth and thoroughly combined, about 1 to 2 minutes. Serves 4.

Party Hats

A NEW YEAR'S BASH calls for outrageous party hats. So set up a table with construction paper, glue, glitter, markers, and other craft supplies and let guests create their own. They can start with a crown, cone, or classic newspaper hat, then build from there, gluing on ornate ribbons, pom poms, or feathers.

New Year's Tree

A FTER YOU TAKE down the ornaments from your Christmas Tree, give it a New Year's makeover. Curl ribbon and make bows and tie them to the branches, along with party horns and balloons. Top the tree with New Year's party hats. This clever idea comes from reader Rhonda Johnstone of Pioneer, California. She points out the convenience of trimming your tree with what's essentially the makings of a New Year's party: "By the time the party's over, the tree will be undecorated!"

New Year's Tree

Stocking Up on Resolutions

Just as fun as making New Year's resolutions is seeing how close you did — or didn't — come to keeping them the year before. For a fun party activity, have guests write out their resolutions on slips of paper (and make predictions for their friends, too). Party guests can take the slips home and follow the lead of the Edgerley family, *FamilyFun* readers in Granville, Illinois. Every year, mom Mary, dad Philip, Emily, 12, Rachel, ten, and Philip, nine, pen their resolutions on New Year's Eve, then tuck them into their Christmas stockings before they're packed away. When the stockings come out of storage the next year, the kids pluck out the lists and put them aside until New Year's Eve when they are shared out loud and replaced with new ones. "It gives you something to look forward to," says Emily.

New Year's Eve

The Bubble Wrap Stomp

10. At midnight, each child should promenade down a flight of steps, number card held high, as the crowd yells out the number. As the last child hits the steps, the steamers should be blowing, the shakers shaking, and the cameras flashing.

The Bubble Wrap Stomp

HANDHELD SHAKERS are perfect for ringing (or rattling) in the New Year, but what if you want to guarantee that your entire party crowd is on its feet and dancing when the clock strikes midnight? Look no further than a packaging-supply store. For just a few dollars, says *FamilyFun* reader Elaine Snyder of Jupiter, Florida, you can pick up several yards of the large-bubbled bubble wrap used for shipping packages. (Or, simply recycle the bubble wrap that comes with holiday gifts.) Just before midnight, unroll the wrap on a hard surface, such as a wooden floor or driveway. When the New Year's countdown concludes, your guests can do the Bubble Wrap Stomp.

Countdown to Midnight

THE BEST COMMOTION on New Year's Eve comes not from the party horns but from excited kids. That's why *FamilyFun* reader Susan Mathews of Minnetonka, Minnesota, developed these countdown cards. During your party, invite the kids to decorate poster board cards by drawing and coloring in the numbers 1 through

Can't wait Till the Midnight Hour?

One advantage of making merry at home is that families with young children can perform some magic and shift midnight to an earlier hour. That way, sleepiness (and all that comes with it) won't undermine the celebration. Here are some fun ways to fool the clock.

☞ Gather all your alarm clocks and set them to go off at a designated time.

☞ Select one candle to be your timekeeper. When it burns down to the quick, the big hour has arrived.

☞ Set a kitchen timer for 30 minutes and turn off all the electric lights. By candlelight, talk about your hopes and resolutions for the year to come. When the bell rings, it's midnight, and everyone flips the lights back on and toasts to the New Year.

Confetti Balloons

To count down to New Year's, the Parmentiers, *FamilyFun* readers in Hudson, New York, host a clock party. Each guest brings an alarm clock, sets it to ring at midnight, and places it on the party table alongside confetti-filled balloons with clock faces. After painting their own faces, kids search for a ticking clock hidden in a room and play "mouse ran up the clock." (To play, a designated "grandfather clock" turns his back to the group and calls out an hour, and the "mice" race to take that number of steps before he turns around. Those who fail return to the starting line. The first mouse to "run up" the clock wins.) At midnight, the alarms ring, balloons pop, and everyone celebrates.

Confetti Balloons

BALLOONS ARE A MUST for a New Year's party with older kids. Not only do they make a big bang when popped at midnight, but — if they're filled with homemade confetti — they also make a festive and absolutely thrilling mess.

To prepare a batch of balloons for your party, set the kids to work punching circles out of brightly colored construction paper with a hole punch (if they aren't quickly captivated by this simple tool, have some store-bought confetti on hand as a backup).

Next, stuff the confetti into deflated balloons using a funnel. If you don't have a funnel, a plastic soda bottle cut in half works fine. For a twist, have the children write fortunes on small pieces of paper and slip them into the mix.

Blow up the balloons and hang them high, but still within reach of the children. A few moments before the appointed hour, hand each child a pin and, on the stroke of midnight, let the confetti fly.

Clock Face-Painting

Holiday Cheer

Valentine Workshop

VALENTINE'S DAY, as far as kids are concerned, doesn't call for roses and champagne. To them, saying "I Love You" means crafting silly cards, eating sweet stuff, and playing red-hot games. On February 14th, invite a group of mushballs under 12 to join in this kid-style celebration of love.

Sweet Nothing Invitations

SEND THIS sweet party messenger — a butterfly valentine invitation — to all your friends. To make one, place shoestring licorice "antennae" between two pieces of stick gum, taping the top and bottom closed to secure the antennae in place. Next cut two heart-shaped wings from construction paper, and write "Happy Valentine's Day" on the front and the party details on the back. Secure the wings in place with a heart sticker. Give the butterfly a face with more heart stickers.

Lovely Decor

ON VALENTINE'S DAY, your house should look as cute as Cupid. Start by outfitting the party room with balloons and streamers in the official colors of love — pink, white, and red. Tape construction paper hearts with romantic sayings to the walls. Finally, dress up the craft and lunch tables with red paper tablecloths, adding a bowl of conversation hearts in the center for nibbling.

Heart-Shaped Animal Masks

LOVE CAN COME in many disguises, as *FamilyFun* reader Lindy Schneider of Bozeman, Montana, and her family prove with these animal masks. (At the heart of each mask is — a heart!) Before your party, cut a pair of hearts from white poster board, making them large enough to cover a child's face. Carefully cut out eyeholes. Glue the two pieces together, sandwiching a tongue depressor or paint stirrer between them. Using this basic shape, invite guests to add elements to make various animal masks. To make the panda pictured at left, tape on paper ears and eyes, a heart nose, and a pink tongue.

Heart-Shaped Animal Mask

Heart Hunt

Valentine Workshop

Hunt for a Romantic Rock

Hold a family treasure hunt for heart-shaped rocks in the stoniest places near you: try a stream bank, a driveway, or the parking lot. The rocks don't have to be perfect — just close enough to paint rosy red for a sweetheart.

Red-Hot Games

KEEP SPIRITS HIGH at your party with a round of Valentine's Day games. Here are four simple ones you can choose from.

Heart Hunt: For little kids, stage a heart hunt, planting conversation hearts (or construction paper hearts) all around the house. The object: Have the kids find as many hearts as they can.

The And Game: This word game is just right for Valentine's Day. It's called The And Game since it's all about words that appear together with *and* in between. I say, "Romeo and …"

Spin Art Heart

Hearts

You say, "Juliet." I say, "Bread and …" You have to come up with "butter." After five, switch roles.

Kind Things: Here's a good game for siblings. Set the timer and see how many kind things you can write down about a person in, say, 3 minutes. You might suggest writing down generous things the person has done or nice things about the way he or she acts, thinks, plays, works, or looks. Done right, this game will clear the air of sibling rivalry for the afternoon.

Hearts: Remember that card game where you either avoid winning any hearts or "shoot the moon" and collect all of them? Hearts is a great one for today. If you don't already know how to play it, you can find the directions in a card game book.

Valentine Crafts

INVITE GUESTS to get a little crafty — and romantic — by making these valentines to take home.

Spin Art Hearts: Put a new spin on the traditional valentine with this salad spinner art sent in by Kellie Weenink, a *FamilyFun* reader in Parma, Ohio. First line the bottom of an old salad spinner with a paper plate. Pour small amounts of red, pink, and purple liquid tempera paint on the plate's surface, close the spinner's top, and whirl away. Remove the plate. Once the paint is dry, cut it into a heart shape (use novelty craft scissors for a different edge). Write a poem or saying on the back and give it to your heart's desire.

Lollipop Mice: These whiskered sweet nothings tote along lollipops, making them the perfect valentines to give to pint-size suckers for love. Since these cards — just like real mice — are easily multiplied, they're a good bet for classrooms and play groups.

From stiff colored paper, cut out a bunch of hearts, about 4 inches across. On each, draw a nose and eyes. Punch four holes above the mouse's nose. Thread a short length of pipe cleaner through the top two holes and another through the bottom two. Lastly, slip a lollipop (either flat or round) down behind the whiskers.

A Lovely Menu

THE FASTEST way to your guests' hearts may be through their stomachs. Hence, your Valentine's Day party foods should be littered with expressions of affection. Serve heart-shaped sandwiches (cut with a cookie cutter) or pizza (shape pizza dough into a heart) along with Love Potion and Painted Heart Cookies.

Love Potion

   ½ cup frozen strawberries
   ½ cup frozen raspberries
   1 cup white grape or apple juice
   Maraschino cherries

Lollipop Mice

Slightly thaw the strawberries and raspberries, then place them in a blender along with the juice. Mix on high until you have a uniform color. Garnish with cherries. Serves 2.

Painted Heart Cookies

With edible paint, you can turn an old staple — heart-shaped cookies — into valentine canvases. First mix up your favorite sugar cookie recipe, cut out the heart shapes, and refrigerate until ready to paint and bake. To make each color of paint, mix 1 egg yolk and ¼ teaspoon water. Add a few drops of food coloring until you've reached the desired shade. Using a clean paintbrush, paint onto the uncooked sugar cookie dough, then bake according to recipe directions.

Love Potion and Painted Heart Cookies

Tiny Treat Bags

Each year the Graham kids, *FamilyFun* readers in Pleasant Grove, Utah, design, package, and label a card-and -treat-in-one valentine for classmates. For the labels, they use rubber stamps on card stock, then they fill small plastic bags with valentine candies. They seal them with a staple — and a kiss.

Easter Party

T HE MAGIC OF EASTER lies not only in the religious traditions but also in the excitement of a new season. With the scent of spring comes renewal — fresh greenery, warm breezes, and tulips in the yard. This Easter, invite friends and family to celebrate all things spring by dressing up like bunny rabbits, nibbling on carrot cake, and running around the yard in an eggs-traordinary egg hunt.

Spring Invitations

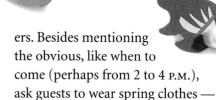

Spring Invitations

F OR SIMPLE, inexpensive invitations, have your kids trace cookie-cutter shapes of chicks or rabbits onto construction paper and decorate them with markers and stick- ers. Besides mentioning the obvious, like when to come (perhaps from 2 to 4 P.M.), ask guests to wear spring clothes — Easter hats optional.

Decorations

Tulips, daffodils, and other early bloomers will go a long way toward sprucing up your house for an Easter party. For extra credit, hang pastel balloons on your walk- way and a dec- orated card- board egg on your door.

Bunny Disguises

Bunny Bag

Easter Egg Hunt

A FEW DAYS BEFORE your party, fill plastic eggs with small toys, jelly beans, and wrapped candies — about 12 eggs per party guest. On the morning of the party, hide all the plastic eggs for the hunt. You may want to divide your yard into two areas — the front yard for the youngest children to hunt in and the backyard for the older kids. Hide the eggs for the younger crowd in low branches, soft, open places, and easy-to-reach crannies. For the older kids, show no mercy when hiding the eggs. Tuck them in pipes, under leaves, and around corners.

Along with the plastic eggs, hide a few special, decorative eggs in difficult-to-find spots. These eggs are not the prizes, but chits the lucky finders carry to the host, who then exchanges them for chocolate bunnies, sugared eggs, or, if you're sugar averse, stuffed animals or Peter Rabbit books.

At the sound of the whistle, send the kids scurrying for Easter eggs. The hunt ends when the last egg is uncovered.

Bunny Bags

IF PARTY GUESTS are going to put all their Easter eggs in one basket, this big-eared Bunny Bag is the one. As guests arrive, invite them to make bags for collecting eggs during the hunt. Begin by cutting a U shape about 4 inches deep down the middle of the top of a paper lunch bag (while holding it closed). Open the bag and cut the sides down even with the bottom of the U. Glue the resulting flaps together, front to back, to create ear loop handles. Glue on two googly eyes. Cut ear, whisker, and teeth shapes from construction paper and glue them on, as shown. Finally, add a cotton ball nose and a cotton tail.

Margie Luttrell's Annual Egg Hunt

Every Easter, a swarm of 50 kids scatters in *FamilyFun* reader Margie Luttrell's yard in Knoxville, Tennessee, scouting for Easter eggs under bushes, down paths, and beneath stones. Beforehand, Margie and a couple of friends fill some 2,000 plastic eggs with candy and prizes and hide half in the front yard for the little kids and the other half in the backyard for the big kids. Friends bring their own baskets and food to share. Margie likes to start the hunt after the guests have sampled the food and the children have begun to paw the ground like racehorses. Then the countdown begins, and egg mania erupts.

Easter Party

Bunny Disguises

AN EASTER PARTY need not be a formal affair, but a few guests may want to wear tails — not to mention ears and noses. Here's how to make them.

Bunny Nose: Cut a cup from an egg carton, leaving a tab of extra material on one side for teeth. Trim the cup's edges and paint the teeth white,

Bunny Tail: Form batting into a cottontail, then sew a length of yarn through it with an embroidery needle. Tie the yarn around your child's waist.

Easter Plates

HERE'S AN ESPECIALLY festive, and disposable, party plate to hold all your rabbit chow, from spring veggies and dip to the Mr. McGregor's Garden Cake at right.

To make one party plate, cut two semicircular ear shapes from the sides of a paper plate. Staple them to the back of another plate, as shown. Make four cuts down the side of a muffin cup and fold two sections to the center to create a bow tie. Staple in place. Add jelly bean eyes. Cut whiskers from a third, smaller plate and teeth from white paper. Place them in the center of the plate with a chocolate kiss nose (until the food is served).

Bunny Disguises

drawing a black gap between them. Glue on a pom-pom nose. For whiskers, cut pipe cleaners into three pieces. Poke three holes on either side of the nose with a pencil, then feed the pipe cleaner whiskers through the holes. Make air vents with a hole punch along the cup's bottom. Keep the nose on tight with an elastic band knotted through holes poked in the cup's sides.

Bunny Ears: Cut out the edges of the egg carton top and glue them to a headband with a glue gun (parents only).

Bunny Ears

Easter Plate

Mr. McGregor's Garden Cake

LIKE HIS COUSIN Peter Rabbit, the Easter Bunny has been known to steal vegetables from Mr. McGregor's patch. On this garden carrot cake, the almond Easter Bunny nibbles marzipan cabbages, carrots, and radishes.

CARROT CAKE:

  3 eggs
  1¼ cups corn oil
  1⅓ cups packed brown sugar
  2 teaspoons baking soda
  2 teaspoons cinnamon
  ½ teaspoon salt
  2 cups all-purpose flour
  1 8-ounce can crushed pineapple in
    natural syrup
  ⅓ cup shredded coconut
  1 cup coarsely chopped walnuts
  3 cups grated carrots (about 4
    carrots)

CREAM CHEESE FROSTING:

  ½ cup unsalted butter, softened to
    room temperature
  ½ cup cream cheese, softened to room
    temperature
  2½ to 3 cups sifted confectioners' sugar
  1 tablespoon fresh lemon juice
    Green food coloring

DECORATIONS:

  3 tablespoons crushed chocolate
    cookies
  Marzipan rabbits and vegetables
    (see recipe at right)

To make the carrot cake, preheat the oven to 350°. Grease and flour a 13- by 9- by 2-inch pan. In a large bowl, beat the eggs, oil, and brown sugar until well blended. In a separate bowl, sift the

Mr. McGregor's Garden Cake

baking soda, cinnamon, salt, and flour, then gradually add it to the egg mixture; do not overmix. Add the pineapple and syrup, coconut, walnuts, and carrots, and beat well.

Pour the batter into the prepared pan and bake for 45 to 55 minutes, or until a toothpick inserted in the center comes out clean. Cool in the pan for 10 to 15 minutes. Invert onto a cooling rack and cool completely.

Meanwhile, mix up the cream cheese frosting. In the bowl of an electric mixer, cream the butter and cream cheese until fluffy. Add the remaining frosting ingredients and beat until smooth.

Ice the cooled cake and sprinkle the crushed cookies on top for "dirt." Add the bunnies and rows of marzipan vegetables. Serves 12 to 14.

Marzipan Decorations

To make the cake decorations, break about 14 ounces of marzipan into balls and knead in dabs of food coloring paste, leaving a few balls uncolored for the bunnies. Next mold the marzipan like clay into orange carrots with green tops, red cabbage, green lettuce, red radishes, and white Flopsy, Mopsy, and Cottontail.

Fourth of July

INDEPENDENCE DAY was the first date to be declared an American holiday, preceding even Thanksgiving. From the start, it sparked unbridled revels with ship cannon salutes, resounding bells, and firecrackers. In this party, we're following those time-honored leads, kicking off July with a day full of high-spirited relay races, a homespun parade, and a feast of summertime foods.

Patriotic Spirit

Over the years, communities have come up with unique ways of celebrating the Fourth of July. Since 1818, the townsfolk of Lititz, Pennsylvania, have illuminated the local park with 7,000 candles. In the 1940s, a two-mile-long picnic table bordered the parade route in Ontario, California. And today on the streets of Bristol, Rhode Island, red, white, and blue stripes replace the yellow traffic lines.

A Grand Old Parade

FOURTH OF JULY parades have been a tradition since the Liberty Bell rang in 1776. Start your party by participating in a local parade or staging your own neighborhood event. Festive hats, makeshift drums, and an independence banner will get the holiday march off on the right foot.

Before the party, make a parade banner on a large sheet of butcher paper. With red and blue markers, write "Happy Independence Day." When guests arrive, have them sign in by adding their names to the mural. Once everyone is accounted for and the sign is complete, elect two people to hold the banner and lead the parade.

Distribute whatever musical instruments you have on hand, including drums, kazoos, pots, pans, and spoons. When the orchestra is assembled, set up a portable stereo or boom box and crank up "Yankee Doodle," "The Stars and Stripes Forever," and so on, encouraging everyone to play and parade around.

Parade Banner

282

Firecracker Hats

WITH THIS QUICK and inexpensive design, you can easily outfit a crowd of paraders with hats that will flutter as they march.

First unfold two full sheets of newspaper one atop the other as if you were reading them. From here, treat them as a single two ply sheet.

To make the brow band, use a ruler to mark a line that measures 3½ inches from the bottom edge of the sheet and fold up along that line. Roll the band up once more and flatten the fold. Paint the brow band blue. When dry, paint broad red and white stripes on the flip side of the newspaper (this will be the inside of the hat). While waiting for the paint to dry, cut star shapes from white construction paper.

Fit the hat by wrapping the brow band (painted side out) around a child's head and taping the overlap securely. At this point, the hat should resemble a tall cylinder. Decorate the brow by gluing on the white stars. Finally, use scissors to fringe the top of the hat, making cuts (an inch apart) that extend halfway down the cylinder.

Firecracker Hat

Coffee Can Drum

Coffee Can Drums

KIDS MARCH to a different drummer when banging on these crafty cans. To make one, use white paint to decorate a piece of red construction paper with stars. Then invert an empty coffee can and wrap and glue the paper around it, leaving an inch of overhang for fringe. Punch two holes into the can's sides with a nail (a parent's job) and string with ribbon. Now grab wooden spoon drumsticks and let the marching band begin.

Flag Face-Painting

Show your patriotic streak at the Fourth of July parade by dabbing on red, white, and blue face paint. Use water-based face paint to draw a flag, complete with stars and stripes, over your child's cheeks, nose, and forehead.

Fourth of July

Egg and Wooden Spoon Race

Stars and Stripes T-Shirts

Set up an area where kids can decorate star-spangled T-shirts. On a picnic table covered with newspaper, set out white T-shirts, cardboard, star fruit (or potato star stamps), and red and blue fabric paint. Insert the cardboard inside the T-shirts to create a flat surface. Then pour the paint into pie tins. Slice the star fruit in half and dry the cut surfaces with paper towels. Dip the fruit (or potato) into the paint and press stars on the shirt. To heat-set the design, follow package instructions.

Balloon Brigade

THIS FAST-PACED race lets winners go out with a real bang. Before the start, each team assembles in single file with the first player in each line holding a balloon.

Balloon Brigade

When the whistle blows, each lead player passes the balloon between her legs to the next person in line. Each recipient in turn passes the balloon overhead to the teammate directly behind her. The balloon is passed alternately between players' legs and over players' heads all the way down the line. When the last person receives the balloon, he or she races to the front of the line and the balloon pass resumes. The relay continues until one of the original lead players regains position at the front of her line and pops the team balloon.

Egg and Wooden Spoon Race

A FEW HARD-BOILED eggs (either plain or decorated), two wooden spoons, and two team flags are needed for this relay. Each team stands in single file behind the starting line and opposite their respective flags, set in the ground about 5 yards away. At the whistle, the first

284

player in each line, balancing an egg on a spoon, races around his team's flag, then back to transfer the egg and the spoon to the next teammate. The recipient races to the flag, and the race continues until one team finishes the course. Anyone who drops an egg must run to the start line for another before resuming.

Popcorn Relay

Popcorn Relay

FANCY FOOTWORK is the ticket to success in this event, which is as much fun to watch as it is to run in. Beforehand, prepare a pair of plastic or paper cups for each runner. Use a tack to poke a hole in the center of each cup bottom. Push one end of a thick rubber band through the hole and into the cup. Then slip a paper clip on the end of the band inside the cup, and gently pull the other end until the clip rests on the bottom of the cup. The rubber band, worn around the foot, holds the cup in place atop the shoe.

Just prior to the race, a member from each team is issued a big bag of popcorn and charged with filling teammates' cups from the moment the starting whistle blows until the relay ends. These individuals stand alongside their teams behind the starting line. Two large, shallow boxes are set 5 yards beyond the starting line, opposite the teams.

When the whistle blows, the first person in each line gets his cups filled, sprints to the team box, and empties his cups into it, trying to lose as little popcorn as possible along the way. He then runs back to tag the next person in line. The new runner heads to the team box, and the first runner goes to the end of the line. The relay continues for 2 minutes, or until one of the popcorn bags is emptied. Then the popcorn in each box is measured, and the team with the most is declared the winner.

Fourth of July

Ring Toss

Ring Toss

FOR THIS GAME, contestants need the tossing skills of a Frisbee player and the good aim of a seasoned horseshoe pitcher.

For the scoring poles, you'll need nine dowels. Set them in the ground in three rows, each composed of three dowels and spaced 2 feet apart. Decorate the planted poles by wrapping them with red, white, and blue crepe paper streamers.

For the rings (three per team), use a dozen sturdy paper plates. You can either purchase colored plates or spray-paint plain ones. Cut out a large circle from the center of each plate. Then place two of the plates face to face and tape them together all the way around the rims. Repeat to make five more rings.

During the game, members from both teams have three attempts each to toss a ring around one of the poles. (It's fun to alternate turns between the two teams.) Kids should be allowed to stand a little closer to the poles than their adult teammates.

A ring that lands around a pole in the nearest row is worth 10 points; a ringer in the middle row earns 20 points; a ringer in the far row earns 30 points. The team that accumulates the most points wins.

Red, White, & Blueberry Shortcake

If you're going to
raise a toast to the
Stars and Stripes,
you'll want to do it
with something daz-
zling and delicious —
like this red, white,
and blueberry float.
Fill a tall, frosty glass
three quarters of the
way with raspberry
soda. Float a large
scoop of vanilla ice
cream on top and gar-
nish with a handful of
blueberries and a
strawberry, festive
decorations, and an
American flag. Serve
with a straw and a
long spoon.

Red, White, & Blueberry Shortcake

T HIS RECIPE MIXES up the
best of the red, white, and
blue — fresh strawberries, blueberries, and whipped cream spooned
over shortcake.

- 5 cups all-purpose flour
- 4 teaspoons baking powder
- ½ teaspoon salt
- 1 teaspoon nutmeg
- ¼ cup sugar
- ½ cup margarine or shortening
- 2 cups milk
- 2 quarts fresh strawberries, sliced
- ½ cup sugar
- 1 pint whipping cream
- 2 tablespoons maple syrup
- 1 pint fresh blueberries

Preheat the oven to 425°. Sift the
flour, baking powder, salt, nutmeg, and
¼ cup of sugar in a large bowl. Using a
pastry cutter, mix the margarine and dry
ingredients until they resemble a coarse
meal. Stir in the milk until the mixture
holds together. Turn the dough onto a
floured surface and pat it into a 1-inch-
thick circle. Use a biscuit cutter to cut
out the shortcakes. Arrange them 1½
inches apart on an ungreased baking
sheet. Bake for 10 to 12 minutes.

Place the sliced strawberries in a large bowl.
Sprinkle with
the ½ cup of sugar. Stir,
cover, and refrigerate
until the berries release
juices and make a syrup.
Next use an electric mixer
to whip the cream and maple syrup in
a chilled stainless steel bowl.

To assemble, split the biscuits in half.
Spoon the strawberries and syrup onto
the bottoms. Cover with the remaining
shortcake halves and spoon more of
the strawberries on top. Top with the
whipped cream and garnish with fresh
blueberries. Serves 10 to 12.

**Fourth of
July Float**

Halloween Party

HALLOWEEN HAS ALWAYS been one of our favorite holidays. The problem is, after all that costume-making, decorating, and anticipation, it's over in a one-hour trick-or-treat spree. With this party, you can make the holiday last much longer. Invite friends to show off their costumes, gobble creepy cuisine, and play wickedly fun games — they'll take home lots of memories along with their candy hoard.

PARTY STATS
Ages: All
Size: 8 to 20 guests
Length: 2 hours
Prep time: 3 hours
Cost: $4 per guest

Haunting Your House

Besides creepy jack-o'-lanterns, every haunted house should have any of the following:

☞ A spooky sound track
☞ Fake spiderwebs
☞ Plastic insects
☞ Monster footprints (cut from poster board or sponge-painted)
☞ A mummy-wrapped scarecrow
☞ Dead flowers
☞ Furniture covered with sheets
☞ Black lights (shining on glow-in-the-dark creatures)
☞ Helium balloon ghosts (drape balloons with sheets and tie at the neck)
☞ Cardboard box coffin

Velcome to our Haunted House

A FEW WEEKS before your Halloween bash, phone friends and invite them to come to your diabolical mansion, dressed in costume, on Halloween Eve or the weekend before or after fright night.

Spooky Decor

MOODY LIGHTING, haunting music, and a few well-placed homemade decorations set the scene for your Halloween bash. Avoid anything with a flame and keep in mind that costumes make kids clumsy — anything fragile or sharp should be moved. Here are a few decorations to get you started.

Giggly Gravestones: It's a not-so-grave sight when guests step into a silly cemetery in your front yard. Cut gravestones out of cardboard, paint them gray, and inscribe them with funny epitaphs, such as Scared E. Cat. On the night of the party, attach garden stakes to the backs of the stones with duct tape and plant them in the yard, tipping some at odd angles for that seventeenth-century look. Partly bury a hat or boots in the front of each stone, so it looks as if the deceased may rise to the occasion.

Furry Spiders: A doorway web filled with furry arachnids is sure to stop guests in their tracks. For each spider, you'll need four pipe cleaners, a four-hole button, and a pair of stick-on googly eyes. To begin, bend a pipe cleaner into a V shape. Push the base of the V up through one of the button holes until it protrudes ½ inch. Then bend the ½-inch length over the top of the button. Use the same method to thread the three other pipe cleaners through the remaining button holes.

Next shape the eight legs by bending the pipe cleaner ends first 1 inch from the button and then again ¼ inch from the tips. Stick the googly eyes onto the button between the front legs. For a web, use a synthetic stretching spiderweb (sold at most novelty shops for under $2). Then set your spiders in the web wherever you like — their legs will stick easily to the fibers.

Furry Spiders

Spooky Decor

Halloween Party

Left Foot Cat, Right Foot Bat

FamilyFun reader Deborah Lee-Quinn of Belleville, Illinois, made this truly twisted Halloween party game, a spooky version of Twister. Using fabric paint, Jonathan, age ten, and Erik, age six, helped mom Deborah paint rows of cats, bats, pumpkins, and ghosts on a 4- by 4-foot piece of felt, then made a corresponding spinner out of poster board. With five kids playing Halloween Twister, it was a tangled web of arms and legs.

Frightening Fun

AT YOUR HALLOWEEN bash, plan more events than you think you need (and some for bad weather, too). In addition to the following games, prepare easy backups: bobbing for apples, painting Halloween murals or pumpkins, or dancing to spooky sounds.

Costume Parade: When all the guests have arrived, organize a terror-raising march in the backyard or around the block to show off everyone's ghoulish gear. Turn on a spooky sound track to start the march — and don't forget to take photographs.

Pin the Wart on the Witch: Hang a picture of a witch at kid's-eye level on the wall, then wad up modeling clay into gumball-size "warts." Blindfolded, kids take turns trying to stick the wart on the witch's nose.

The Mummy Wrap: Divide the kids into teams of two, give each pair a roll of toilet paper, and instruct one member of each team to race to wrap his partner, mummy style, at the sound of a screech. Kids must use up the whole roll, avoiding the head and wrapping arms separately from the torso. Once wrapped, the mummy yells "mummy wrap!" Award the winning team, reverse partners' roles, and start again.

Boo Am I? To put a frenzied twist on a traditional game of charades, write out clues for Halloween characters on slips of paper (Frankenstein, a mummy, a mad scientist, Dracula, a skeleton, a cat, a bat, a rat, and so on). Put each slip inside white "ghost" balloons, blow up the balloons, and set them aside. Divide the kids into two teams. The first player has three minutes to choose a balloon, pop it, read the clue inside, and silently act it out until her team guesses the clue. The child to guess correctly picks the next balloon.

Eyeball Relay: Before the party, make the eyeballs (you'll need at least six for each team). Use colored markers to draw irises, pupils, and bloodshot veins on Ping-Pong balls. To play, set a chair across the room from each team. Have the first player on each team cup his hands and fill them with eyeballs. On cue, those players must race around their team's chair and back to hand off their eyeballs to the next teammate in line. Eyeballs that are dropped in the transfer must be retrieved before the second runner can head for the chair. The first team whose members all complete the course wins.

Eyeball Relay

Costume Parade

Ghost Storytelling: In a jack-o'-lantern-lit room, a ghost (parent in costume) gathers storytellers into a circle and starts spinning a spooky yarn into a handheld tape recorder: "One night, Mr. Bonapart heard the sound of heavy footsteps in his attic. With every step, the house rattled …" She then passes the tape recorder to a child, who improvises what happened next ("The man couldn't take the noise, so he went upstairs with a bat…"). Once each child has had a chance to speak, the ghost rewinds the tape, and the gang listens to the story. Older kids enjoy the added challenge of pulling an object (a feather, dog collar, mirror, and whatever else you can round up) out of a box and incorporating the item into the story.

Freaky Hair

This activity will make your guests' hair stand on end. Spread out a white sheet on the floor or on a bed, then have a child lie down on it. Help the child fan out his or her hair (have a wig on hand for the crew-cut contingent). Invite the child to make his or her most gruesome Halloween face while you take a Polaroid picture from directly above. When the photo develops, write the child's name on it, use it as a place card for the party table, and then send it home as a party favor.

DEVON

Halloween Party

Spider Pretzels

It's easy to make these arachnid treats, and they look positively lifelike crawling all over the table. Spread two crackers with peanut butter and insert eight pretzel stick legs into

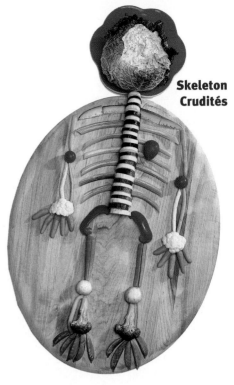

the filling. With a dab of peanut butter, set two raisin eyes on top.

Monster Operating Table:

In this gooey game, a parent made up as a monster sits at the end of an operating table as young physicians (party guests) examine his ghoulish guts. To make the body, arrange food on a picnic table to resemble a skeleton, minus the head (which, after all, belongs to a dad).

For arms, thighs, and shins, use zucchini; a turnip, split in half, makes excellent kneecaps. Use toothpicks to pin a celery rib cage together; secure dried apricot toes to celery feet; and attach baby corn fingernails to hotdog fingers. Just below the rib cage, pile cooked spaghetti (small intestines) and licorice ropes (large intestines). Below the intestines, fill a pie plate with Jell-O (guts). Add water chestnut gallstones and a water balloon heart.

Skeleton Crudités

When the organs are in place, secure them to the table with duct tape. Top with an old sheet and cut slits so the kids can reach in and touch the organs without being able to see them. Next position the live monster as close to the head of the table as possible, sitting on a chair. To create the illusion that the head is connected to the body, drape a second sheet over the monster's shoulders. Now invite the guests to operate on his guts.

Creepy Cuisine

A HALLOWEEN PARTY cries out for a perfectly inelegant menu. Start with Skeleton Crudités followed by deviled egg sandwiches cut with Halloween cookie cutters. For dessert, serve up the Witch's House Cake.

Skeleton Crudités

To make the vegetable platter, prep the freshest vegetables you can find the day before the party and store them, soaked in water, in the refrigerator. When you're ready, just drain and pat dry, and arrange on a platter as shown above. For

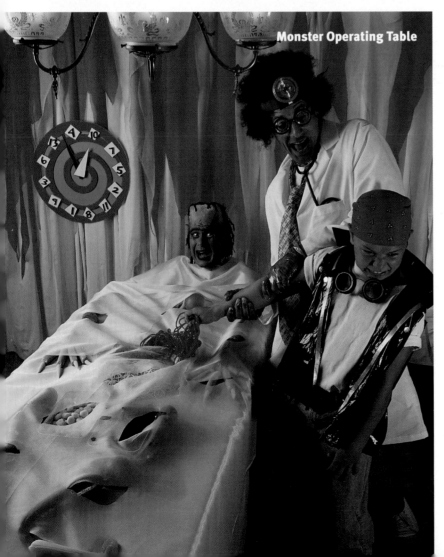

Monster Operating Table

a gruesome noggin, fill a cabbage head with your favorite dip for brains.

Witch's House Cake

When guests dig into this devilishy delicious cake, it will be love at first bite.

- 3 baked devil's food cakes: a 13- by 9- by 2-inch, an 8-inch round cake baked in an ovenproof bowl, and a 6-inch loaf
- 4 cups chocolate frosting
- 1 cup orange frosting
  Decorations: green gumdrops, chocolate graham crackers and cones, peanut butter sandwich cookies, black shoestring and twist licorice, chocolate kisses, mini chocolate chips, green hard candies, mini marshmallows, and chocolate-covered raisins

Cover a large cutting board with foil. Place the 13- by 9- by 2-inch cake on top to create the "graveyard." On one end, place the bowl-shaped cake "hill." Ice the graveyard and hill with chocolate frosting. Cut a 2- by 3-inch rectangle, about 1 inch deep, on top of the hill to accommodate the house.

Turn the loaf cake into a house by cutting the corners off one end to form a peaked roof. Place the house in the 2- by 3-inch slot and "paint" with orange frosting. Tile the roof with chocolate graham crackers and frosting. Add scary details: windows made of broken chocolate cones with orange icing grids and a peanut cookie door with a candy doorknob. Surround the house with shoestring licorice barbed wire. Add a flying witch (a gumdrop face with a chocolate kiss hat on a licorice broomstick).

To create gravestones, break peanut cookies in half and pipe on spooky sayings with orange frosting (R.I.P.,

Boo, and so on). Secure in the muddy frosting. Next make ghosts in the trees (cut crooked branches in a piece of licorice and add mini marshmallow ghosts with mini chocolate chip eyes), then plant the trees in the mud. Next draw a crooked path from the base of the cake up to the witch's door with a toothpick. Outline the path with chocolate-covered raisins, then sprinkle with broken green hard candies. At the entrance, add a chocolate graham cracker drawbridge. Finally, outline the yard with broken chocolate cone fencing. Set the house in a place for all to see — and scream about.

Witch's House Cake

Monster Paws

Your kids won't wait to get their hands on these popcorn-stuffed party favors, recommended by *FamilyFun* reader Julie Peters of Lakewood, Colorado. Begin with washed clear plastic gloves (available at beauty supply stores). Stick one candy corn at the tip of each finger, pointy side up, for fingernails. Fill the glove with popcorn. Tie a bow at the wrist with ribbon.

Thanksgiving Feast

PARTY STATS

Ages: All
Size: 8 to 20 guests
Length: 4 hours
Prep time: 3 hours
Cost: $5 per guest

THIS THANKSGIVING, we're dishing up the perfect dressing for your family's turkey day — a collection of easy-to-make decorations and treats for your holiday table, ranging from personalized Pilgrim place cards to chocolately Pilgrim hats. Plenty, we think you'll agree, to satisfy the whole Thanksgiving crowd.

Pilgrim Place Cards

HERE'S A POP-UP card design your kids can use to transform their thumbprints into Pilgrim portraits that resemble your dinner guests. Then everyone can find his or her place, and face, at the dinner table.

Cut out a 5- by 4-inch rectangle from the card stock for each place card plus 1 extra. Fold each card in half so that the 4-inch edges meet and flatten the crease. Then reopen all of the cards.

In the center of the extra card, draw a Pilgrim hat, positioning it so that the top is above the fold and the brim is just below it, as shown. Cut it out and use it as a template, tracing it in pencil onto the centers of the remaining cards (again, trace the top of each hat above the fold and the brim just below it).

Once all of the hats are drawn, have your child lightly coat her thumb with skin-toned tempera paint and print a Pilgrim's head below each hat (have her practice a few times on scrap paper first).

When the paint is dry, your child can use the markers to color in the hats, draw on collars, add facial features and hairdos that resemble those of specific family members, and print their names. Then she can adorn each hat with a glitter-glue buckle.

Finally, use a craft knife to cut along the outer edge of each hat top but not around the brim (a parent's job). Refold the cards, gently pulling up the hat tops to stand upright, as shown, and they're ready to set in place on the dinner table.

Pilgrim Place Cards

key Hats

Thanksgiving Feast

Kernels of Thanks

Every Thanksgiving, the Suits family of Zeeland, Michigan, sets the table with a few Indian corn kernels at each place. Before dinner, everyone takes a turn telling what he or she is thankful for while dropping the kernels into a little basket (one thought per kernel). "As we hear what each family member is grateful for," says Diane, "we think about how blessed we truly are!"

Turkey Hats

PUT A FEATHER in your cap (and everyone else's at your holiday feast) with this festive chapeau.

Scissors
Brown paper bags
Cardboard (cereal box)
Glue stick
Colored construction paper
2 small white pom-poms
Black permanent marker

From the brown paper bags, cut a circle 3½ inches in diameter for the turkey's head. Next, cut a 3-inch-wide band to fit around your child's head. From the cardboard, cut a strip 5 by 1½ inches to use for a neck. Fold it three times accordion style, then glue one end to the back of the paper circle.

For a beak, fold yellow construction paper and cut out a small double triangle (1½ inches along the fold). Cut a rounded *L* from red paper for the turkey's wattle. To create eyes, draw a black circle on each pom-pom with the marker. Glue the eyes, wattle, and one side of the beak to the head. Let them dry. Then, glue the loose end of the neck to the center of the headband.

Indian Corn Napkin Rings

HISTORIANS SAY the Pilgrims might not have survived their first winter after settling in North America if local Indian tribes had not taught them to grow corn. That's why we think these corny napkin

Turkey Hats

Indian Corn Napkin Ring

rings make a fitting addition to your holiday table. The colorful kernels are stamped with a pencil eraser — a technique even young kids can easily master.

Craft knife and ruler
Cardboard tissue tubes
Red, yellow, and blue acrylic or
   tempera paints
Paper or plastic plate
New pencil with an eraser top
Newspaper

Using a craft knife, cut the tissue tubes into 2½-inch sections (a parent's job). You'll need 1 for each napkin ring. Trim the edges smooth with scissors.

Next, pour small amounts of the 3 paint colors onto a paper or plastic plate. Now show your child how to dip the pencil eraser into some paint and practice stamping corn kernel shapes onto newspaper.

Once he's mastered the printing technique, have your child hold the bottom of a tube section and print rows of kernels all around the top half, mixing the colors. Then have him set the tube on end to dry while he prints the tops of the other tubes in the same manner. After the paint dries, he can pick up each napkin ring and print kernels on the unpainted half.

Thanksgiving Treats

IF YOU WANT to hatch a novel holiday dessert that your kids can help make, these tasty treats fit the bill. They're also great for classroom parties.

Gobbling Good Cupcakes

24 frosted cupcakes
24 Nutter Butter cookies
2 to 3 tablespoons of white frosting or decorators' gel
Mini chocolate chips
Fruit leather
Wooden toothpicks

To make each turkey, press the lower portion of a Nutter Butter cookie into a frosted cupcake for the bird's head. Use tiny dabs of frosting to stick on mini chocolate chip eyes and a red fruit leather wattle. For the turkey's tail, use a butter knife to cut out a dozen feather shapes (about 3 inches long by ¾ inch wide) from fruit leather. Lay 6 of the

feather shapes on a flat surface and place a wooden toothpick atop each so that one end extends about ½ inch below the feather. Layer another feather shape atop each of the first ones, sandwiching the toothpicks between them. Press the 2 layers together to make them stick, then fringe the edges of the feathers with a butter knife. Now your child can stick the colored feathers into the cupcake behind the cookie head.

Marshmallow Pilgrim Hats

24 chocolate-striped shortbread cookies
12-ounce package of chocolate chips
24 marshmallows
Tube of yellow decorators' frosting

Set the chocolate-striped shortbread cookies stripes down on a waxed paper–covered tray, spacing them well apart. Melt the chocolate chips in a microwave or double boiler. One at a time, stick a wooden toothpick into a marshmallow, dip the marshmallow into the melted chocolate, and promptly center it atop a cookie. Using a second toothpick to lightly hold down the marshmallow, carefully pull out the first toothpick. Chill the hats until the chocolate sets, then pipe a yellow decorators' frosting buckle on the front of each hat.

Table for Four

When *FamilyFun* reader Eileen Allen offered to host Thanksgiving at her home in Draper, Utah, her kids were thrilled until they realized they would have to sit at the kids' table. So mom Eileen suggested they decorate it. Brent and Adam wrapped the table legs with crepe paper and then made canvas place mats. Eileen picked up silly straws, candy kisses, and napkin holders. Needless to say, the kids' table was the most popular seat in the house.

Christmas Carnival

**PARTY
STATS**
Ages: All
Size: 8 to 20
guests
Length: 2 to
3 hours
Prep time:
3 hours
Cost: $4 to $6
per guest

THE ENTHUSIASM that takes hold of kids from November to December makes them the perfect guests for a holiday celebration. Our gathering capitalizes on those high spirits with a round-robin of the season's best — quick crafts, silly games, and the merriest snacks this side of the North Pole.

Invitations

**Christmas Carnival
Invitation**

THIS SNAZZY Christmas tree collage makes a charming party invitation — but its real beauty lies in the fact that kids of all age groups, from toddlers to teens, can enjoy crafting it. Simply cut angled shapes from tissue paper, construction paper, leftover wrapping paper, or your children's recycled artwork, then glue them onto a picture of a tree on another piece of paper. Write the party details on the inside in green ink. You can either color-copy the invitation or handcraft one for each family.

Deck the Halls

IN ADDITION to the tree (which is a party must), you and your kids can deck the halls, walls, and stairways with sprigs of holly and mistletoe, Christmas lights, and jingle bells. For a sweet wreath, tie an assortment of hard candies in their wrappers and a small pair of scissors to a ready-made wreath. As party guests arrive, they can snip off the sweets one at a time.

**Sweet
Wreath**

Santa's Workshop

KEEP THE LITTLE elves busy at your party with one or two of the following holiday crafts.
Cardboard Gingerbread People: For a clever ornament, invite guests to decorate cardboard "cookies." To make one, trace a holiday cookie cutter on corrugated cardboard and cut with an X-Acto knife (a parent's job). Then invite the kids to decorate the cookies with puffy paint.
Holiday Garlands: Set out bowls of stringables — popcorn, beads, pinecones, buttons, or anything else that can be poked with a needle. Offer guests heavy-duty thread and let them dig into the bowls and string garlands.

Christmas Carnival

Christmas Carnival

Handy Tote

Handy Totes: Let partygoers create a tote bag for hauling home all their party loot, from favors to holiday crafts. For best results, plan this activity early in the party before things get rollicking, and have kids work one at a time. Near a sink, cover your work surface with newspaper. Pour tempera paints in pie plates and have enough small paper bags with handles to go around. Offer each child a smock, then let her customize the front and back of a folded bag. Once dry, stuff the bag with party favors — candy canes, snow globes, ribbon candy, or homemade ornaments and garlands.

Gift Wrap: While you have the paint out, let kids craft gift wrap. Tape a sheet of newsprint or butcher paper onto a basement wall and let kids paint with handprints. Once dry, cut the paper into sections for each guest to take home.

Handy Totes

Cheese Ball Snowman

This cheesy little guy is almost too cute to eat, but he makes a perky companion to a plate of crackers or mini bagels.

2 8-ounce packages cream cheese (for the head and body)
Raisins (eyes, mouth, buttons)
Piece of carrot (nose)
Crackers (hat)
Parsley sprig (optional, for hat)
Fruit leather (scarf)
Pretzels (arms)
Canned baby corn (pipe)
Toothpicks

From the cream cheese, fashion two balls for the head and body. (Note: Do not warm the cream cheese to room temperature.) Add face, buttons, hat, and scarf. Break pretzels and use the center sections for arms. Make the corncob pipe from half an ear of baby corn and a toothpick. Tip: For extra flavor, dress up the cream cheese with confectioners' sugar and lemon juice or feta cheese and garlic powder.

Reindeer Gear: Your crew can prance right into party mode by adorning themselves in the latest North Pole couture: easy-to-make reindeer antlers. Before the party, cut red poster board into 1½- by 24-inch-long strips for the headbands and cut brown poster board into 6- by 9-inch rectangles for the antlers (two for each child). Put out pencils, scissors, a stapler or two, glue and glitter, and, if you like, red face paint.

Help each guest wrap a strip around his or her head for a comfortable fit, remove it, and securely staple the ends. On the brown poster board, each child can outline a pair of multi-branched antlers and then cut them out. Kids who want spiffier antlers can add glue and glitter; less patient reindeer can just staple the antlers to the front of the headband. Use face paint to finish off each reindeer's costume with a big red nose.

Crudi-tree

This make-ahead centerpiece is not only spectacular to look at, but it's also a tower of healthy, sugar-free nibbling. Start with a 12-inch, green Styrofoam cone and use toothpicks to attach vegetables (broccoli florets, cucumber slices, olives, sugar snap peas, cherry tomatoes, and sliced red, yellow, and green peppers). Top the tree with a yellow pepper star. Serve with your favorite vegetable dip. Tip: Be careful using the toothpicks — try pressing them in with a thimble. Also, don't worry about covering every inch of the cone at first. Go back later and stuff bits of broccoli (without toothpicks) into the bare spots.

Reindeer Gear

Christmas Carnival

Tree-sicles

These treats are made with your favorite sugar cookie dough. Roll the dough to a ⅛-inch thickness and cut with tree-shaped cookie cutters. Sandwich a craft stick between two cookies and bake as usual. (Note: The cookies are thick, so baking may take longer.) Cool and frost with green frosting, then add icing, candy, and sprinkles. Tip: Separate the decorating goodies into cupcake holders and give each child his own assortment to use.

The Reindeer Games

ONCE YOUR GANG has finished making crafts, it's time for silly games and contests of skill (and the chance to score a few prizes). The following events include several that kids like to play over and over, plus a few one-timers that work best with the whole group. Before the big day, be sure to lay in a supply of inexpensive prizes, such as candy canes, stickers, marbles, and rubber balls.

Snowblowers: A good set of lungs and coolness under pressure are essential for this contest. To set up, tape large paper cups to one side of a table so that the cup openings are level with the table's surface. Fill each cup halfway with small prizes (candy canes, colored pencils, stickers, bright erasers) and clear away any chairs so players have an open pathway at both sides of the table. Give the first two players paper towel tubes and explain that when you place a Ping-Pong ball in front of each of them, they must blow through the tubes like a snowblower. (Point out that a gentle breath is all it takes to get the "snowball" rolling.) Each contestant will have 15 seconds to direct the ball across the table and into one of the paper cups; if the ball goes over the edge first, that player's turn is over. Each winner gets to pick one prize from the cup — and the playing continues until each cup is empty.

Stuff the Santa: This merry game pits teams against one another in a race to create the stoutest Saint Nick of them all. To play, you and your kids will need to inflate an ample supply of balloons and borrow or buy a red, one-piece union suit in Santa's size — extra large.

Contestants are divided into teams of four to six players. Draw candy canes to determine which player will don the suit over his or her clothes; the player selecting the longest candy cane is "Santa." Teammates are given the task

Snowblowers

Stuff the Santa

of stuffing the suit with balloons. Remind the players that a gentle touch is essential for keeping balloons intact. Set a timer for 2 minutes and see how many balloons the team can stuff into the suit before the time is up. The next team of Santa stuffers must try to top the previous record, but first give old Santa a chance to show off his lumpy physique.

Full of Beans: Pique your guests' curiosity with this classic puzzler: How many red and green jelly beans are in the glass jar? During the party, each contestant must write his or her name and best estimate on a slip of paper and drop it into a box with everyone else's guesses. At the end of the party, read off each estimate and record it on a large sheet of paper. Then, with great flourish, pull out a sealed envelope with the answer in it and announce the correct number. The winner is the person (or persons, in the case of a tie) whose guess comes the closest. For the brilliant deduction, the winner takes home the candy jar and its contents.

Full of Beans

Cookie Swap

For an easy holiday party, invite guests to a cookie swap. Karla Davison of Fairfax, Virginia, had her sons deliver invitations to nearby friends, asking them to make two dozen cookies for party day. Karla then displayed the cookies at her house and had each child talk about his or her contribution. After games and crafts, everyone chowed down — and took a bag of cookies home to share with Mom and Dad.

Hanukkah Party

E VERY HANUKKAH, the Wallace family of Saratoga, California, brightens up their home with a Festival of Lights party. The premise is simple: friends and family are invited to bring a menorah and share in the lighting together. Barbara, the mother of two boys, says, "To have our home filled with all of these menorahs, especially the ones that hold memories, is a wonderful way to celebrate the holiday.

Hanukkah Hand Invitations

T O MAKE A MENORAH invitation, trace both of your child's hands onto blue paper, overlapping the thumbs to make the shammes candle in the middle. Next glue the paper cutout onto a sheet of white paper folded in half. Light up the flames with a gold glitter crayon. Write the party details inside the card, including a request that guests bring their own menorah to light. Anything goes, whether it's a menorah made at Hebrew school or a great grandmother's prize menorah.

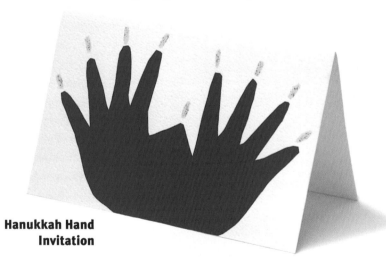

Hanukkah Hand Invitation

Lighting the Menorah

T HE MAIN EVENT at the Wallaces' party is when everyone illuminates the menorahs. They light them at the kitchen table (draped with a nonflammable tablecloth), then put one menorah in the dining room windowsill, one at the kids' table, and the rest all around the house.

With so many menorahs, all of the kids get the chance to light a candle. "There's something magical about lighting the candles, especially for kids," says Barb.

Playing Dreidel

INVITE GUESTS to spin the dreidel — and try to take home the pot. Explain that the dreidel top is decorated with the first four letters from the Hebrew phrase *Nes gadol hayah sham,* which means "A great miracle happened there." To play this game of chance, everybody begins with an equal amount of chocolates, coins, or peanuts. Before each round, players ante up. The players spin and follow directions based on the letter that's faceup when the dreidel stops:

נ *(nun)* — take nothing from the pot
ג *(gimel)* — take the whole pot
ה *(hay)* — take half the pot
ש *(shin)* — add two items to the pot

You can play for a set number of rounds or until someone has won everything.

Chocolate Menorah

Playing Dreidel

BRIGHTEN — and sweeten — your family's Hanukkah celebration with this double-chocolate menorah.

1¼ cups semisweet chocolate chips
½ cup white chocolate morsels
⅓ cup heavy cream

Melt ¼ cup of the semisweet chocolate chips in a microwave-safe bowl, about 1 minute on high. Using a clean paintbrush, drizzle the chocolate on the inside of one regular and eight mini foil muffin cups. Next melt the white chocolate morsels in the microwave and paint over the drizzled chocolate. Place the mini cups in a mini-muffin pan and the large muffin cup in a custard cup. Freeze for 5 to 10 minutes, or until hardened.

Meanwhile, make the ganache filling. Heat the heavy cream in the microwave until it comes to a boil, then stir in 1 cup of chocolate chips until melted and smooth. Spoon the ganache into the candy cups. Refrigerate for 1 hour, or until set. To assemble the menorah, place the candy cups on a large platter or board with the largest cup in the center. Insert candles into each cup, then light in the traditional manner. Serves 9.

Week Of Guests

In Santa Fe, New Mexico, *Family Fun* reader Miriam Sagan's family celebrates Hanukkah with the traditional rituals — lighting the menorah, frying latkes, and giving gifts. They also follow an old European custom of inviting a mix of people to their house every night of the holiday. Word gets around, so when one of their guests can't make it, someone else is sure to call and say, "Hey, we heard you need people on night number six, and we're volunteering!"

Party Resources

Party Locations

For a change of pace from the home party, consider taking the kids out. Not only will an alternative setting spare wear and tear on your home (and your nerves), but the kids will have a blast, too. Once you've settled on a location, call and find out if they offer party packages or group discounts. Here are some locations to consider:

- Bowling alley
- Ice or roller skating rink
- Radio, television, fire, or police station
- Pizza parlor or local restaurant
- Planetarium
- Ceramics studio
- Children's museum
- Farm
- Circus, zoo, or aquarium
- Kids' gymnastics or sports center
- Movie or theater matinee
- Nature center
- Miniature golf or batting center
- Playground
- Basketball court or baseball field
- Local park or pool
- Beauty parlor
- Water or theme park

Party Supplies

Birthday Express
11220 120th Avenue NE
Kirkland, WA 98033-4535
1-800-4-BIRTHDAY
www.birthdayexpress.com
For busy parents, this mail-order (and online) catalog is a real time-saver. You can purchase complete party packages, from the invitations to the favors, for popular children's party themes, such as Thomas the Tank Engine, Madeline, and Winnie the Pooh. Call, write, or e-mail for a free catalog.

M&N International
P.O. Box 64784
St. Paul, MN 55164-0784
800-479-2043
www.mninternational.com
This 200-page mail-order catalog features hundreds of party decorations and accessories for every holiday of the year, from the back-to-school season to Fourth of July. Call for a free catalog.

MeadowLark Party Shoppe
2 Beistle Plaza
Meadowlands Mall
Shippensburg, PA 17257
717-532-3535
www.party-here.com
MeadowLark, a mail-order party-supply company, specializes in theme decorations and party kits with more than 13,000 items to choose from. Visit their outlet store in Shippensburg, Pennsylvania, or call, write, or e-mail to order the $10 catalog (which includes a 25 percent-off coupon).

Party and Paper Retailer Magazine
www.partypaper.com
If you're looking to find a party-store in your area, check out this on-line resource. Click on your state in the retail locator for a handy listing.

Party and Paper Worldwide
www.partypro.com
Shop in this online party-supply store as if you were shopping in a super party warehouse for "Birthday in a box" packages, piñatas, paper supplies, and much more.

Party Favors

Oriental Trading Company, Inc.
P.O. Box 3407
Omaha, NE 68103
1-800-875-8480
www.orientaltrading.com
This 100-page mail-order catalog is overflowing with party favors, prizes, and gifts for children's birthday and holiday parties. Many of the items can be ordered in bulk. Write or call for a free catalog.

The Nature Company
www.naturecompany.com
1-800-627-9399
This retail chain offers a selection of nature-themed toys and favors, such as tumbled rocks, rubber balls, spyglasses and magnifiers, tops, and plastic animals. Call or use the on-line store locator to find a store in your area.

MediBadge, Inc.
P.O. Box 12307
Omaha, NE 68112
800-228-0040
www.medibadge.com
If you're looking to fill a treasure chest with favors, stickers, erasers, and tiny plastic toys, check out this mail-order catalog. MediBadge supplies children's novelties in bulk to medical and dental offices—and to the public. Call for a free catalog.

Zany Brainy
888-WOW-KIDS
www.zanybrainy.com
Zany Brainy specializes in educational toys for kids, but they also carry stickers, rubber stamps, science favors, children's books, and craft supplies. Call or e-mail to locate a store in your area, or to order a free catalog.

Cake and Candy Resources

Wilton Enterprises
2240 W. 75th Street
Woodridge, IL 60517
800-794-5866
www.wilton.com

Wilton is the ultimate source for all your cake-decorating needs, from novelty cake pans and cookie cutters to food coloring paste and cake decorations. Call or write for the $9.99 catalog, or to find a local distributor.

King Arthur Flour

P.O. Box 1010, Route 5 South
Norwich, VT 05055
800-872-6836
www.kingarthurflour.com
This mail-order catalog features unbleached flours, baking pans and supplies, colored sugars and sprinkles, marzipan, and cake-decorating tools. Call for a free catalog or visit their retail store in Norwich, Vermont.

Sugarcraft

1143 South Erie Boulevard
Hamilton, OH 45011
513-896-7089
www.sugarcraft.com
This online cake-decorating, cookie-making, and candy-supply catalog features over 10,000 items, from cake pans and candy molds to sugar flowers and edible images. Order items on-line or visit their retail store in Hamilton, Ohio.

Wizard Cupcakes, page 183

Rental Sources

American Rental Association

www.ararental.org/consumermain.htm
If you're short on plates, tables, and chairs, or you'd like to rent a moonwalk or cotton candy maker, head to a rental store in your area. To find one, simply enter your Zip Code in this on-line search engine.

Taylor Rental, Grand Rental Station, or TruServ

www.taylorrentals.com
This national rental company has more than 600 retail stores in the United States. Check the Yellow Pages under "rental service" or search the on-line guide to find addresses and phone numbers of rental stores in your area.

Rental Prices

If you'd like to add punch to your block parties or large gatherings, consider renting any of the following items. To find a rental store in your area, see the sources at left (prices may vary).

◆ Helium tank: $10 to $25
◆ Karaoke: $45 to $60
◆ Bubble maker: $20 to $30
◆ Fog maker: $10 to $50
◆ PA lectern: $30
◆ Chairs: $.65 to $2 each
◆ Tables: $4.50 to $20 each
◆ Table settings: $.30 to $.50 per piece
◆ Moonwalk: $75 to $140
◆ Popcorn cart: $30 to $45
◆ Snowcone maker: $35
◆ Cotton candy machine: $40 to $50
◆ Grill: $35 to $85
◆ Dunk tank: $100 to $200

Hiring Party Entertainers

An entertainer, whether he's a magician or a clown, can add an exciting element to a birthday or holiday party. To find one in your area, check the Yellow Pages under "entertainers," or read or post ads in the newspaper and on library bulletin boards.

Once you have someone in mind, set up an interview. Ask him or her what the show includes and the approximate duration of their act. You may also wish to see a videotape of a performance or request references.

The following is a list of entertainers you might consider hiring for your party (review it with your kids).

◆ Police officer or firefighter (call the station for information; some firefighters or police officers may be willing to bring their vehicles)
◆ Disc jockey
◆ Musician
◆ Naturalist (with animal friends)
◆ Clown
◆ Magician
◆ Storyteller
◆ Puppeteer
◆ Costumed character
◆ Farmer who offers pony rides
◆ Mad scientist
◆ Ballerinas
◆ Game coordinator

Index

Dinosaur Cupcakes, page 191

Racetrack Cake, page 189

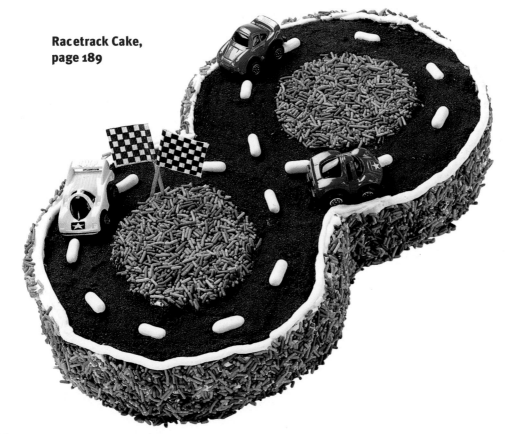

Bubble Wrap Stomp, page 272

Strawberry Smoothie, page 270

**Take-Home
Tackle Box,
page 209**

Art & Photography Credits

Special thanks to the following *FamilyFun* magazine photographers, illustrators, and stylists for their excellent work.

PHOTOGRAPHERS:

Robert Benson: *Back cover (bottom right); 17; 60; 67; 68; 69; 70 (upper left); 161 (middle left); 184 (middle and bottom left); 185-187; 204; 205 (bottom); 206; 207 (bottom, middle, and upper left); 268; 289; 292 (bottom left); 293 (upper right)*

Paul Berg: *Cover (left middle & left bottom); 28; 79 (upper right); 87; 239 (upper left); 295, 296 (bottom left); 305 (bottom right)*

Robert Bossi: *230; 260 (bottom); 261 (upper right); 262-265*

Michael Carroll: *18 (bottom right); 49 (upper right); 61; 64 (upper left); 72 (upper left); 95 (upper right); 98 (bottom right); 122; 123 (top); 148 (top right); 155 (upper left); 290 (bottom right), 291, 292 (upper right and middle left)*

Faith Echtermeyer: *212 (bottom left and middle)*

Alan Epstein: *18 (bottom left); 20 (bottom right); 21(upper right); 22; 27(bottom left); 219 (middle and bottom); 220 (bottom)*

Peter Fox: *208 (bottom left); 222 (bottom); 237; 238; 251; 276 (bottom left and upper left); 298 (bottom left)*

Jim Gipe: *123 (bottom right); 164 (bottom right); 171; 298 (middle right); 304 (bottom)*

Thomas Heinser: *160 (middle right); 251-253; 254 (bottom and top right); 255*

Jacqueline Hopkins: *Cover (bottom center); 16; 179 (bottom); 180 (top left); 181 (top right, middle, bottom right); 294 bottom right; 296 (top right), 297*

Tom Hopkins: *37(upper left); 38 (top); 52; 53; 54 (bottom); 56 (upper right); 62 (bottom); 65 (upper right); 78 (bottom right); 80; 81; 85 (upper right); 86; 90 ; 92; 93 (upper right); 94 (upper right); 95 (bottom right);*
97; 98 (upper right); 99; 100; 106 (bottom right); 110 (bottom left); 114 (upper left); 124 (top left); 125 (bottom right; 126 (upper left); 150; 151(upper right); 152; 153; 154 (upper right); 160 (middle left); 161 (top left); 176; 178;192 (bottom and middle right); 193; 195; 196 (bottom right and upper left); 197; 199 (middle and bottom right); 200; 201 (bottom and upper right); 231 (left and right bottom); 232-233; 234; 235 (upper right); 257-258; 298 (upper right and two right); 299-303

Ed Judice: *Back cover (top right); cover (top right); 147; 160 (bottom left, middle right, upper left, and bottom); 161 (bottom right and middle left); 173; 182 (bottom left, top right); 183 (middle right); 189 (bottom right); 190-191; 194; 198; 201 (2 top left); 203; 214 (bottom left); 216 (bottom left); 217; 223 (middle right and 2 bottom); 224 (bottom left); 226; 249 (2 bottom right); 261 (bottom right); 266; 274 (middle and bottom left); 275; 276 (middle); 277 (top and bottom right); 288 (2 bottom and upper right); 290 (bottom, right side, middle left, and top); 298 (bottom left)*

Michael Kevin Daly/Corbis: *304 (middle right)*

Rob Lang: *222 (upper left)*

Brian Leatart: *Cover (top left); 25; 39 (bottom right); 43 (upper right); 49 (bottom); 52; 54 (upper left); 55; 59 (bottom right); 74; 76; 82; 91 (top right); 102; 106; 108; 113; 118; 130 (bottom); 134 (upper left); 142; 146; 239 (bottom right); 282 (bottom); 283-286; 287 (upper middle)*

Lightworks Photographic: *4-15; 19; 20 (bottom left, upper right); 21 (bottom); 24 (bottom left); 27 (top & bottom right); 31 (bottom); 32 (bottom right); 33 (upper right); 34 (bottom right); 35 (bottom); 36; 40;41; 42; 44; 45 (center); 47; 48; 50; 51; 57; 58; 63 (bottom left); 64 (middle left); 66; 73; 75; 77; 78 (top left); 84; 85(middle right); 89; 94 (bottom left); 96; 103; 104; 105; 106 (upper left); 109; 110 (upper left); 112; 114 (bottom left); 115; 116; 117 (bottom); 119; 124*

New Year's Eve party, page 271

Also from FamilyFun magazine

★ **FamilyFun magazine:** a creative guide to all the great things families can do together. Call 800-289-4849 for a subscription.

★ **FamilyFun Homemade for the Holidays:** 150 festive holiday crafts, recipes, gifts, and parties (Disney Editions, $14.95).

★ **FamilyFun Tricks and Treats:** a ghoulish group of 100 wickedly easy costumes, crafts, games, and foods for Halloween (Disney Editions, $14.95).

★ **FamilyFun Birthday Cakes:** 50 of our cutest and most creative birthday cakes (Disney Editions, $10.95).

★ **FamilyFun Cookies for Christmas:** a batch of 50 recipes for creative holiday treats (Disney Editions, $9.95).

★ **FamilyFun Crafts:** a step-by-step guide to 500 of the best crafts and activities to do with your kids (Disney Editions, $24.95).

★ **FamilyFun.com:** Visit us at **www.familyfun.com** and search our extensive archives for great ideas, practical advice, and fun stuff to do.